Praise for Peter Guralnick's

FEEL LIKE GOING HOME

"The most emotionally and intellectually satisfying rock book yet to appear." — ROBERT CHRISTGAU, *Village Voice*

"We feel the passion of Guralnick's love for the music and also the real personalities of the bluesmen he interviews." — NELSON GEORGE, *Billboard*

"A powerful, personal book about blues, rock 'n' roll, and the musicians who play it. . . . It brought me closer to every figure it sought to illuminate. . . . Guralnick's capacity to draw out his subjects is one of his most admirable qualities as a chronicler. In all the articles that I have ever read about Muddy Waters, I have never seen anything so moving as the statement he made at the end of his interview with Guralnick." — JON LANDAU, *Rolling Stone*

"Nobody digs deeper into what makes [these musicians] tick, and nobody conveys their achievement with more grace, details, and empathy." — JOHN MORTHLAND, *Music & Sound Output*

"The author cuts so close to the bone you almost want to turn away for fear of learning what you don't want to know. Essential reading." — DAVID McGEE, *Record World*

"Few music works delineate the history of blues and rockabilly as intelligently or as tenderly." — CHRIS MORRIS, *Los Angeles Reader*

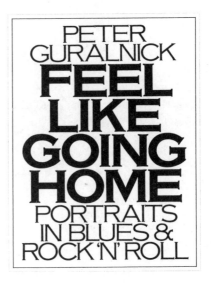

PETER
GURALNICK
FEEL
LIKE
GOING
HOME
PORTRAITS
IN BLUES &
ROCK 'N' ROLL

CANONGATE

ALSO BY PETER GURALNICK

Lost Highway
Sweet Soul Music
Nighthawk Blues
Searching for Robert Johnson
Last Train to Memphis: The Rise of Elvis Presley
Careless Love: The Unmasking of Elvis Presley

This edition first published in the UK in 2003 by Canongate Books,
14 High Street, Edinburgh EH1 1TE

First published by Outerbridge & Dienstfrey, 1971

10 9 8 7 6 5 4 3 2 1

Copyright acknowledgements appear on page 263
Photograph on preceding pages by Val Wilmer

British Libray Cataloguing-in-Publication Data
A catalogue record for this book is available on request
from the British Library

ISBN 1 84195 281 5

Printed and bound by
CPD, Ebbw Vale, Wales

www.canongate.net

For my grandparents, Philip and Rose Marson,
and for Jacob, their great-grandson

I started writing about music as soon as anyone would listen. Long before the existence of *Crawdaddy!* or *Fusion* or *Rolling Stone* I wanted to do a history of Sun Records; I had mapped out a biography of Skip James. I had this intimation that what I was interested in could be of importance to other people, too.

When I did start writing serious uncritical pieces about my heroes in blues and rock 'n' roll, my intentions, I thought, were of the purest. I sought to publicize the artists; I wanted to call the attention of others to what seemed to me worthwhile; I tried to repay a little the enormous debt I owed to these musicians for opening up my universe.

Nothing ever turns out to be that simple. Writing, of course, is its own reward; in publication lie the pitfalls. It's flattering, after all, to see your own name in print. You become aware of the small degree of power that you exert. And although I have never written any piece out of anything less than personal enthusiasm, it is impossible to avoid becoming manipulative at least to a certain extent. At some point you even begin to get paid.

This book sprang originally out of a suggestion made many editors and over two years ago. A large publisher, riding the crest of the new youth market, wanted "the definitive history of the blues". I wasn't interested in that. Even ignoring my own lack of qualifications for the job, I tried to explain the breadth of the subject, also that it had been covered, probably as well as it could be, in Paul Oliver's *Story of the Blues*. My objections were waved aside. Develop your own treatment, I was told. Well, ultimately, this book is the result.

It is a book of profiles intended to show a kind of historical progression. This progression I hope will be obvious from the profiles themselves and from the very abbreviated history in Chapter II which traces the development of the blues from traditional country roots up through Memphis and Chicago and into the first heady days of rock 'n' roll. Rock 'n' roll, of course, I took to be an extension of the blues tradition, and I am sorry circumstances prevented me from including Little Richard or Chuck Berry as an example of the black artist's adaptation of his own cultural experience for white popular consumption. The stories are interrelated in any case, and undoubtedly the reader will make his own connections as well.

Much more important than any specific progression, however,

are the musicians themselves. Every one of them is an artist I've known and admired, if only from afar, for years. Every one of them is, I think, a significant artist; every one of them deserves your attention. What I wanted to do was to present them in a way in which they had not been seen before, within the context of their own time and world. I wanted to explore in some ways how that world shaped them and how they in turn shaped it.

Obviously there are limitations to this kind of approach. Their experience is, in almost every case, foreign to my own, and I have had to make certain imaginative leaps even to begin to comprehend it for myself. It's an experience, on the other hand, in which I have steeped myself for the last twelve years, and I thought it important for this reason to give the reader a little bit of a clue to my own background and bias, the viewpoint by which the framework is necessarily limited. Chapter I, "Rock 'n' Roll Music", is an attempt to do just that and, I hope, in the process to suggest a kind of portrait of an era. Because it is that era, after all, which not only killed off the blues as a popular music but has now resurrected it, fifteen years later, out of guilt perhaps and out of necessity.

In the end, though, it's the music that counts. If this book moves you to listen, if it causes you to pay at least that minimal tribute to each artist's work, then it will have served some real purpose. Otherwise it's just empty rhetoric, and everyone knows we don't need more of that.

Peter Guralnick
Newburyport, Massachusetts
May 21, 1971

9

ACKNOWLEDGEMENT

For their continuing help and encouragement in doing this book I would like to thank: Dick Waterman; Bob Koester; Jim and Amy O'Neal; Bruce Iglauer; Paul Garon; Jon Landau; David Evans; Richard Allen, Curator of the Archive of New Orleans Jazz at Tulane University; Bob Smith; Parker Dinkins; Terry Pattison; Carl Moxey; Peter Wolf; Jack Viertel; Fred Davis; David Gessner; Steve Frappier; John Grahm; and my editor Bob Somma.

The chapter on Johnny Shines is based on interviews by Jack Viertel as well as myself; the chapter on Muddy Waters utilizes material kindly supplied by Carl Moxey; extensive background information on Robert Pete Williams was supplied by Dick Allen and the Archive of New Orleans Jazz; Bruce Jackson's interview with Skip James was an invaluable expansion of my own. I am indebted to Loren Coleman and Ralph Bass in particular for showing me around the Chess offices.

And, of course, most of all I would like to thank the artists themselves for their generous sharing of time, memories, and hospitality.

Val Wilmer

CONTENTS

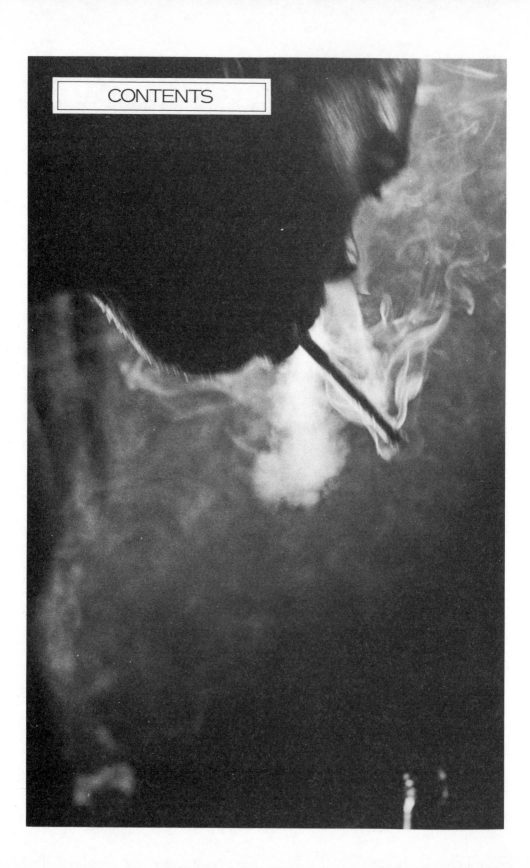

Val Wilmer

CHAPTER 1
ROCK 'N' ROLL MUSIC
GROWING UP AND COMING DOWN

I

Like nearly everyone I knew I was unsure how to react to rock 'n' roll. I was twelve when Elvis scored his first success, and he wasn't much older. The excitement, the exhilaration, the *novelty* of that moment is something it would be impossible to recapture.

"Hail, hail, rock 'n' roll/Deliver us from the days of old." Rock 'n' roll *did* deliver us from the days of old in more ways than it could ever know. Its energy was explosive. It introduced us to a culture whose existence we had never previously suspected. It served as a vehicle for vague proletarian yearnings. It confirmed to us our own reality. Looking back on it from the vantage point of the present it seems hard to believe we ever lived through an era in which values were so circumscribed and distinctions so sharp. But those were the boundaries of our world. It was a world in which "crazy mixed-up kids" was a household word and dirty boogying an act of social defiance.

I don't mean to dwell on the era, because I don't know too much about it. Pegged pants and ducktail haircuts, raised collars and switchblades: these seem like familiar landmarks, but I don't know that they're anything more than the nostalgic by-products of an era. Growing up in it you don't imagine that what is going on around you can be of any great importance; afterwards nearly everything seems of equally momentous significance. From the viewpoint of the present, though, it seems to me that the overwhelming feeling my friends and I shared was that we must be doing something terribly wrong. We measured ourselves against the judgment of our elders and believed what they told us even when it rang false to our own experience. There were at that time certain immutable standards, and if they said that rock 'n' roll was a passing fad, like swing and Frank Sinatra, it seemed unimaginable that it was not.

That's why our first reaction was necessarily so ambiguous. There was, at least among my acquaintances, not the faintest suspicion of any Woodstock nation, not the least idea that there was anyone even remotely resembling us out there. We believed pretty much what we were told, though we sensed that it was wrong. Harry Belafonte had a hit with "Day-O" and calypso had supplanted rock 'n' roll. The next year it was Pat Boone with a clean-cut ballad or two, and the year after that by *Time's* report thrill-crazed youth had gone on a gospel kick which would never actually materialize. When the treacle period of the late fifties and early sixties engulfed us we recited the familiar litany, by now grown stale from repetition: Elvis in the Army, Buddy Holly dead, Little Richard in the ministry, Jerry Lee Lewis in disgrace and Chuck Berry in jail. We mourned the passing of our youth, but took it as our due. It was this, I think, as much as anything else that contributed to the considerable staying power of our culture: that we were not overburdened with self-righteousness.

Lightnin' Hopkins/Val Wilmer

The great thing about it, in the beginning at least, was that there seemed to be no one in control. It was *our* music in more than just name not because it represented some kind of pure aesthetic (rock 'n' roll has always been the most commercial of musics) but because it was for the most part beneath the contempt of those who were marketing it. Almost by accident it sprang out of an industry that was only beginning to discover itself, and as a result it grew up free and unencumbered, its success not only uninstructive but actually counter to good business methods.

"Like all great folk artists," read the liner notes of the first Lightnin' Hopkins album I ever bought, "like Ives, Lightnin' Hopkins improvises easily." To the record producers teenagers had just about the same status as blacks thirty years earlier and just about the same appeal, too. They represented a huge but totally unpredictable market subject to whims of taste and fancy no sane person could sensibly predict. "In selecting the songs for this new album," boasted the liner notes to Little Richard's second LP for Specialty, "Little Richard tried to top his first album ... [and] included some unreleased material especially for his fans' parents who still may not 'dig the beat.' He feels that if they'll only listen to songs they remember like 'Baby Face' and 'By the Light of the Silvery Moon' done up in the Little Richard style, they'll enjoy this new album, too!"

With advocacy like this who could blame us for a certain schizophrenia of our own? The first time I heard Little Richard's "Tutti Frutti" was on the car radio on the way to school.

> A-wop bop a lu bop a lop bam boom
> Tutti frutti, oh rooty
> Tutti frutti, oh rooty

it burst out at us. Our first reaction, I think, was one of chagrin. Somebody's father was driving, and he expressed our discomfort before we could ourselves. What command of the English language, he said and switched stations. We all laughed self-consciously because it was, after all, our fault.

Jackie Wilson's "Lonely Teardrops," The Diamonds' "Little Darling," The Platters, The Penguins, The G Clefs all met with similar reactions. We didn't know what to make of this new music for the simple reason that we had never been exposed to anything like it before. Our first encounter with Elvis Presley was no different.

> You ain't nothin' but a hound dog
> Crying all the time.
> You ain't nothing but a hound dog
> Crying all the time.
> You ain't never caught a rabbit,
> and you ain't no friend of mine.

Even the irony of a male singer voicing these sentiments escaped us at the time. What do you think of Elvis Presley?, was the first business of social exchange, and your answer defined you politically, morally, sociologically. It was a little like asking a ten-year-old if he liked girls. You gave the answer you were expected to give – a sour look, a turned-up nose. You conformed to type.

Obviously mine is a very limited experience. Not everyone reacted with the same ambiguousness, and rock 'n' roll appealed from the first to a huge audience which immediately claimed it for its own. I think that my experience was not isolated, however, because, whatever your outlook at that time, for all the youthful gestures of rebellion, you expected some day to take your place in adult society. You were aware of growing pains and stages that you were going through, and what doubts you had could be smoothed over by the certainty of the future and the reassurances of your elders. If rock 'n' roll had had no other value it would have been enough merely to dent the smug middle-class consciousness of that time and throw into confusion some of the deadening rigidity of that world.

For that was what it unmistakably did. To keep a comb in your back pocket was both a declaration of independence and an expression of political solidarity. Here we were, irretrievably middle-class, but what were we doing then in our baby blue jeans, our collars turned up, and torturing our hair into modified DAs? We went to the Big Beat shows, and if we did not we bitterly resented having listened to our parents' warnings and the humdrum security of our lives. We hung out on streetcorners and swaggered into the House of Pizza, got thrown out of bowling alleys and movie theatres and buses, picked fights we could never win.

What I think was happening quite clearly was the convergence of two warring cultures. Just as James Dean and Marlon Brando came to represent our unarticulated hurt, just as it was *The Catcher in the Rye* and *The Stranger* that gave us our literary heroes — existential ciphers that refused to speak when spoken to — rock 'n' roll provided us with a release and a justification that we had never dreamt of.

The very outrageousness of its poses, the swaggering sexuality, the violence which the radio of that day laid at its door, its forbidden and corrupting influence — that was the unfailing attractiveness of rock 'n' roll. The hysteria of its terms, the absurdity of its appeal — Fats Domino bumping a piano offstage with his belly; Little Richard's outlandish screams and "jungle rhythms"; Jerry Lee Lewis' vocal gymnastics and theatrical virtuosity; Elvis's very presence and Carl Perkins' "Get off of my blue suede shoes"; with Chuck Berry all the while merrily warning, "Roll over Beethoven" — how could we deny it entrance into our lives? The ease with which you could offend the adult world, the sanctimoniousness of public figures and the turnabout that came with success ("Presley will never appear on my show," said Ed Sullivan, shortly before Elvis's series of $50,000 appearances), above all the clear line of demarcation

between *us* and *them* made it impossible for us to turn our backs and ignore this new phenomenon. So from the first we were hooked. We were addicts without even knowing it.

II

But then rock 'n' roll died. It was over before it even had a chance to slyly grin and look around. In its place came a new all-synthetic product. I was only in the ninth grade when we entered what was then called the Philadelphia era of rock.

Even then we knew it was a fraud. Dick Clark's Brilliantine good looks, the sterility of *Bandstand* (but where are you now, Justine?), and the block which had been lucky enough to produce Frankie Avalon, Fabian (who at least articulated the right sentiments: Turn me loose and I'm a tiger) and Bobby Rydell. What we did at the age of fifteen was to retreat into the past. The past year or two.

It's hard to remember the limits of our world at that time. For the longest time I had exactly two long-playing records. My mother gave me Elvis Presley's first and, perhaps to make up my debt to him, I went out and bought Little Richard's on my own. We listened to Jumping Joe Smith and Arnie "Woo Woo" Ginsberg and occasionally, late at night, Symphony Sid, but we simply were not exposed to that much music. Instead, we played the records that we did have over and over until we knew the words to every song, and could anticipate each riff and drumroll.

Buying a record in those days was quite a production. To begin with, of course, there weren't many out and even fewer places to find them. But then, too, it was a commitment of taste; your self-esteem was on the line, your whole reputation could stand or fall on a single $3.00 purchase. I don't know how many times we'd sit scrunched over in the listening booth at Briggs and Briggs, playing the same record over and over again and trying to avoid the sales-lady's cold eye. That was standard operating procedure, though, and you never purchased a record before thoroughly evaluating the consequences. It was a tortuous process sometimes, but perhaps as a result there are few records from that period that I find myself regretting ownership of today. Of course I could hardly afford to. Even if I didn't like the record, the investment of time and energy would tell me otherwise. So this had to be a foolproof process.

Singles, of course were a different story, and we all had scattered selections. Even so, the only people I knew with extensive collections of 45s were girls who went to every Tony Perkins movie. Or worshipped Elvis, or Tab Hunter. And we were rightfully scornful of that.

We considered ourselves not fans but connoisseurs. We could sit around and speculate endlessly on the reasons for Elvis's artistic decline, Little Richard's intellectual capabilities (he had entered Morehouse College, it said in the liner notes to his second album), Gene Vincent's amputated leg or Carl Perkins' speculated insanity. It was only by accident that we discovered Elvis's matchless Sun sides on the RCA albums (put out while he was in the Army). The legend of Sun Records was a whole new phenomenon in itself. And we assembled our own selection of Golden Oldies to recall or invoke new memories.

Towards the end of high school we painstakingly put together a rock 'n' roll tape of these selections. Elvis had twelve, Jerry Lee ten and Little Richard eight. In our hierarchy that made Elvis king, Little Richard and Jerry Lee Lewis princes, and Carl Perkins, Chuck Berry, Fats Domino, and Gene Vincent archdukes. And that was our high school yearbook.

Blues grabbed mamachild, tore him all upside down
Robert Johnson

The only alternatives to rock at that time were cool jazz and folk music along the lines of The Kingston Trio. Fancying ourselves beatniks we flirted with the one; out of snobbishness undoubtedly we toyed with the other. Folk music never offered either the high spirits or the surging energy of rock 'n' roll; it did provide us with an introduction to Josh White and Leadbelly, though, and it was in this way that I first stumbled on to the blues.

The blues captured me initially by its directness of impact. I had never known a more searing expression of emotion. "The blues is a low-down shaking chill." From my first exposure to it, through

Little Richard/Sepia magazine

a friend and through Samuel Charters' book, *The Country Blues,* I found myself enthralled in a way I had never experienced before; it struck some responsive chord which I cannot explain even today.

There are lots of reasons, of course, why blues should attract a white audience of some proportions. There is, to begin with, the question of colour. Most of us had never known a Negro. That didn't stop us, however, from constructing a whole elaborate mythology and modeling ourselves in speech and dress and manner along the lines of what we thought a Negro would be. Norman Mailer has expressed this attraction well in "The White Negro." It was, really, the whole hipster pose. But it was also, as Eldridge Cleaver has pointed out, that rock 'n' roll represented not only an implicit social commitment but the explicit embrace of a black subculture which had never previously risen to the surface, so that we were set up, really — I was, anyway, along with my friends — for the adoption of a purely black music and a purely black culture.

Blues offered the perfect vehicle for our romanticism. What's more, it offered boundless opportunities for embroidery due to its exotic nature, the vagueness of its associations, and certain characteristics associated with the music itself. For one thing it was an undeniably personal music; whatever the autobiographical truth of the words, each singer undoubtedly conveyed something of himself in his song. Then, too, the lyrics in addition to being poetically abstract, were often vague and difficult to understand; the singer made a habit of slurring syllables or dropping off the end of a verse, and the quality of the recording, often from a distance of thirty-five years, added to the aura of obscurity. The life of the singer, too, was shrouded in mystery. Blind Lemon Jefferson, Sleepy John Estes, Jaybird Coleman, Funny Paper Smith and Bogus Blind Ben Covington: bizarre names from a distant past about whom literally no facts were known. We were explorers in an uncharted land.

But most of all there was the vitality of the music itself. I knew it immediately, I still hear it today. And while I have gone on to any number of ancillary enthusiasms, it remains central in my life. For lesser attachments there are always explanations, but blues appealed to something deep-seated and permanent in myself, it just sounded right to me.

We never imagined we would see any of these shadowy figures from our mythology. We never dreamt that Son House, Skip James, Bukka White, Sleepy John Estes, all would be rediscovered. Part of the attraction, I'm sure, was that they were all tucked safely away in the past. For, as far as we were concerned, there were no contemporary blues singers. Encouraged by what we had read and helped by our own bias, we believed country blues to have stopped still with the Second World War and Lightnin' Hopkins, in Sam Charters' words, to be "the last of the great blues singers". We couldn't be bothered with such corruptions of style as amplification and popularity; we cavalierly dismissed Howlin' Wolf and Muddy Waters, as Charters had in his book. Instead we contented ourselves (at first anyway) with dubs from ancient 78s and our own elaborate fantasies. Robert Johnson we pictured as the tortured poet and tormented genius; Blind Lemon Jefferson froze to death in a snowstorm in Chicago. On Blind Willie McTell our imaginations really went to work. A sensitive, oddly wistful singer, he was, to us, a figure of mystery and determination, who had tenaciously clung to a recording career which stretched back to 1927. In 1935 he disappeared from sight only to resurface on some 1940 Library of Congress recordings. Then he was not heard from again until 1948 when, according to Charters, he just walked into the Atlantic recording studio and cut a record as great as any of his early sides. In 1961 Prestige announced an album of last sessions, but we didn't believe it. We expected him to walk in the door at any moment. Such was the stuff of which our dreams were made.

The first blues singer that we saw in the flesh was Sam "Lightnin'" Hopkins. He appeared at Harvard at the Agassiz Theatre in a concert with Cisco Houston. He was received with that air of reverential silence which has come to characterize these gatherings, and he was hailed to us as "the epitome of the cool Negro" by a boy with a very posh accent. What contempt we lavished upon that preppie then, but really, I think, he was just voicing our secret sentiments.

Gradually blues became an all-consuming passion and music a very important element in our lives. It cemented old friendships and made new ones. It became the principle vehicle for conversation and subject of discussion. This was at a time – 1961, '62 – when popular music was almost universally scorned. Blues was respectable enough, but no one could understand how we could go on listening to Chuck Berry and Little Richard, and among blues purists our fantasies of a comeback for Bo Diddley and Jerry Lee Lewis seemed almost perverse.

I think a not untypical incident will illustrate some of the confusions of that period. The first time we saw Bo Diddley he was appearing at Boston College in 1964 in an afternoon concert. Receiving equal billing with him were The Rooftop Singers, who had recently had an enormous hit with a very innocuous version of Gus Cannon's "Walk Right In". Just as the concert was due to begin The Rooftop Singers announced that they would not go on. Bo Diddley was a rock 'n' roll singer, and they were folk artists dedicated to their art. The start of the show was delayed about an hour, and eventually it had to be announced that the programme was worded wrongly, that two separate concerts were to be given here today, the first by The Rooftop Singers. Then, leaving no room for doubt, they did a full concert performance, and Bo Diddley did not go on till after five, when he responded with a two-hour show of his own.

It didn't matter that Bo Diddley proved infinitely more entertaining to the audience and that The Rooftop Singers were heckled off the stage. What was at stake was Integrity, and, difficult as it now is to believe, integrity was thought to reside entirely within the acoustic guitar or banjo or stringed instrument. That was what gave blues its respectability, of course. It was linked almost entirely in the public mind with the folk revival of that time. It was even called Folk Blues, and its chief appeal to an audience obsessed with sterile images of its own virtue was its unassailable purity.

As for us, we dreamt of a day when all musics would be equal, even as we envisioned the dawning of a new era of equality and social justice. Elvis Presley, Fats Domino, Carl Perkins, all would be accorded their place in the pantheon. On a more mundane level we could imagine that Jim Jackson's "Kansas City" might be updated by someone like Elvis, that "Trouble in Mind" might become a new popular standard. Little did we dream that something like this would actually happen, that a group like Canned Heat, named after a Tommy Johnson song, would enjoy considerable success with a revival of Henry Thomas's "Going Up the Country", complete with pan pipes. We didn't even know if anyone else was listening at the time. We just kept to ourselves, forming a tight self-contained little enclave with private quotes and private fantasies and a blues lyric for every occasion. Some of our finest moments came from such occasions as these, when you could say to a girl, "Honey honey honey honey honey/Get up off of that money" in the face of her bewilderment and our own smug satisfaction.

IV

I just got back from my tour over in England
Everybody talking about the rocking crave
*   over in England*
Well come on over, baby
Whole lotta shakin' going on.

                                                    Little Richard, 1964

I was in England in 1963, the year The Beatles first burst into prominence. *Melody Maker* posed the question, "Can The Beatles Make it with the U.S. Market Where Cliff Richard Failed?" and there was a great flurry of excitement in Miller's, the local music shop, the day "Twist and Shout" came out. For us, though, The Beatles were of minimal importance. Like Dylan before them they just seemed another imitation of American blues and rhythm and blues artists. What was important to us was the seriousness with which the British took blues and rock 'n' roll. Jerry Lee Lewis made the Top Ten in Cambridge with his version of "Good Golly Miss Molly", and his tour was highly touted in the musical press. In the short time that we were there tours were undertaken or proposed for such singers as Chuck Berry, Little Richard, Jerry Lee, Fats Domino and the second American Folk Blues Festival, which consisted of Sonny Boy Williamson, Muddy Waters and Big Joe Williams among others, none of whom we had had the opportunity to see at home. We bought records by Gene Vincent in Sweden and Speckled Red in Holland and came across a recognition of American genius which we had never encountered before. Not the least of which came from The Beatles themselves.

We haunted Dave Carey's Swing Shop on the outskirts of London, where you could not only pick up rare transcriptions by singers like Kokomo Arnold, Peg Leg Howell, Barbecue Bob, but actually engage in conversations with someone who knew and loved the music. In France we paid our respects at Bert Bradfield's

Carl Perkins and Paul McCartney/courtesy of Carl Perkins

Treasury of Jazz and listened to him mouth the lyrics of every Carl Perkins song we put on the record player. In Soho the salesgirl said, "Oh, that's the one where he chuckles, isn't it?" when we asked for Jerry Lee Lewis's "Mean Woman Blues". And we met a part-time mailman who played nothing but rock at his wedding and had rushed off from the reception to see Little Richard or Jerry Lee perform in person. Lots of crazy people, just as crazy as we were. We cut our own tour of the continent short to come back and Rock! Jive! Twist! Across the Channel with Jerry Lee Lewis. Which unfortunately we missed, and which for the second year in a row was denied landing at Bordeaux because of the rowdiness of the party. But I did get to see Gene Vincent, all dressed in leather from boots to gloves, leather jacket, leather vest, and leather pants, and flanked by sinister henchmen who escorted him on and offstage in tight formation to hide the limp in his walk. I sat through two boring hours of well-meant English tribute to hear a ten-minute set which culminated, of course, in "Be Bop-a-Lu-La" and a stiff-legged vault of the microphone wire. It was worth it.

When I came to England I had visions of settling there. I was disillusioned with the whole American system and thought the English much more respectful towards writers and democratic institutions. But after eight months of clipped speech and exaggerated politeness, after eight months of *articulateness,* I realized that what I was hungry for was hamburgers and ice cream sodas and baseball and bigness. Just like Chuck Berry said:

> *I'm so glad I'm living in the U.S.A.*
> *Where hamburgers sizzle on an open grille night and day*
> *Anything you want, they got it right here in the U.S.A.*

V

Dig these rhythm 'n' blues!
Chuck Berry

I think our development just about paralleled that of The Rolling Stones. When they first appeared they were a blues group almost exclusively, and one of the things that most appealed to us about them was that their taste corresponded so exactly with our own: Chuck Berry, Bo Diddley, Muddy Waters, and Little Walter. On their first American tour they made the obligatory stop in Chicago, and when they appeared on *Shindig* they brought along Howlin' Wolf and sat mutely at his feet while he shook and writhed, jumping up and down till it seemed as if the small stage would collapse, taking Wolf, Stones, and *Shindig* dancers along with it. With the debut of Wolf on network television and the popularity of his "Little Red Rooster," if only in The Stones' version, we were in our heaven.

But if The Stones merely served to confirm our belief in the blues, in soul music they played a truly educational function. I don't think I'd ever heard of Solomon Burke before The Stones recorded "Cry to Me." And though we listened to WILD, the local soul station, for whatever blues they might play, we were largely indifferent to the rest of the music. Otis Redding, Don Covay, Wilson Pickett, Marvin Gaye — these were just indiscriminate names to me before The Stones singled them out and deposited them in our homes (just as they deposited blues in the guise of rock 'n' roll for their larger audience) in songs like "Hitchhike," "Pain in My Heart," "Have Mercy." Because whatever else they have been, The Stones have always proved the best advertisement for American black music outside of the music itself. Where a group like The Beatles retreated quickly into studio seclusion and, more important, never really did anything to see that their influences were recognized, The Stones from the first have paid their respects.

They have recorded songs by artists as prominent as Muddy Waters and as obscure as Slim Harpo and the Reverend Robert Wilkins. They have showcased blues and rhythm and blues artists like Buddy Guy and Junior Wells, B.B. King, and Chuck Berry and even allowed themselves to be upstaged by James Brown (on film) and Ike and Tina Turner in person. It would be difficult to imagine many other performers paying such explicit dues, but then The Stones have always had a sense of high drama.

Of all their contributions to my own education, though, I would say that the one for which I was most grateful was the presence of James Brown in The Stones-headlined *T.A.M.I. Show* film. James Brown, of course, we had heard of, we knew his music a little, and his reputation as an entertainer preceded him. Nothing that we heard could have prepared us for what we saw even in the grainy, far-away

Mick Jagger with Howlin' Wolf

quality of the film. The dynamism, the tireless energy and unflagging zeal, the apocalyptic drama of his performance were all unprece- dented in our experience, and when we emerged from the theatre we had the idea that we could skate one-legged down Washington Street, defying gravity and astonishing passers-by. The Stones after that performance had been nothing more than an anti-climax, and we watched in silent approval as the blacks trooped out one by one, leaving the field to the latecomers.

We saw James Brown lots of times after that, in Providence, at the Arena, at the Boston Garden. And we started going to the r&b shows at Basin Street East and Louie's Showcase Lounge and the seasonal showers of stars, lonely white figures in a sea of black faces, isolated, quite solitary individuals in a mass of hand-slapping friends.

We took these shows as ceremonial occasions, really, for which we wore our best clothes and were put on our best behaviour. There was something exhilarating in being a part, however peripheral, of a community which engaged in such public celebrations of the spirit, and we soaked up a little bit of the warmth of that world, the excitement and colour of mutual recognition and greetings, great waddling old ladies flinging their arms around each other, children moving to the music, and hipsters bopping up and down the aisle. And then it was Star Time, Ladies and Gentlemen! although a great deal of the time the star wouldn't show or you couldn't hear anything over the crackling PA system or there would be some unexplained interminable delay or some terrible comedian would tell second-hand crude and raucously received jokes. None of it seemed to matter, though; no one seemed to mind very much. For most of the audience these were social occasions above all else. As for us we were fascinated by the whole swirling drama of that world, we delighted in the music and the exchange, the unashamed emotionalism and the whole panoply of the performance.

Solomon Burke with his great corpulent presence and gold cummerbund tied about a bulging waist. Otis puffy and in electric green. Joe Tex preaching and Rufus Thomas walking his dog. Little Anthony and the Imperials with their acrobatic displays and Moms Mabley croaking a message of tolerance and integration. Above all, the preaching, at gospel shows and secular revues alike, and the audience testifying in a body with "That's right!" and "Tell the truth!" and hands raised in a preview of the clenched fist salute. A

sense of real solidarity that might not survive the evening itself.

I can't say that we were ever exactly comfortable in these surroundings. In the beginning we were for the most part ignored, but by the time that Otis Redding died our presence was more and more openly resented and we frequently met with cold stares and hostile words. Whenever a fight broke out we started edging away for fear that its focus would shift to us, the conspicuous outsiders, and we went out of our way to avoid confrontations.

Stokely Carmichael kept telling us we had nothing to worry about, if we were afraid to set foot on the streets of Roxbury it was only because we were honky racist cowards. Why shouldn't he, after all, be just as afraid to enter the lily-white suburbs? Well, I didn't know about that, but I did know our situation was increasingly precarious. I kept excoriating myself for being a racist, but it didn't drown out my fear.

The last show we were going to see was James Brown at the Boston Garden in 1968. Two nights before the performance Martin

Luther King was assassinated. The show went on anyway, James Brown was widely credited with having cooled racial tempers in Boston, and it was a situation upon which everyone was to be congratulated — James Brown for his sense of responsibility and for performing the public service that he did; Mayor Kevin White for having allowed the show to go on at all; and Channel 2, the local NET outlet, for broadcasting it two or three times consecutively in an attempt to keep the kids off the streets. We stayed home and watched on TV, as James followed the by-now-familiar routine, mesmerizing the live audience with his grace and agility and the ritual conclusion of his act. At the end a couple of kids jumped up on stage, and then some more, and for a moment as the cops moved in it looked as if the fragile peace was about to be shattered after all. But James Brown indignantly motioned the cops back, his face furrowed with concern, as he pleaded with the kids, "Hey wait a

James Brown with valet, 1964/Don Paulsen

minute, wait a minute, that's not right. You ruining everything, you making me ashamed of my colour. What's it coming to if I can't get respect from my own people?"

We were far from it all, afraid to go out on the streets that night, and sorrowing in our own way for the death of a man and the death of a promise which held out nearly as much hope for us as whites as it did for any black.

VI

You say that music's for the birds
You can't understand the words
Well, honey, if you did, you'd really blow your lid
Baby, that is rock and roll.

The Coasters, 1959

The Man Can't Bust Our Music

Columbia Records, a Division of the
Columbia Broadcasting System, 1970

That was the difference of a decade. And perhaps it is the difference of a world. It is in any case indicative of the change in attitudes which took place and the difficulty rock 'n' roll would have maintaining itself as an effective counter-culture today. In the end everything gets absorbed into the cultural mainstream, and rock 'n' roll was no different. Today there are just too many other outlets for disaffiliation for it to serve a truly subversive function. They've even gone and changed the name, and what was once a kind of secret metaphor (like "ball" and "Miss Ann" and "brown-eyed handsome man") has become instead just another explicit Anglo-Saxon epithet.

Maybe it's wrong to question such a state of prosperity. With the success of The Beatles and The Rolling Stones all our old heroes were brought back to life. Not just Skip James and Son House but Chuck Berry and Little Richard, Carl Perkins and even Elvis himself awakened from his long Hollywood slumber. We made mad dashes of up to 250 miles to see Muddy Waters at Hunter College, Chuck Berry in his New York Concert Debut, Bo Diddley at the Ebb Tide and Jerry Lee Lewis at Canobie Lake Park in Salem, New Hampshire.

And, oddly enough, we were never disappointed. The old-time glamour, the practiced way in which they manipulated their audience, the thorough professionalism of a performance that hovered on the continual edge of hysteria never failed to appeal to a sense of ourselves that was rooted deeply within us. And yet that, too, in the end proved futile, as Little Richard got wrapped up more and more in the frenzy of his own claims and each artist confronted an audience that demanded not music so much as instant nostalgia. The spectacle of Chuck Berry relentlessly grinding out his old hits became more depressing than exhilarating after a while, and for all the exuberance of the performance, for all the mastery of the stage art an inescapable bitterness crept into the music itself.

The white artists have had a slightly better time of it, as they have one by one returned to the country field from which they first emerged, sometimes with notable success. Elvis Presley, of course, never had to look back, nor did Johnny Cash. But for Carl Perkins, Roy Orbison, Conway Twitty, Marty Robbins, Sonny James, there will always be a home in country music, whatever the fluctuations of the pop marketplace. And Jerry Lee Lewis, for a brief spell chief claimant to Elvis's throne, has remained a legend in the country field.

They're better off there. They're in touch with a real market that has stayed loyal to the kind of music they've played over the years. They're removed, too, from the scrutiny of the critics, and from books like this one which can only feed the growing self-consciousness of a music that was originally meant to deny the rigidity of claims. And they're playing to an audience of men and women very much like themselves, who grew up on a diet of hillbilly songs mixed in with Negro blues and made of rock 'n' roll at one time the truest kind of folk music.

Rock 'n' roll today, to my mind at least, is a middle-class phenomenon almost exclusively. What for us was a liberating act — like getting your licence or getting laid for the first time — has become part and parcel of the times and created a whole new set of definitions of its own. It is admirably eclectic, it offers a dazzling variety of choices within its own terms, and it has become in the process something a great deal more serious and infinitely less important.

That's why all attempts at revival are bound to fail. To bring it back you'd have to bring back the Eisenhower Era and the McCarthy Hearings. You'd have to bring back gang wars and the high school hop and all the crippling inhibitions of that time. For me rock 'n' roll was just what The Coasters said: a secret message delivered with a sneer and taken with a grain of salt. For us it was a source of endless energy and boundless amusement, and that it can have become camp in our time is only evidence of the terrible attrition of time and the voraciousness with which our culture devours its young.

At some point, obviously, the romance wore off. I'm sure there are lots of reasons. Getting older. Writing about music. The absence of political panaceas. The terrible surfeit of material. Just knowing too much. There are lots of things I don't like about some of the music — the loudness, the self-congratulation and lack of professionalism — but the one thing I find insufferable is that rock 'n' roll should become in its turn the same respectable and bland emulsifier that pop music was for us in 1954.

The Rolling Stones alone have retained the star image. It isn't always benign (as witness Altamont), but they are undeniably rock 'n' roll stars. And they sing rock 'n' roll music. The Beatles, whatever you may say of them, never really did that. Dylan is into something quite different. And Elvis is a ghost from a recollected past. But The Rolling Stones give us rock 'n' roll in all its glory, pimples and adolescent defiance, energy and endemic bad taste, with all the beauty and all the painful ugliness.

On their 1969 American tour they did the *Ed Sullivan Show* in somewhat muted form except for a blues that featured acoustic and slide guitar.

> *The blue light was my blues*
> *And the red light was my mind.*

It was Robert Johnson's "All My Love in Vain", thirty years after Johnson himself had died, resurrected on national TV in front of fifty million viewers. I thought to myself, what if Johnson himself were around to see this, and I could fantasize that he was alive somewhere in Mississippi or out in L.A. watching a TV he still owed payments on, and thinking — what? The only consolation must be that the music has been preserved.

CHAPTER 2
BLUES IN
HISTORY
A QUICK SKETCH

I

Blues takes in a lot of territory. If you confess to a liking for it, you open yourself to any number of responses. Oh, Louis Armstrong, someone will say. Bessie Smith. B.B. King. Ten Years After. Any one of them will be correct, because within a fairly narrow framework there exists a real multiplicity of styles. But if it's *country blues* that you're talking about, despite all the exposure and attention which have been lavished on the blues in recent years, it's unlikely that you're going to be able to make yourself clear. Because, somehow or other, this music, which is the background for all the flourishes and refinements and the underpinning for nearly all of today's popular music, has been obscured in each new phase of its development. Country blues, which was at first considered too disreputable to record, remains to this day too funky in a pejorative sense to merit serious attention.

Classic blues, it's true, was recorded first. The first blues to have been put on record seems to have been Mamie Smith's "Crazy Blues" (1920) and W.C. Handy, Clarence Williams, Perry Bradford all copyrighted and formally "composed" blues for the great women singers (Bessie Smith, Bessie Smith's mentor Ma Rainey, Clara Smith, Victoria Spivey). These blues were common property long before they were set down on paper, however, and if the recording of the classic blues singers stimulated a new period of growth for the country blues, W.C. Handy himself admitted, "Each one of my blues is based on some old Negro song of the South, some old song that is part of the memories of my childhood and my race. I can tell you the exact song I used as the basis for any one of my blues."

Instrumental jazz started out as the articulation of that same feeling, an ingenious approximation of the human voice. Certainly it went on to become something quite sophisticated of its own, but listen to Charles Mingus, or Coltrane, or Miles Davis and you'll hear wordless blues that go back to field hollers and slavery times. Ornette Coleman, the most committed of modernists, worked in countless rhythm and blues bands around Fort Worth; just a few years ago Charles Lloyd was boasting of his association with Howlin' Wolf twenty years before in West Memphis. Almost no black musician of any prominence will deny his roots or his blues heritage.

There are many popular misconceptions about the blues. For

Val Wilmer

37

Son House, Skip James and John Hurt/Dick Waterman

one thing it's thought to be an intensely personal music. Now, obviously, in certain instances it is. Robert Johnson sings as feelingly and with as direct an emotional thrust as can be imagined. Skip James was a unique and idiosyncratic stylist. Robert Pete Williams today invents blues which are free to the point of occasional anarchy. These are exceptions, however, to the general rule. For blues, like business, baseball, and other American inventions, is a highly conservative institution. Its structure is rigid, its lyrics derivative, and there is little place in its canon for oddness or eccentricity. "Don't pester me with your jazz or your how high the moon spodee-do. I don't play nothin' but blues," says Howlin' Wolf. And for most musicians that just about covers it. Blues is a twelve-bar structure, three-line verse, the words rhyme and most frequently derive from a common pool of lyrics or "floating verses". To Furry Lewis the most important thing is to rhyme the verses up. "It got to be rhymed up if you call yourself being with the blues. If it ain't rhymed up it don't sound good to me or nobody else." Each singer has his own individual way of expressing himself, but there is a common thread of ideas as well as lyrics which enables almost any blues player to sit in with any other, and some of the most notable collaborations on record have been the result of chance studio meetings which would not have been possible in any other music.

We thought of blues, when we first took it up, as protest music. This, too, seems a vast misconception, even though much of the literature on the subject continues to see it as a reflection of sociological conditions and a commentary on the black man's lot. Most blues unfortunately don't even deal with the subject, and, unless passing references and veiled allusions can be said to constitute a body of protest music, blues is for the most part singularly free of even the most casual reference to these conditions.

Lightnin' Hopkins, it's true, could deal with such considerations quite explicitly in "Tim Moore's Farm." Whether this derived from personal experience or, as is more likely (from the evidence of Johnny Shines' brilliant "Mr. Tim Green's Farm" and numerous Texas versions), from a commonly shared folk tradition, there is no question that it was deeply felt and sharply observed:

> *Now Mr. Tim Moore's a man*
> *He don't never stand and grin*
> *He just say, keep out of the graveyard*
> *I'll save you from the pen.*

Skip James, too, dealt with uncharacteristic bluntness with the Depression in "Hard Time Killing Floor Blues":

> *Now the people all drifting*
> *From door to door*
> *Can't find no heaven, I don't care where they go.*

There are other songs that might be cited, but they are, really, isolated instances and blues for the most part confines itself to a very restricted range of subjects: women and whiskey but rarely social conditions; sexual but never political innuendo.

Blues as poetry. That was another well-intentioned romance on our part. There are blues singers, it is true, who might be considered poets. Robert Johnson, for instance, chooses his images with sufficient care to bear repetition on the printed page. Johnny Shines, too, employs often startling imagery, and the explicit autobiography of Sleepy John Estes (or on a more instinctive level Robert Pete Williams) is at its best a vivid, strikingly "poetic" document. Most blues, however, consist of no more than a series of unrelated verses strung together at random, and for most blues singers the words are of only secondary importance. Skip James, for example, as intimate and personal a singer as he is, fails to put a distinctive stamp on most of the blues *lyrics* that he sings. Singers like Howlin' Wolf and Elmore James and even Muddy Waters seem to care scarcely at all for the words that they are singing. What meaning there is they convey not through words but through feeling and intonation. Elmore James sounds constantly on the edge of hysteria. Wolf

Sleepy John Estes/Val Wilmer

suggests menace with his magnificently expressive voice. It's not that what they sing is trivial exactly. It's just that it does not entirely reflect what they are singing about.

What almost every blues does possess is a shared feeling for love and loss. Wit and irony, paradox, a metaphorical reclamation of reality — these are the property of nearly every blues singer. In this sense the blues might be considered poetry, but it is the tradition, not the individual blues singer, which is the poet. Lines like "Did you ever dream lucky, wake up cold in hand?", "They arrest me for forgery but I can't sign my name," "You can read my letter but you sure can't read my mind/Well, you thought I was loving but I was leaving you all the time," and phrases like "laughing just to keep from crying," "easy rider" and "old-time used-to-be" show up in song after song, and the grimly ironic personification of the blues ("Good morning, blues, blues how do you do?") tells a story as true as any individual invention.

What is blues then? Well, it's a lot easier to keep on saying what blues is not. It isn't necessarily sad music. It doesn't tell a story. It neither makes nor alludes to minor chords. It is for the most part self-accompanied. It follows certain basic progressions (I-IV-V-IV-I or tonic, subdominant, dominant chord patterns). It is not a music of particular technical accomplishment. In the end you come back to the familiar conundrum; if you have to ask, well then you're just not going to understand. Because blues after all is little more than a feeling. And what could be more durable or more fleeting and ephemeral than just that?

II

What is popular has never corresponded to what is good. Or at least what is judged after the fact to be worthwhile rarely turns out to have been especially prized at the time. There is a mythology that black audiences are more discriminating than white, and in the sense that they have foreshadowed all the trends in popular culture from walk and talk to hip life style, there is a certain element of truth in that. On the other hand, I have seen black audiences as hoodwinked as white by the shallowest kind of trickery. And I've seen singers like B.B. King or Bobby Bland, ignored and humiliated by their own people, put on a show that obviously reflected their reception, then perform brilliantly with the encouragement of whites. It is largely a question of fashion, I suppose, and fashions have a habit of making the rounds.

Blues is certainly no exception. It was, to begin with, a popular music. Its very popularity in fact influenced recording trends and tended to place upon it a far greater emphasis than it enjoyed in the community. It has always been a commercial vehicle, and particularly so because it is so adaptable a form.

In the twenties jug bands were popular; in the thirties it was the hokum bands. Tampa Red must have gone through thirty versions of "It's Tight Like That," a banal repetitive melody that persists to this day. Ragtime, minstrel music, and even female impersonations (in the person of Frankie Jaxon, Tampa Red's associate) were always immensely popular while a country singer like Arthur Crudup confesses, "I never thought about making money by music, other than recording."

Of the more straightforward blues singers, Big Bill Broonzy virtually dominated the thirties both on his own records and on the records of friends like Jazz Gillum, Sonny Boy Williamson, and Washboard Sam. Artists like Blind Willie McTell or Robert Johnson, for instance, were virtually unknown, and in fact there is scarcely an instance of a blues singer with a distinctive personal style who has achieved widespread popularity. Since the war, of course, Muddy Waters, Howlin' Wolf, and particularly Lightnin' Hopkins and John Lee Hooker gained considerable followings. But it was B.B. King — like Lonnie Johnson before him, a much more urbane singer and guitarist — who really captured the mass audience, first of blacks, then of whites. Blues to this day remains too parochial a concern; country blues, at least, presents too rough and forbidding an exterior to reap the rewards that more sophisticated practitioners from Leroy Carr and Peetie Wheetstraw down through Charles Brown and Louis Jordan have enjoyed.

There is ample evidence in addition that the record companies tailored their artists to suit existing trends. Blues itself, for example, is only one of many forms of country music that were popular at the time. Reels, jigs, fiddle tunes, and two-step dance music all abounded at the picnics and country frolics that were the principal focus for musical entertainment at the start of the century.

42

Furry Lewis/Dick Waterman

It was blues that caught the public's fancy, however, and the recording of blues to the exclusion of all other forms undoubtedly led to the extinction of the pre-blues forms. It is only in recent years in fact that the emergence of songsters like Mance Lipscomb, sixty-six years old when he was first discovered in Navasota, Texas, and Mississippi John Hurt, who first recorded for Okeh in 1928, has indicated the vast recesses of that tradition. But blues singers, for the most part, sang blues exclusively on record. (There were exceptions: Henry Thomas, a Texas songster who played the panpipes and was nicknamed "Ragtime Henry"; an older singer like Peg Leg Howell or Frank Stokes, who would slip in a reel or buck dance or minstrel tune once in a while.) In many cases it is likely that their popularity simply ran out, and what we are left with are the one or two songs which they or the field scout considered their best numbers. Of all the country blues singers only Charley Patton and Blind Lemon Jefferson indicated on record their true range of talents and revealed a truly extensive repertoire. To our great good fortune their popularity was such that they got to record a great number of songs in an uncharacteristic variety of styles.

Blind Lemon Jefferson, a native of Wortham, Texas, travelled extensively all through the South. He is remembered as far east as Virginia and the Carolinas, and he seems to have been a formative influence in the lives of nearly as many white musicians as black ones. Just how important an artist he really was can be seen from the number of reminiscences you encounter even today from musicians who could have been no more than small children when he died in 1929. And perhaps more to the point, it must be remembered, he was not appearing in vaudeville houses or theatres, he was playing in the streets in front of the local grocery or feed store or just at the biggest crossroads for crowds far fewer in number than would have filled a small theatre.

What Blind Lemon Jefferson sang was, of course, blues. Because he was one of the first country bluesmen to record, many of his lyrics would seem to have originated with him. But whether this is so or not, he was a striking and individual singer with a high piercing voice and a singular talent for blues poetry. "Black Snake (Mmmmm, black snake crawling in my room)" was his most famous number, and in it he combined the familiar double-entendre of the blues with a richer kind of imagery. Due to considerations of time and undoubtedly because of musical conventions of the day there was little room in his music for guitar solos or instrumental embroidery, but his sprung-rhythm single string guitar work was distinctive and immediately recognizable and gave rise to a whole school of bluesmen who came to imitate the form if not the tone of his idiosyncratic playing. He did record "Hot Dogs," a ragtime piece and some pre-blues like "Begging Back" and "Shuckin' Sugar" as well as his justly renowned hymn, "See That My Grave Is Kept Clean."

Lemon's music was echoed in its day by the work of Texas artists like Little Hat Jones, Texas Alexander, Alabama-born Edward Thompson and, more recently, by Alexander's cousin, Lightnin' Hopkins. In his guitar style, too, Lemon influenced the Texas native Aaron "T Bone" Walker, whose deft single-string guitar work became the standard in post-war blues, influencing in its turn Mississippi-born B.B. King, and through King almost all of the contemporary school of black and white blues players. There is no question of the brilliance of Jefferson's style, and the state of Texas deserves a whole book in itself — which it is going to get in a definitive study by Paul Oliver and Mack McCormick. But it is, in a sense, a dead end, a back-water tradition which developed on its own. Except for the rather tenuously developed B.B. King line, Texas has remained a kind of isolated pocket in history.*

Not so with Mississippi. The blues we hear today are almost all Mississippi-derived and -influenced. Muddy was born in Mississippi.

*Walker, after all, worked with the big bands, and an equal case might be made for the influence of Lonnie Johnson's jazz-like phrasing on him, as indeed King points to Django Reinhardt as a formative influence.

Blind Lemon Jefferson/Blues Unlimited

So was Wolf. Elmore James, Jimmy Reed, John Lee Hooker, Skip James, Sonny Boy Williamson, Elvis Presley — all spent their formative years in Tunica, Ita Bena, Tupelo, taking as a matter of course the harsh terms of a world which seems so far removed from us today. Nor is it simply a matter of geographical situation. Singers like Bo Diddley and Otis Rush, who grew up in Chicago, carry with them their Delta roots. Memphis singers like Furry Lewis, Frank Stokes, Robert Wilkins show unquestionable stylistic debts. There is in fact a clear stylistic progression from Charley Patton through Muddy Waters and Johnny Shines right up to the present day. Son House, Robert Johnson, Elmore James, all are in the direct line of descent. And while it might be stretching a point to see it as a matter of pure inheritance, it is something much more than a convenient grouping. For our purposes I think it is enough to say that the blues came out of Mississippi, sniffed around in Memphis and then settled in Chicago where it is most likely it will peacefully live out the rest of its days.

III

Charley Patton was born in 1891 on a farm outside Edwards, Mississippi. The facts of his life are vague though the research of Bernard Klatzko and Gayle Wardlow has turned up a sister and the last of his common-law wives. He appears to have spent most of his early years, like nearly every one of the Mississippi blues singers, on the plantations, and it was at Will Dockery's, where he lived until around 1921, that he came in contact with Tommy Johnson, Roebuck Staples, Willie Brown. Unlike most blues singers, who made their living from sharecropping or driving a tractor or working a section gang, Patton towards the end of his life anyway seems to have lived off his music. He moved from plantation to plantation, playing at picnics and country suppers and the jook joints out in the logging and turpentine camps. It was a rough life, a violent life, and Patton seems to have gotten into his share of trouble. He moved around a lot, though, and built up a considerable local reputation.

All the blues singers remember him. "Oh, he was a great man," said Bukka White upon his own rediscovery. "I always wanted to be like him when I was a kid a long time ago and I said if I ever live to get halfway grown I wants to come to be a great man like ol' big Charley Patton." Son House, too, recalls him vividly, if in slightly less exalted circumstances:

> I remember one night Willie [Willie Brown] and I and Charley were to play at the same place and Willie and I were late, but Charley had gotten there kind of early. And the guys got off the centre kind of early, too. Got to fighting and shooting off those old owl-head pistols. Well, Willie and I got near to the house, and we heard such a gruntin' and a rattlin' coming up through the stalks, and I said, 'Wait a minute, Willie. Hold it. I hear something coming up through the cotton field. Don't you hear it?' He said, 'Yeah. It's something.' We were always suspicious, you know, about animals. Out in the country around there it wouldn't be anything to see a teddy-bear or something. So we got the idea we wanted to hurry up and get to the road where we could see it. Finally, who should pop out to the roadside but Charley! He looked and saw us and said, 'I'll kill 'em all. I'll kill 'em all.' Me and Willie started laughing and told him, 'How you gon' kill 'em all? We heard you running.'*

House is an old man today himself, and his memories are sometimes a little jumbled. If his factual data is of doubtful accuracy, the mood is undeniably authentic.

What is undoubtedly most difficult to envision about the blues is the context in which it took place. The barrel houses and jook joints, and packed steaming rooms jammed with couples doing the lindy and two-step, the slow drag and buzzard lope, the hard-drinking, boisterous, fierce and exultant atmosphere — these are almost as difficult, I think, for a young black audience as a white one to imagine. It's something that exists almost entirely peripheral to our experience and a visit to a Chicago gin-mill — crowded, grimy, noisy, full of good times — is the closest approximation you can get to the experience, and only a rough one at that. "What I mean about this," Otis Spann told Paul Oliver, "when a musician — they all know one another — they all gets to a place and they sits down to a piano and they starts to barrelhousin'. And what I mean by barrel-housin' — barrelhousin' it mean store-porchin', and store-porchin' it means one man be playing a piano, and when he start to playin' he done either lost all his money at the gamblin' table or he don't have

---

*This is from Julius Lester's fine interview with Son House (which originally appeared in *Sing Out,* Vol. XV, No.3), as are all other quotes by House.

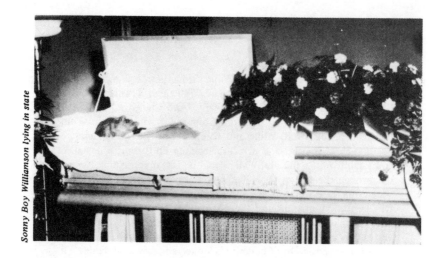

enough money to get in the gamblin' game! When coloured people wants to have places to go ... in Belzoni, Mississippi the only places they *could* go is to a honkytonk on the weekend, and so they gits down to the honkytonk and they have a wonderful time amongst theyselves. They have fish fries and they have gamblin' in the back, and sometimes they be fighting in the back and in the front and so forth. But they be fightin' 'mongst theyselves and don't nothin' ever happen, you understand ..." And this, I think, is what he is talking about. It is the atmosphere in which the blues developed, the world in which the music grew up, and the vitality without which it cannot survive.

Charley Patton was ideally suited for this milieu. A slight light-skinned man, he was endowed with a powerful rasping voice and a real propensity to entertain. Some blues singers think less of him for this. Son House, for example, considered him a kind of clown. He would rap on his guitar and throw it up in the air, his vocal asides have the air of vaudeville commentary, and he was not always overly scrupulous about the sense of his blues. He was the best kind of entertainer, though, for these crowded dances and balls: powerful, extroverted, durable, and compelling. And he was immensely popular all through the Delta region.

What is perhaps most surprising about Charley Patton is that he got a chance to record as much as he did. Local reputation, of course, meant something. But Mance Lipscomb, Henry Stuckey, Bubba Brown, all had extensive local reputations and never got on record at all. Someone like Blind Lemon Jefferson travelled so widely that it might have been expected that he would come to the attention of some record company. But Charley Patton was discovered exclusively through the agency of H.C. Speir, a Jackson record dealer and talent scout who discovered Son House, Skip James, and Tommy Johnson as well. How he came to Patton we don't know, but Skip James describes an audition in his Jackson store which drew over one hundred local contestants, with each given a few minutes to sing a verse or two of his number one song. And Speir, with his remarkable eye for talent, could scarcely overlook Patton.

The first title that Paramount released was his signature tune, "Pony Blues." In the course of the next five years Patton recorded nearly seventy titles, including spirituals, ragtime, pre-blues, bottle-neck pieces and popular songs of the day. Mixed in among these are place names, people's names, dates, drinking incidents, all memorialized as part of a sometimes explicit, often confusing autobiographical narrative which is further obscured by Patton's habit of trailing off in the middle of syllables and lines. Close listening more than rewards attention, however, and all in all Charley Patton's recorded work represents perhaps the best documentation of any country blues singer (except for Blind Lemon Jefferson) and the breadth of his repertoire on record exceeds even that of Jefferson.

Perhaps more to the point, Patton was a superb artist. There are traces on record of the kind of clowning that Son House complains about, but the tone for the most part suits the dark brooding qualities of his voice. Charley Patton, on record, is among the most intense of blues singers. He sometimes growls more than sings, which makes the business of understanding lyrics even more difficult. It contributes as well to the overwhelming force of his vocals. He played guitar in a number of styles, always strongly percussive, and he showed an extraordinary sense of dynamics, alternating between a harsh whisper and a rasped shout, slurring a word or purposely dropping a syllable, introducing spoken interjections, and making full use of a voice whose range comes across even on the scratchiest of records made under the most primitive of recording conditions. That he was the most powerful of performers is borne out by the fact that he still retains this ability to move us today, that there remains this intensity and force even across so wide a gulf of years and culture. When you listen to Charley Patton today you can't help but conjure up not only the commanding presence of the man himself but the strong suggestion of a world that has all but passed.

IV

"We'd all play for the Saturday night balls, Willie and I and Charley. Them country balls were rough! They were critical, man! They'd start off good, you know. Everybody happy, dancing, and then they'd start to getting louder and louder. The women would be dipping that snuff and swallowing that snuff spit along with that corn whiskey, and they'd start to mixing fast, and oh, brother! They'd start something then!"

Son House had a deeper, more regular and pleasing voice than Charley Patton. His songs were more rhythmically accented and less subject to Patton's unpredictable flights of fancy. They were at the same time no less powerful or intense, and when Charley Patton died in 1934 it was House who was his principal heir.

House was born around 1902 just outside of Clarksdale. He spent a good part of his boyhood in Louisiana, where his father played in a marching band. It wasn't until he came back to Mississippi, though, around 1926, that he really got interested in the blues or even took up guitar. There he came under the influence first of James McCoy and Willie Wilson and then of Charley Patton. When he met Patton he was twenty-seven years old and had only been playing the guitar for three years, performing mostly the pieces of Wilson and McCoy.

Together with Patton and Willie Brown (who generally just seconded or "complemented" on guitar) he's still remembered around the Delta. Howlin' Wolf has credited him as an early influence and Muddy Waters recalls how impressed he was. "Seem like everybody could play some kind of instrument and there were so many fellers playin' in the jukes around Clarksdale I can't remember them all. But the best we had to my ideas was Sonny House," he told Paul Oliver. "I was really behind Son House all the way." There are many similarities to Waters, of course: the heaviness of tone; the

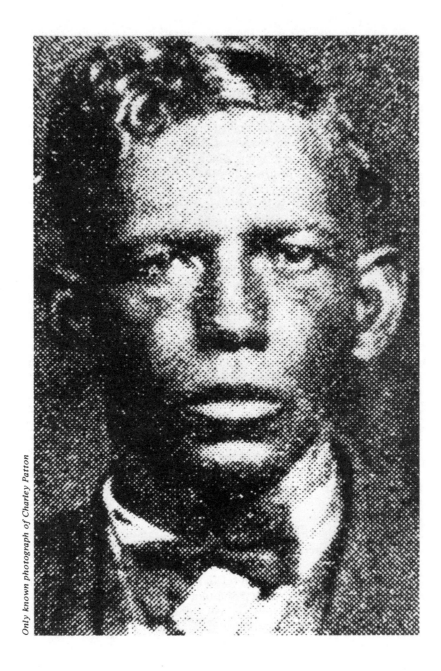

Only known photograph of Charley Patton

stolid insistence on the beat; the dark coloration of voice. But House put a degree of passion and intensity into his singing which differs from Muddy's more phlegmatic emotional manner. Indeed each song becomes for him an almost transcendent experience.

He first came to record through Charley Patton. Patton brought him to H.C. Speir, and Speir packed them all up — Patton, House, Willie Brown, and a teenage pianist named Louise Johnson — and sent them up to Grafton, Wisconsin. There Patton did four numbers and House recorded ten titles which met with little commercial success. After that he returned to Mississippi and the Saturday night balls and fish fries with which he enlivened his life. During the day he was a tractor driver Willie Brown sharecropped, but "Charley wouldn't do either one. He'd try to be slick. He'd take up with the white folks' cook. He was a slicker, you know."

House came to record again for the Library of Congress in 1941 by accident. He happened to be in Lake Cormorant when Alan Lomax passed through there on a field recording trip, and when he came back a year later Lomax took the trouble to look him up. As a result we have fifteen superlative sides, among which is a fine adaptation of Patton's "Pony Blues."

In 1943 he moved to Rochester and took a job with the New York Central Railroad. About a year later Willie Brown joined him. Brown left to go back home, though, and in 1952 died of the effects of alcohol. "I got a telegram from his girl that Willie was dead. I said, 'Well, sir, all my boys are gone.' That was when I stopped playing. After he died I just decided I wouldn't fool with playing any more. I don't even know what I did with the guitar."

He was rediscovered in 1964 by white blues enthusiasts and with some prompting returned to performing. Although his voice remains strong he suffers from a tremor which reduces his guitar-playing abilities and an apparent incapacity to recall more than nine or ten songs. Because of this every performance is something of a traumatic experience both for him and for the audience (it's as much a question whether he'll survive as whether he'll get through a coherent set). But on his good days he recalls a little bit the music of the Delta thirty years ago and what it must have been like for Muddy and Johnny Shines and the blues singers of our own day to hear him and Charley Patton, with Willie Brown seconding them on guitar. His music is still marked by a fixed and insistent rhythm, a powerful if repetitive guitar accompaniment in the familiar bottle-neck style, and that exceptional vocal control which he claims to have gotten from his years as choir director. His voice remains, with its deep resonance and rich tonal variety, one of the most glorious vehicles which the blues has ever seen, and some of his most affecting pieces today are sung *a capella*.

What he is most remembered for now, however — and undoubtedly what captures the imagination of his young audiences — is that he was the teacher of Robert Johnson. This is not, of course, strictly true. Just as he learned from Charley Patton and a whole variety of sources, what Robert picked up from him was by no means the extent of his musical education. But he was undeniably in the direct line of descent from Patton and House to Muddy Waters and Elmore James. And he represented the fruition, the perfect crystallization of an entire tradition.

"We'd all play for the Saturday night balls and there'd be this little boy standing around. That was Robert Johnson. He blew a harmonica then, and he was pretty good with that, but he wanted to play a guitar. His mother and stepfather didn't like for him to go out to these Saturday night balls because the guys were so rough. But he'd slip away anyway." He'd sit at their feet, by House's account, and play during the breaks. "And such another racket you'd never heard. It'd make the people mad, you know." Then he went away, and Son didn't see him for a while. When he came back they let him sit in one evening on a bet. "So he sat down there and finally got started. And man! He was so good. When he finished all our mouths were standing open. I said, 'Well, ain't that fast! He's gone now!'"

Not much is known for certain about Robert Johnson: House's recollections; Johnny Shines' reminiscences about two years they spent together hoboing around the country; Muddy Waters' affir-mation of his influence; the fragmented memories of blues singers like Henry Townsend and Honeyboy Edwards — that's about all. Not even a picture exists, although Johnny Shines recalls that he had a bad eye and looked a lot like the contemporary Chicago blues singer, Buddy Guy*. But he was undoubtedly, for all the conflicting claims

*In the early 1970s folklorist Mack McCormick discovered wives, sisters, children, and several other living relatives of Johnson's, as well as a handful of photographs. As of 1988 only one of these photographs had been published—once officially, and then by Steve LaVere—but McCormick's long-awaited book should clear up many of the mysteries of Johnson's life and death.

that are made about him, the most important and most influential of all the country blues singers.

One reason for the widespread nature of his influence was that he travelled so much. Unlike Blind Lemon Jefferson and Charley Patton, he never got to record a great deal (his entire recorded output is confined to two Texas sessions in 1936 and 1937; when Vocalion sought him for a third he was already dead); but he travelled even more extensively than either one. Johnny Shines recalls playing all through Texas, Arkansas, and Tennessee. "Then in the spring of '37 we hit Kentucky, Illinois, Indiana, Michigan, Windsor, Ontario, then Michigan again, and New York." Contrast this to a singer like Arthur Crudup, who never left Mississippi except to record, or Johnny Shines himself for that matter ("I just considered that I was tagging along.") and you get a pretty good idea of why he should have reached so many people. He came into town, unlike Blind Lemon, without prior publicity. He quickly made a reputation for himself, however, and it is a question whether he left more disciples or broken-hearted women behind.

It was a woman who was supposed to have done him in some time around 1938 or 1939. The story is that she poisoned him; Son House heard that he had been stabbed to death. It doesn't really matter. When he died, as when he lived, he was undoubtedly alone.

There are any number of reasons for the reputation he has achieved since his death. There is, to begin with, his music. Then there is his tragic death and the lack of any real knowledge of the facts of his life. Almost as much as either of these elements, however, is the fact that Robert Johnson fulfilled in every way the requisite qualities of the blues myth. Doomed, haunted, dead at an early age; desperate, driven, a brief flickering of tormented genius.

Not one of his songs fails to bear out these romantic associations. "Got to keep moving, got to keep moving, blues falling down like hail/And the days keep 'minding me/There's a hellhound on my trail." "I got stones in my passway, and my road seems dark as night." "Me and the devil was walking side by side/I'm going to beat my woman till I get satisfied." "Early this morning when you knocked upon my door/And I said, Hello, Satan, I believe it's time to go."

In his brief lifetime Robert Johnson absorbed a good many influences — Lonnie Johnson, the Delta bluesmen, Kokomo Arnold,

Elmore James

Scrapper Blackwell. What made his work unique, however, was an uncommon ability to synthesize these influences and a poetic sensibility which drew its inspiration from highly disparate sources and transformed them into a startling new blend. Every one of his blues is a carefully worked out composition, and the lyrics are the highest flowering of the blues language.

The music is more than a match for the words to which it is set. His voice — more accessible in its light, clear, slightly nasal tone than Charley Patton's or other Delta bluesmen — possesses a passionate intensity which is emphasized by the choked manner into which he will sometimes fall. Son House didn't like his voice, apparently because it was not always fully under control, but this is testimony as much to his emotional engagement with his material as any lack of native ability. Johnson was, according to House, a much better guitarist than singer, and from his records it is evident that he was highly accomplished in a number of styles. The most striking of these, however, was the familiar bottleneck style of the Delta, which he adapted to the nervous rhythms of his music with devastating effect. "This sound affected most women in a way that I could never understand," said Johnny Shines. "I said he had a talking guitar and many a person agreed with me."

That he was a deliberate, highly conscious artist is borne out by the extent and breadth of his repertoire. It has come down to us over the years in the adaptations by countless singers of such songs as "Dust My Broom," "Sweet Home Chicago," "Stop Breaking Down," and "Rambling on My Mind." Robert Jr. Lockwood and Walter Horton in "Little Boy Blue" both took a song that Johnson sang but never recorded and made it into a post-war standard, and Lockwood's version of another unrecorded Johnson blues, "Take a Little Walk with Me" is a classic. ("I only know two women who might have been very close [to Johnson], and that was Shakey Horton's sister and Robert Lockwood Jr.'s mother," said Johnny Shines, and Lockwood calls himself Junior after the man he claims to have been his stepfather.) Just a year or two ago The Rolling Stones adapted his "All My Love in Vain" and used it as one of the most effective vehicles on their album, *Let It Bleed.*

Elmore James took Robert Johnson's "Dust My Broom" and made a career of it. James, a contemporary of Johnson's and Johnny Shines', apparently ran with him just after Shines but didn't get to record himself until 1950. His version of "Dust My Broom" (recorded for the Trumpet label in Jackson, Mississippi with Sonny Boy Williamson on harp) followed Johnson's lyrics very closely and incorporated a riff which Johnson used frequently in his bottleneck recordings but which had not appeared in the original of that particular song. James during the fifties became very popular – his slashing bottleneck style, the wild surge of energy and a taut almost hysterical voice approximated the feeling if not the form of Johnson's art – and he was for a time widely influential. It was through him undoubtedly that songs like "Rambling" and "Crossroads" became virtual standards in the South fifteen years after their creator's death, and he contributed along with Muddy Waters,

Johnny Shines, and Robert Jr. Lockwood in Chicago to keeping the whole Delta tradition alive.

There were, of course, sidetracks along the way. Arthur Crudup grew up in Mississippi and never played in any definable tradition Tommy McClennan and Robert Petway approximated the rough-voiced vocal tones of Charley Patton but didn't play bottleneck guitar at all. Tony Hollins strongly influenced John Lee Hooker, who in turn is one of the most successful and most individual of

Bukka White / David Gahr

58

post-war stylists. Other blues singers like Skip James and Robert Pete Williams (a Lousiana bluesman who has few links to any recognized tradition) grew up almost altogether apart from the influence of their contemporaries. There was, it's true, a Bentonia school which grew up around James's music, but Williams developed his blues virtually unobstructed and both represent a case of cultural isolation and the idiosyncratic nature of the blues.

Bukka White and Big Joe Williams, too, were both extremely arresting and significant artists, but they don't seem to have influenced anyone appreciably. White, inspired by Charley Patton, put together one of the most moving, personal and autobiographical documents in the history of the blues when he recorded for Vocalion in 1940, shortly after his release from prison. The delicate bottleneck, the haunting, almost impressionistic lyrics are among the highest achievements of the blues. Williams, in more recent years a striking reincarnation of Charley Patton with his thick heavy voice, bass-slapping accompaniment and strong country rhythms, has for years played his battered self-styled invention, the nine-string guitar, and travelled back and forth across the continent, the image of the itinerant blues singer even into his seventies. He is a great and powerful blues singer demonstrably within the Mississippi tradition, yet without visible heirs.

More important from the standpoint of influence was Tommy Johnson, a Jackson blues singer around whom a whole school grew up. Johnson, in fact, a native of Crystal Springs, is the only real rival of Patton in terms of influence, and just who originated the melody line for Patton's "Saddle My Pony" has been the subject of hot debate among blues researchers for some time now.

He represents quite a contrast in terms of style to Patton. Quiet, subdued, essentially lyrical, with a highly developed sense of melody and an intricate guitar part which varies little from song to song, his music is characteristically punctuated by a wordless and moving falsetto cry.

> *Canned heat, oh canned heat, mama,*
> *Canned heat is killing me*

he sings in one of his better-known songs, and it is that same sense of wistful regret which marks all his compositions. Unlike Patton or

59

Jefferson or even Robert Johnson (whose twenty-nine titles make at least a respectable legacy), Johnson recorded very little for a singer of his eminence. Virtually every song that he did record, however, became something of a classic, and some measure of his popularity may be gained from the number of versions of his songs that were released by artists as popular as Floyd Jones in the fifties or the Mississippi Sheiks in his day and the fidelity with which singers like Roosevelt Holts and Shirley Griffith will today recall his songs. "Big Fat Mama," "Big Road Blues," "Maggie Campbell," "Cool Drink of Water" — each one is a carefully worked out and beautifully achieved arrangement. Every one has permanently entered the language of the blues.

One of the singers most influenced by Tommy Johnson was, oddly enough, Howlin' Wolf. Oddly, because Wolf was to begin with almost a pure product of Charley Patton — one of the few younger singers who could match the intensity in Patton's voice with an equal ferocity of his own. It seems a double irony that he should have been so taken with Johnson's lyrical style in that he never met Johnson himself and seems scarcely aware of the authorship of some of the Johnson songs in his repertoire. Johnson did not make much of an impression except with his music, but there is no question that Wolf absorbed a great deal from this alone. The songs themselves, the falsetto cry (Wolf's howl), the peculiar delicacy mixed in with Patton's rough vocal tones make a unique and compelling combination, and Howlin' Wolf achieved in his own way a strikingly independent synthesis of Mississippi styles which would influence even more widely the music of another generation.

In 1943 Muddy Waters moved to Chicago. Johnny Shines had already arrived two years earlier gandy-hopping on his way to Africa. Upon his father's death Wolf moved to West Memphis in 1948, five years after John Lee Hooker had arrived in Detroit from a job cleaning out the W.C. Handy movie theatre on Beale Street. With them the music of the Delta moved into the cities and with it the peculiar solitude and cultural isolation out of which the blues had grown was forever shattered.

We'll never know what Howlin' Wolf's music of the thirties sounded like. Son House remembers him playing around 1938 in the streets of Robinsonville with one of the first electric guitars House had ever seen and a rack harmonica. By the time he was recorded, though, he had formed a band and already had a chance to absorb the boogie style of Memphis which permeated so much of John Lee Hooker's work. It was this boogie style – jump tunes, overamplification, driving rhythms, country time – incidentally, out of which rock 'n' roll was to grow. Sam Phillips, the man who recorded virtually all of the Memphis singers – Wolf and Walter Horton, Little Junior Parker and B.B. King – went on himself to start Sun Records, a blues label until record No. 209 which featured a white singer from Tupelo, Mississippi doing a blues tune by Arthur "Big Boy" Crudup. Elvis Presley was in the Memphis tradition – he sang a vibrant up-tempo jump-styled number featuring his own voice and a heavily amplified lead guitar – but his success hastened the death of the blues. As rock 'n' roll gained greater and greater success, with black as well as white audiences, the existence of a separate, highly specialized music for a very limited segment of the population came more and more into doubt. Rock 'n' roll broke down cultural as well as racial barriers.

The story of Chess Records in Chicago is no more than an illustration of this process. A white-owned, black-oriented company whose success was ensured by the popularity of Muddy Waters' Delta-styled blues in the late forties and early fifties, their focus was completely changed by the advent of rock 'n' roll. Singers like Chuck Berry and Bo Diddley (like Little Richard on Specialty, a gospel-styled blues singer screaming pop-oriented lyrics) represent the reaction by blacks to a white adaptation of their own music. Chuck Berry and Bo Diddley are in essence blues singers, but with the success of their novelty styles there was no place for singers like Muddy and Wolf and, until their discovery by a white audience in recent years, they were leaders looking for their people, preachers who had been deserted by their flock.

It's a process which is saddening but as inevitable as time. Big Joe Turner, musing on the vagaries of a career which saw him start out as a Kansas City shouter, become one of the founding voices of rock 'n' roll, and today return to a semi-obscure kind of limbo, once insisted, "For a fact rock 'n' roll ain't no different from the blues, we just pepped it up a lot. Man, that music was in the blues bag all the time ... It's all trends," he went on. "They come and go. It seems like every twenty years the world jumps off and gets happy. It's going to explode again. You just be there when it jumps.'

61

CHAPTER 3
MUDDY WATERS
GONE TO MAIN STREET

I

Muddy Waters lives in a carefully maintained brownstone in a neighbourhood that's going downhill. You let yourself in by a low iron gate and climb the stairs to a glass front door. A coloured cleaning man, stooped over and humming to himself, answers the bell. Mister Waters, he calls. Visitor for you. Muddy is lying in bed in a back room on the ground floor. He is watching TV. You see that, man? says one of his visitors. That damn dog fixing to run away. Naw, man, says the other, who is wearing a dashing wide-brimmed circuit preacher's hat. He going to get help. Muddy, stolid-looking even under ordinary circumstances, grunts and shifts in bed. He's just recovering from a painful automobile accident ("I was almost destroyed," he tells his visitors, shaking his head. It obviously preys on him, because later he comes back to it, saying, "I love to travel, but this accident taken a lot out of me. I mean, you don't never know when it's coming, that's the heck of it. I was just trying to make it home, man.") He wears a black do-rag on his head, black silk pajamas, and a brightly coloured kimono which stands out against his dark glistening skin. He has high Indian cheekbones, striking, almost oriental features, and an impassive expression which serves effectively to mask just what he is thinking.

His visitors glance over at me with some mistrust. They are about thirty-five or forty, probably neighbours, somewhat in awe of the man, Muddy Waters. I playin' lead guitar now, one of them says. Oh yeah? Muddy tilts his heavy head. I didn't know you was playing any guitar at all. Muddy is a man of something less than ordinary loquaciousness, but his words when they come come all in a rush, accompanied often by a strained, almost nervous chuckling. I'm just trying to decide what kind to get, Guild or Martin. They're both good, Muddy reassures him. Of course he uses the Guild himself because of the advertising tie-in. The man nods rapidly two or three times and stands up. Well, we gonna be going. You come back real soon, says Muddy. Next time we gonna bring you something. The other man nods. You just bring yourself, Muddy says graciously. They shake hands all around, and Muddy prepares to answer my questions. It's probably his fifth or sixth interview since he got busted up. He's been home from the hospital for two months now, and he's getting restless. Every afternoon he goes out for a ride. "I ain't been home like this in years," he says. "Ordinarily you come home, the time slip by like it's no time. But like this, it kind of gets on your nerves."

II

Muddy is one of the few blues singers who has made it. He plays jazz clubs and the college circuit and has established a white audience which, if it is not as large as B.B. King's, is certainly just as loyal. When blues was the popular music of blacks he was a popular artist, and he has been driving a Cadillac for years. Around Chicago his name is legend (like B.B., Elmore James, Wolf, and even Junior Wells he has his own imitator, Muddy Jr., currently working the clubs), his influence has been almost universally acknowledged, and in the last ten years he has gained something of the international status of a Louis Armstrong in jazz or a Ray Charles or James Brown in contemporary rhythm and blues.

And yet his life is not so different from the average and less successful bluesman's. He doesn't have a jet or a retinue of personal retainers. He owns his own home, but it remains in the heart of Chicago's South Side in a section that's been steadily deteriorating for the last ten years. Inside the walls are all panelled and there are plastic slipcovers on sofa and chairs, but there's no way of shutting out the street outside and a recurrent topic of conversation is the decline of the neighbourhood and the decline of the South Side in general. His neighbours all refer to him with respect; to the livery driver across the street "I guess he's the king of the blues." But it's said with a deprecatory chuckle and until very recently his dominion, for a monarch, was exceedingly small. For years he played the dingy neighbourhood joints and bars and even at the height of his popularity he was working seven nights a week in clubs like Smitty's, Pepper's, and Gary's F&J Lounge, with occasional forays into the South. It wasn't until his first trip to England in 1958 that he became aware of a larger audience, and he still expresses honest amazement at the extent of his success. "I went up to Montreal," he told a Chicago newspaper reporter. "There were men and women of all ages [in the audience]. Some of them was older than me. I look at them and I say, What the hell is this thing? What is going on?"

He is subject in many ways, too, to the limitations of the world in which he grew up. Lacking any real education, he has developed a kind of wariness both in his personal manner and in his professional dealings. Without ever showing any open hostility he retains an inscrutable look and a cautiousness of expression which protects him from committing himself too quickly. He never says more than he means, and even in conversation with friends he seems to maintain a guarded watchfulness and will take the listener's part more often than not.

He is the same up on the bandstand. He hasn't got any act, he avoids elaborate announcements, and he will rarely resort to theatrical gesture or false histrionics. He presents a song straightforwardly, gets what he wants from the band by a word or a glance from his hooded eyes, and both in public and in private always carries himself with an enormous dignity. He is, it is obvious, an extremely proud man, and sometimes it is not difficult to imagine that the titles which have been bestowed upon him for his singing were not in fact his by earlier possession. For Muddy Waters carries himself with all the dignity of a king.

III

He has come to accept all the questions and interviews pretty much as a matter of course. He no longer seems surprised by your interest or by your knowledge of his early life. He is if anything just a little bit amused, and some of his answers are tinged with the slightest trace of mockery. He does not, however, expand very freely, and, while he is always courteous in conversation, it becomes necessary to piece together his story from various accounts.

He was born McKinley Morganfield in Rolling Fork, Mississippi on April 4, 1915. "I was the second boy child," he told Paul Oliver, "but my daddy — his name was Ollie Morganfield — went right on makin' children. My daddy was a farmer; he raised hawgs and chickens. Grew watermelons." He was born in the Delta, but he grew up in Clarksdale about one hundred miles away, where his grandmother raised him after his mother's death in 1918. He was called Muddy Waters at an early age, he says, because he liked to play in the near-by Deer Creek, but Sunnyland Slim remembers him in

Early Waters band: includes Spann on piano and Rogers on guitar

Clarksdale ("he used to 'muddy' on Saturday and sell fish on Saturday nights") and claims that this is how he got his name. Muddy himself recalls the suppers and Saturday night fish fries. "Well, I played everywhere I could," he told Oliver. "Everybody used to fry up fish and had one hell of a time. Find me working all night, playing, working till sunrise for fifty cents and a sandwich. And be glad of it."

Like many other blues singers Muddy started out on harmonica and didn't take up guitar until the age of seventeen. By then he was married (Robert Nighthawk, another noted blues singer, played at his wedding; "I couldn't play nothing next to him") and with a friend named Scott Bohannon formed a band which included Henry Sims, Charley Patton's old fiddle player. "We played jook joints, frolics, Saturday night suppers, we was even playing white folks' parties when we was around home. No, I was leader. Son Sims had made a record for himself, I believe, he was really what you call a pretty ancient man, but I did most of the singing." In the course of playing he was, naturally enough, exposed to a great deal more music, and at some point early in his career he heard Son House. "I had been learning guitar from this Scott Bohannon. I thought he could play. But then I saw Son House and I realized he couldn't play nothing at all. Son House played this same place," he told Don de Michael, "for about four weeks in a row, and I was there every night. You couldn't get me out of that corner, listening to what he's doing."

He came into contact with Robert Johnson, too, and though they never met his style was very much a blend of the two. His thick heavy tone, the dark coloration of his voice and his firm almost stolid manner were all clearly derived from House, but the embellishments which he added, the imaginative slide technique and more agile rhythms, were closer to Johnson. "I consider myself to be, what you might call a mixture of all three. I had part of my own, part of Son House, and a little part of Robert Johnson. Robert? No, I seen him at a distance a couple of times, but I never actually seen him to play. I regret that very much, because I liked his style. I thought he was real great from his records. Beautiful. Really, though, it was Son House who influenced me to play. I was really behind Son House all the way."

In 1940 Muddy went up to St. Louis "just to sniff around." In 1941 he joined up with a Silas Green tent show and travelled around some, playing harmonica and singing a little. It wasn't until 1943, though, after he had already been recorded by Alan Lomax for the Library of Congress, that he left Mississippi for good. He was twenty-eight years old, and he never looked back.

IV

"I wanted to get out of Mississippi in the worst way, man. Go back? What I want to go back for? They had such as my mother and the older people brainwashed that people can't make it too good in the city. But I figured if anyone else was living in the city I could make it there, too." In the years since then he has returned very seldom and then only to visit his father. For years he scrupulously avoided the state even in his tours of the South, and a hint of the exhilaration he must have felt in leaving comes out in his voice even today.

Chicago in 1943 was not an easy town to get a start in. "Blues was dying out," Muddy says. "There was nothing happening. Well, a few things. Big Maceo and Tampa Red, Sonny Boy Williams, but not

Son House/Dick Waterman

too many help you. It was pretty ruggish, man." He will not admit, though, to feeling any discomfiture or being in any way deterred by the bleak conditions of the city. He got a day job driving a truck and at night played the house rent parties and then the smaller clubs, getting paid off in whiskey and looking to make a name for himself. Around 1945 Big Bill Broonzy introduced him at Sylvio's, and he was given his first electric guitar by his uncle, Joe Brant. In 1946, probably through Big Bill, he recorded for Lester Melrose at Columbia. The sides were never released, but in late 1947 he was heard by Sammy Goldberg, the Chess brothers' black talent scout. He was driving his uncle's coal truck when a friend, Antra Bolton, sought him out, located him, and sent him over to the Chess studio where Sunnyland Slim had arranged for him to record his first session for Aristocrat.

Only five years had elapsed between his initial recording and his recording for Aristocrat which the Chess brothers, immigrants from Poland, had only recently started. The first titles were not particularly successful. "I kept my job until I had a couple of records out. I was playing seven nights a week and working six days, making, I think I was getting on my job $38 or $40 a week. On my job. I was making $35 a week from playing seven nights, $5 a night. It's good to know these things." Then in 1950 they changed the name of the label to Chess, and both Muddy and the record company had their first real success. "Rolling Stone" was Muddy's first release, and it was a hit.

"Hit" at that time meant you sold probably 60,000 copies in the race market and almost exclusively around Chicago, Gary, St. Louis, Memphis and the South. There was no distribution on the coast, there was no radio air play, and the money that was involved would certainly seem small by today's inflated standards. Even so it was enough to make Muddy Waters a star.

It probably didn't change his life all that much. In the first few years undoubtedly he continued to play the same small clubs and lounges. Other musicians came around and sat in, but it wasn't until around 1949 that he had developed sufficient confidence to form his own band, and his records up till then consisted of just himself playing guitar, Big Crawford's or Willie Dixon's bass, and occasionally Little Walter on harmonica. To the extent that he had graduated from house rent parties his life was changed; to the extent that he no longer worked a day job and had finally come to consider himself a professional musician his outlook was different; but more than anything else what gave Muddy Waters a sense of his own arrival was the fact that he was known.

"Years ago," he was quoted in a conversation in *downbeat.* "I'd say back in '47 or '48 — Little Walter, Jimmy Rogers, and myself, we would go around looking for bands that were playing. We called ourselves The Headhunters, 'cause we'd go in and if we got a chance we were gonna burn 'em." "Sometimes," he told me, "we'd come in and win the contest, they'd have an amateur contest with a prize, but

Jimmy Rogers

the guy would come up to me after he found out who I was and say, Uh-uh, Muddy, you's too heavy. You can work for me if you wants, but you's too heavy to be in the contest." He recalls those days with relish but then adds, "Of course I ain't like that no more. I know different now. Cause you can't be the best. You can just be a good 'un."

He can afford to be magnanimous today. Of all the singers from that period he and Howlin' Wolf alone have survived, and there seems little question at this point that both will continue to occupy a position of some importance in the blues. Their celebrated rivalry, though, shows no sign of abatement and indicates in its own way the sort of competitive state which must have existed for the blues singer in Chicago twenty years ago. "There are certain people," says Wolf, making it quite clear who he is talking about, "who think they are better than you are." "Wolf?" says Muddy disdainfully. "I was here way before Wolf. I had this town sewed up in my hand."

Maybe so. By 1952, when Wolf came up from Memphis, Muddy was a nationally established recording star who had already had three of the nine records he was to place on the r&b charts in *Billboard's* Top Ten. His band included Little Walter and Jimmy

Rogers, recording stars in their own right, and in fact he got Wolf his first job in Chicago.

1954 was his big year. He had three records in the Top Ten, including two of his biggest hits, "Hoochie Coochie Man" and "I Just Want to Make Love to You." If it had stayed a race market he probably would have remained a star for another decade. But the market changed when rock 'n' roll came in and after 1956 Muddy never had another hit.

V

What is it that can have contributed to his extraordinary success up to that point? Johnny Shines, Elmore James, Homesick James, Robert Jr. Lockwood, all were playing and singing in a style that was similar to Muddy's. The blues of Robert Johnson had in fact turned out to be as influential and as popular as any previously existing style. But Muddy Waters alone turned that style into a vehicle for personal popularity, and fifteen years later it is Muddy Waters alone who retains any wide personal following.

"It was sex," says twenty-seven-year-old Marshall Chess, whose father Leonard discovered Muddy. "If you had ever seen Muddy then, the effect he had on women. Because blues, you know, has always been a women's market. On Saturday night they'd be lined up ten deep."

"He had that drive," says Marshall's uncle Phil who started the Aristocrat label with his brother. "A guy like Johnny Shines? He was a run-of-the-mill singer. But Muddy had that drive."

"I like to think I could really master a stage," says Muddy. "I think I was a pretty good stage personality, and I knew how to present myself right. No, I never developed an act of any kind. I just had a natural feel for it."

Undoubtedly all of the above statements are true. More than any other blues singer I've ever met Muddy is single-minded in his purpose and can channel all his impressive energy towards a single highly specific end. He is, in addition, of course, an exceptionally creative musician, whose compositions and recordings over the years have been as remarkable for their consistency as for their brilliance. But more than anything else what seems to me the key to Muddy

Waters' success has been his ability to organize and maintain a succession of bands which have almost perfectly reflected the very personal kind of music which he plays. Virtually alone Muddy Waters developed the ensemble style of play which has come to characterize the omnipresent school of Chicago blues.

When he started out he was, of course, accompanied by only one or two other instruments, and he continues to express a preference for this kind of music. "I think I done it right, man. I was playing blues like I knowed them, and all that bass playeı have to do was follow." He prefers, too, the "true sound" of the acoustic guitar and would, he says, if he had the choice, return to playing as a solo performer. But it was necessary in order to be heard in the noisy clubs and taverns of Chicago to take up an amplified instrument. And it was necessary, to achieve any kind of success in the big-band-oriented rhythm and blues market, to put together some kind of group.

This was not as easy as it might at first appear. Because for one thing the blues is not exactly a formal music with regular time signatures and predictable chord changes. For another, working with a group posed some very real conflicts in presentation and style. "See, my blues is not as easy to play as some people think they are. Cause here, this is it, I may have thirteen beats in some song, and the average man, he not used to that kind of thing. He got to follow me, not himself, because I make the blues different. Do that change thing when I change, just the way I feel, that's the way it went. I mean, you take that song, 'Just To Be With You.' Now that's a good blues tune, and I made it just the way I felt, sometimes I play thirteen, sometimes I play fourteen beats. And I got just about as good time in the blues as anyone."

It was as much a problem for nearly every country blues singer who recorded after the war. Elmore James worked for much of his career in an inappropriate big-band setting, and Johnny Shines, who remains to this day almost entirely a solo performer, never achieved any widespread popularity. It took Howlin' Wolf ten years to develop a group which could adequately reflect his very fierce brand of music, and John Lee Hooker never learned to work with a band at all, although some of his biggest sellers came from a hesitant alliance between himself and several other instruments. Muddy, though, not only developed a group to complement his sound; he put together a band which could actually extend it.

His first recorded group consisted of himself, Jimmy Rogers on second guitar, Little Walter's harmonica and Elgin Evans on drums. Together about five years off and on, it was without question his finest group, but it was, in addition, a blues band which has not been equalled to this day. For, apart from Evans, each member of the group was not only a distinctive vocalist but an outstanding soloist in his own right. They possessed as well a kind of wordless understanding which enabled them to function as a perfect musical unit, alternating brilliant solos with tight ensemble work in a fusion that few groups of any sort ever attain.

Jimmy Rogers, who was born in Georgia in 1924, came up to Chicago probably around the same time as Muddy and joined a group which consisted of Muddy and another guitarist-drummer, Baby Face Leroy, around 1949. While Muddy's guitar generally took the lead, Rogers was absolutely essential to the band, executing bass runs and fill-ins with an unerring touch and echoing Muddy's slide at all times with uncanny precision. Together he and Muddy worked out intricate patterns of counterpoint and rhythm which have been captured only intermittently in the years since Rogers left the band. It was Muddy, too, who brought Rogers into the studio and produced several of his early records, often at the end of his own sessions. He played on several of his friend's hits, including "That's All Right," the song by which Rogers came to be known, and in fact Jimmy Rogers was a very popular musician around Chicago in his own right for several years. He quit the music business altogether, though, in 1959, and Muddy has seen him only intermittently since then. "The last time I seen him was at Little Walter's wake. Why he quit? I don't know, this is a hard thing for me to answer. He just didn't have that willpower, I guess, you know it take willpower to stay out there, man. Because if things get hard, you know sometimes it ain't all kick out there, some people just can't wait on it. Last I heard he was working in a second-hand clothes store."

Walter, of course, everyone knows. Born in Alexandria, Louisiana in 1930, he gave the following summary of his early life. "I was about eight years old, I left home. About ten I come into St. Louis and stayed a while. Got to play around a few shoe-shine stands, pool rooms, you know. Then I left St. Louis, came to Chicago, I was still too young to get in the clubs and play. So I had to get me a little set-up on the street. Which the name of the street

Little Walter/Val Wilmer

was Maxwell Street in Chicago, and we played every Sunday in the daytime, start out about nine in the morning, quit about four in the evening. So I would keep going, have a few coins until I got of age, and then I started playing with some of the older fellows, you know, that was in the clubs. And I met Muddy in '47." Coming from anyone else that kind of account might very well seem suspect, but Little Walter fulfilled in many ways the stereotype of the doomed bluesman, tough, suspicious, self-destructive, and alcoholic. Probably the single most innovative performer in the history of the blues, he was a veteran by the time he started recording at seventeen and an old man when he died in 1968 at the age of thirty-seven. "He could have been the biggest," says Howlin' Wolf. "I don't like to say nothin' about nobody, but that boy could have been tops in the blues field. Young, good-looking, the women all go for him. But too much of that liquor and too much of that other stuff, that pot and stuff, brought him down."

"Liquor's the thing that'll get you," Muddy says. "Well, I imagine, I guess if you get too much of anything I don't think you can make it all the way. Just enough to give you a gauge, then you got a lot of nerve and you feel good. Sure, I used to be a good liquor drinking man. But when the doctor told me to come off the liquor, I said, This is it. No more whiskey."

It is in talking about Walter that Muddy's traditional reserve will break down. "When I met him he wasn't drinking nothing but Pepsi Cola. Just a kid. And I'll tell you, I had the best harmonica player in the business, man. Oh man, I wished you could have seen him. While you're recording, he be dashin' all around you everywhere, changing harps, you know, running all around the studio, but he never get in your way. He put a lot of trick things in there, getting all different sounds, aww he was the greatest. He always had ideas."

That was the thing about Little Walter. Although he was probably the first to amplify his harmonica, and while he introduced sounds which were a product as much of the studio as of his chromatic and Marine Band harmonicas, it was not so much his technique as the unerring logic of what he played that pays tribute to his genius. He introduced sounds that no one had ever heard before: the big horn-like sound and sudden swooping moans, the haunting echo and the unrelenting attack of his playing, his mastery of the more difficult chromatic, all were tributes not only to his technical skill but to his musical judgment and taste as well. For like everyone else in the band he was capable of laying back when it was time to lay back and filling in with perfect tact and delicacy when someone else was taking a solo.

In 1952 his first record on the Checker label came out (he had earlier recorded for Parkway and Ora-Nelle, two obscure Chicago labels, mostly on guitar) when the band was on tour in Louisiana. It was a harmonica instrumental called "Juke" which was destined to go to Number One on all the rhythm and blues surveys. "He heard that record on the radio," Otis Spann recalled shortly before his death, "next thing you look up and Walter was gone. See, you get a record out, you figure well, now I get something. But that's wrong, that record may go no further than across the street. After that we went back together again for a while, but it wasn't never the same. There wasn't but four of us carrying it on."

Spann himself joined the band in 1951, twenty-one years old and just out of the Army. He and Muddy have always claimed to be half-brothers, though just what their exact relationship was has never been made clear. They could not have been closer musically, and Spann's piano was the driving force in Muddy's band almost from the time he joined it until his death in 1970. "A lot of people want to know how Otis got to play the blues *so* good," Muddy told Don de Michael. "They never knowed this particular thing: he used to come to my house and park in front of the door with a bottle of whiskey, and I'd sit there and teach this man, tell him exactly what to do with the piano when I was singing the blues." "That's the truth," Spann chimed in. "Ride around, be daybreak before we got home. Sit there talking. I don't believe there'll be another musician, up to date, that can follow my brother Muddy singing, because he's a 'late' singer. If you don't wait for him, he's not there." "He know my music better than any man alive," Muddy said to me. "We better raise up another before it's too late."

Spann, too, left the band but not until 1968 when his wife's professional ambitions seemingly prodded him to go out on his own. Had Muddy encouraged him in the move? I asked. Muddy's eyes narrowed. "Well, if he feel like that. If you feel like that you go. See, everybody looking for a name in this business. Everybody looking for a star name. He may be playing sideman, but in his mind he wish he was the star. So everybody looking for a break, you know, when that comes, well let him go. Find somebody else somehow. Of course a real good man like Little Walter, Jimmy, Otis, them was extra to me. But you have to get you another man, you just keep trying.

"Well, see, I was dividing the singing all the way through. Some leaders, they hold back their sidemen, you know, he's afraid the sideman may get more hands, more rounds of applause than he do. And it look like they jealous of that. But me, it makes me no difference. I always have believed, if somebody can shine put the light on him, let him shine. I think that's about the right thing to do, don't try to do it all yourself. And back then we was like brothers anyway. Just like family. We always had laughing and talking and had our own little thing going to have fun whilst we were on the bandstand. Oh, it went hard when they left. It goes hard, man, when you get used to one sound and you got to go out and get another one. Seems like to me I had more trouble since I been getting these newer bands."

But he *has* put together new bands and the bands have always reflected his sound. The music has always built around his dark almost plodding voice and, except for a brief period in the late fifties, featured his dramatic slide guitar. The piano fills in with dark rolling chords on the slower songs and drives the band on the faster numbers. There are always one or two guitars to second Muddy's slide with rhythm and those patented bass-run fill-ins and to take the lead on the more modern-styled numbers. He has had a succession of harp men who, if they have never really taken Little Walter's place, have always provided more than adequate commentary. And bass and drums keep a steady rhythm, nothing too fancy, as Muddy cocks his head or stamps his foot impatiently if anyone gets off the beat.

Just about everyone who plays modern Chicago-styled blues has passed through Muddy's band at one time or another. Walter Horton, Junior Wells, Willie Dixon, James Cotton, Hubert Sumlin, Earl Hooker, and Buddy Guy have all played and recorded with Muddy. Like Bill Monroe in bluegrass and Miles Davis in jazz, his band has been a kind of proving ground for young musicians, and if he has never assembled a group which is the equal of the first it is more because there is no one to replace Little Walter — it would be impossible to duplicate a musical partnership like Muddy's and Jimmy Rogers', like Muddy's and Otis Spann's — than through any

Otis Spann/Val Wilmer

lack of trying. For Muddy retains an implacable determination to maintain the high standards which he has set for himself.

"I believe all the time I can learn a guy how to do something. I look for a guy that can play *pretty* good and then we get him and rehearse him and try to get him to play *my* sound. The Muddy Waters sound." Often he will prefer the musician who shows a feeling for his kind of music to one who is more technically adept. "Well now, you take Luther," he said, referring to Luther Johnson, a young guitarist who played very much in his style. "He don't play anywhere near as good as Sammy Lawhorn. But Sammy, he's not a deep bluesman. He play a lot of guitar. But he don't have that blues feel. Now Luther, he'll get that whining sound. You can feel it."

Keeping a blues band together, though, is not just a matter of musical direction. It requires diplomacy and firmness sometimes, psychology and an absolute sense of direction. Because blues is not a particularly remunerative field, sidemen are always going off on their own, and in the last few years Muddy has seen James Cotton, Otis Spann, and Luther Johnson leave to form their own bands. Musicians get tired, too, of having to furnish the same sound night after night or just of life on the road. There are any number of reasons why a musician will leave the band (Jimmy Lee Robinson became a Black Muslim and Pee Wee Madison was in jail for a while; George Smith got homesick for Los Angeles, and George "Mojo" Buford, his successor, went home to Minneapolis), and the leader always has to be prepared to deal with the unexpected and to cope with whatever contingency might happen to arise.

And there is, of course, always the problem of liquor. Blues grew up in the taverns and jook houses, and there isn't a blues singer you could name who has not been at one time, anyway, a fairly heavy drinker. Muddy has quit drinking himself, but it remains a problem with certain members of his band. At one time he was without the services of a regular drummer after Francey Clay, who had worked with him for the past several years, went out to join Cotton (whose own drummer, Sammy Lay, had just quit to form a group of his own) and S.P. Leary, Clay's replacement, proved to be capable enough when sober but not sober enough of the time. Muddy carried him for a while, but several times you'd see him send Leary down from the stand (Luther Johnson would take over the drumming chores; Lawhorn would play lead and Muddy rhythm), and eventually, of course, he had to replace him. "Well, you see," he admits a little sheepishly, "he was lushing. I tried to make it smooth enough over, so that people wouldn't, you know, know what was happening. I didn't want to give him a let-down too hard. But he was just a little too heavy in the head, I guess a lot of people knowed that."

James Cotton/Val Wilmer

It all seems a little bit like a juggling act sometimes, but over it all Muddy presides with the imperturbable calm of a beleaguered chief. Other leaders resort to threats and physical chastisement (one prominent singer is supposed to have knocked out his guitarist's front teeth, and Little Walter frequently brandished a gun), but Muddy seems to rely upon the respect his musicians obviously feel for him and upon his immense personal dignity.

There's no question that operating as a kind of administrator has taken its toll. "I feel like it have taken a lot out of me. You see, you got to have this on your kind all the time, instead of thinking of one thing you're thinking about where's the next job or what you're going to do next. I used to come up with some good songs, you know, but I can't get down with it, 'cause I can't think no more I got too many things on my mind. I'm the man having a hard time with material now, and I used to think up some *good* things, man."

At the same time he feels an obvious affection for his musicians and takes great pride in the accomplishments of his "boys." In recent years he has A&R-ed sessions for Spann and Luther Johnson as well as a couple of albums for his band and one for Big Mama Thornton. If you ask him if he enjoys it he'll tell you, "I don't think so. It ain't too cool for me, man. Cause you trying to tell someone something, and maybe they'll think your ideas is too square, you know, I'd rather for them to have their own ideas and let someone else do that work and I'll do my real job." It has not deterred him in any case from making the effort on his friends' behalf, and despite his disavowal he has even contributed five or six songs to Spann's and Luther's sessions, including a beautiful "Looks Like Twins" and a deeply moving tribute to Martin Luther King.

He no longer attempts to record his own material at Chess. "I coulda recorded that on my own," he says of a Spann song, "but I ain't gonna ruin the song. Because they got this old funny thing going, man, every time I go in to Chess to record I got to record with another band. And it ain't that they're not good players, those boys can play just about anything, they some of the top-notch guitar players in Chicago, but they can't get that blues sound. And my band can get pretty blue. I'll tell you, man, I don't know what's happening, it almost make me kind of case-hardened, cause I just ain't got the spirit to record. These boys are top musicians, they can play with me, put the book before 'em and play it, you know. But that ain't what I need to sell my people, it ain't the Muddy Waters sound. And if you change my sound, then you gonna change the whole man."

VI

Chess in fact has had very little idea of what to do with Muddy for the past ten or twelve years. His records probably continued to sell pretty steadily until 1960, but since then he has had nothing even resembling a blues hit. The "race" market that was once there has shifted, and the company has reacted predictably enough by trying to cash in on one contemporary trend (from Muddy Waters Folksinger to the Muddy Waters Twist) after another. Everyone at Chess speaks very highly of Muddy (Marshall Chess refers to him as "practically my godfather" and Muddy says he and Leonard were "very close. Pretty close."), but when it comes to the music they seem to have no feel for the blues form and Muddy's group is regarded about as highly as a band of itinerant gypsies.

Their cynicism may have affected Muddy for a time. There was a period in the late fifties and early sixties when, he says, he lost interest in the music. He was still playing seven nights a week in the clubs, he made regular swings through the South, and his records were on the jukeboxes. More and more, though, he let the band do all the work. He featured Spann and James Cotton increasingly on vocals, and he himself gave up playing the guitar because, he confesses, "the band sounded so good to me, I didn't think I have to play."

It may have been that he was getting tired of the routine. It's tough work playing in the clubs and, as he said to Pete Welding a few years ago. "I'm getting older and I don't want to work too hard. You know, getting up there and working six hours a night and putting everything you got into that, you won't be no good ... I do three, four songs and that's it. And I put everything I got in it. But you can't do that all night."

More likely, though, he was just exercising the star prerogative. For a singer like Muddy, for any singer coming up through the ranks, it's immensely important to establish that he is somehow different, it's essential to indicate in some way or other that he has made it. "You take a guy off a plantation," reminisced B.B. King in an interview with Stanley Dance about his own early days, "who has been getting twenty-five dollars a week and put him where he's getting twenty-five hundred — well, I don't know how to describe it! The first thing I wanted to do was to get some of the things I never had, like clothes, I wanted a nice automobile, and, believe it or not, I never had enough sweet potato pies. That lasted quite a long time, but now I have a Volkswagen at home, and that's what I drive. Then, it had to be a Cadillac, and to me that proved I was popular. You see, I used to read about the stars in Hollywood, and their bodyguards, and how when they came out the whole street stopped and the people gathered around them. That was how I felt it should be. I was the star, and I had to have everything the star was supposed to have."

Muddy never made it as big as B.B. But certainly he was faced with the same problems of adaptation. And he was affected in other ways, too, which a singer like Johnny Shines, who was never confronted with success at all, either its problems or its rewards, could never know.

For one thing his music changed. With the success of songs like "I Just Want To Make Love to You" and "Mannish Boy" (his 1956 answer to Bo Diddley's "I'm a Man") Muddy turned away increasingly from the dark, almost introspective blues which he had brought up with him from the Delta to a music of raw force, sometimes frightening power and surprising intensity. These new blues — shouted, declamatory, explicit, sexual — were better adapted to working in the clubs, and they were Muddy's way of keeping up with the times. At the same time they demanded a different manner of presentation, and there seems little question that this, too, contributed to the development of a new style. He was at any rate in 1960 a different kind of artist than he had been ten years before, a fact which Paul Oliver underlines in a description which gives the flavour of a typical performance:

> At that time Muddy worked on Tuesdays at the F&J Lounge in Gary, Indiana and he took Valerie [Oliver's wife], myself, St. Louis Jimmy and Joe Brant along with him in his Cadillac. The car radio was on — turned up to maximum volume as a record of Howlin' Wolf's came on ... turned down ... then up as J.B. Lenoir was heard, Muddy's ears detecting every blues item in the mixed bag with the radio nearly at "off." On our way to the job he talked quietly and the band was already working when we arrived. The Lounge was entirely for Negro steel-mill workers and servicemen; white people never visited it. We sat unobtrusively but near the band, and throughout the evening had a stream of interested, friendly people come up to chat with us.
>
> As the music warmed up Muddy began to comment, give encouragement, working himself up to a pitch of excitement that made a tremendous impact when he fronted the group. There was no doubting who was king — the effect was stunning. And frightening too. The sheer physical drive of band and blues singer chilled the spine. Muddy roared, leaped, jerked in fierce and violent spasms. When he came off the stage he was in a state of near-trance and the sweat poured off him. It was close on half an hour before he had unwound himself sufficiently to drive us home on the great "skyway" in Chicago, and for most of the following day he lay in a shaded room with an ice-pack on his forehead. Few people probably realize how much he gives of himself when he works and how long he needs to get over a session which generally lasts till four in the morning.*

His life may have changed, style may have changed, but there seems little question that Muddy retains the same fierce commitment which originally moved him. As Paul Butterfield said of him: "If Muddy is the richest man in the world he's still got the feeling, he's

*Paul Oliver, "Muddy Waters," cf. Bibliography.

still the man." And, if any further testimony were needed, Muddy himself told Sheldon Harris, "I been in the blues all of my life. I just got to love 'em. I enjoy 'em, feels 'em. Sure, I can kinda take care of myself now, but I still got that feelin'. I'm still delivering, 'cause I got a long memory."

Muddy doesn't play the taverns anymore. He doesn't work much around Chicago, and he probably hasn't set foot in the F&J Lounge for years. Like only a handful of other blues singers he was swept up first in the folk boom of the early sixties and then in the wake of the British blues revival. The Beatles, Eric Clapton, Chicago-born Paul Butterfield, and most of all The Rolling Stones (who took not only their name but a considerable amount of their early repertoire from his music) have all acknowledged their debt, and Muddy at this point is probably as well known in the white community as in the black.

He has made the transition with remarkable ease. Far more than any other blues singer that comes to mind he seems at home with his new audience, and he treats his latter-day career almost as a kind of challenge. It was the discovery of this larger audience in fact which led, Muddy insists, to his renewed interest in the music. 'Well, see, in a hard liquor club ain't too much coming for you. The people are out to have a good time, they drinking and dancing, oh they'll enjoy what you putting down, they'll like it, but they don't give too much attention to it. Now with white people when you play something good you really get appreciated for it. You get more of a push-off." Every blues singer will tell you this, but most clearly prefer the reassuring atmosphere of the clubs where they can relax and exchange banter among friends and acquaintances. Most blues singers build up a loyal local following, which extends sometimes no more than a few city blocks, and then hold on to it often at the expense of wider fame. Some are afraid to travel, many are just suspicious of white people, but all are afraid in one way or another of the dangers of permanent dislocation. Muddy on the other hand almost seemed to welcome it.

His first tour of England in 1958 was something of a disaster. The English were not ready for amplified blues apparently, and by all accounts Muddy just about blasted them out of the hall. His second tour in 1963 was much more successful, and since 1964 he has been back on numerous occasions, to be welcomed each time as something of a conquering hero. He speaks today of "the thrill of going overseas for the first time" and confesses that he had had no idea of the existence of that vast new audience up till that time.

Paul Butterfield/Charles Sawyer

His renewed popularity had more tangible results as well. He took up guitar again some time in the early sixties largely at the behest of his new audience and at the urging of Otis Spann. He dispensed with many of his newer songs (which he is inclined to dismiss as "commercial gimmicks") and with a great deal of the flamboyance of his stage act, too, and he went back to playing in a way that was much closer to his original style. His band broke up briefly in 1961, but since then he has put together one group after another to reflect his non-commercial, non-gimmicky sound. And he has come to the point today where he is booked almost exclusively into clubs like the Electric Circus, the Jazz Workshop, the Kinetic Playground, and the college festivals.

It is a situation about which he cannot help but have mixed feelings. He thinks a great deal of the white kids who have tried so hard to understand his music. He can't see them as blues singers, though. "I think they're great people, but they're not blues players. Really, what separates them from people like Wolf and myself, we're doing the stuff like we did way years ago down in Mississippi. These kids are just getting up, getting stuff and going with it, you know, so we're expressing our lives, the hard times and different things we been through. It's not real. They don't feel it. I don't think you can feel the blues until you've been through some hard times."

He's come in for a great deal of criticism himself for carrying white musicians in his band. Paul Oscher was with him on harp for a few years, and while it wouldn't be beyond Muddy to calculate the commercial advantage of Oscher's colour, he had an obvious pride and an almost paternal affection for the boy. "Now Paul's gonna be a *good* bluesman. He's already a good bluesman, he gets a lot of response even when I take him to a black club. Naw, we never had any real trouble. One time in Cleveland we was playing for the black, we was playing for the city, you know, and they was getting a little

Muddy Waters/Val Wilmer

funny, you know, acting violent. We didn't even let him play that day, we just sent him on over to one of them big restaurants, let him eat and drink coffee till we get through playing. That's the onliest time that I can recall."

Most of all, though, he is confused and upset by the disrepute into which his music has fallen among blacks. He is aware, certainly, of the anomalies of his own position, and he appears to feel vaguely guilty about it. "I don't hardly play for a black audience any more. Now and then I have a booking in the black. But not too often. It's not that I don't want to play for my peoples. I *love* to play for my peoples, man, but I just been busy." And he is a man who, like many another great artist, seeking recognition as well as reward, has been forced to go outside of his own community to get it.

He has become, ironically enough, something of a model for the young singers in the process. Artists like Buddy Guy and Junior Wells, who patterned themselves after Muddy when he was king and they were just starting out in Chicago, are emulating him today in their attempts to build a popular following. And, even though he doesn't get around the city much any more, he retains the respect and remains the dean of all Chicago blues singers.

Muddy has always taken his responsibilities very seriously. When he came to Chicago it was Sonny Boy Williamson and Big Bill Broonzy who gave many of the younger men their start. Since Big Bill's death in 1958 Muddy has reigned virtually unchallenged.

"I have helped many more people than have given help to me." Howlin' Wolf, Chuck Berry, Otis Spann, Paul Butterfield — the list of singers whom he has helped and actively encouraged over the years is virtually endless. Somewhere, you know, there is still a glint of the competitive spark which drove him once to go out and challenge everyone on the South Side to "cutting contests." Muddy has mellowed over the years, though, and without ever sacrificing any of the drive which originally impelled him he seems at this point a benign, almost beneficent figure.

He has never forgotten any of the people who have helped him either. His uncle, Joe Brant, who gave him his first electric guitar, lived with Muddy until his death in 1963. His "half-brother," Otis Spann, stayed for years in the basement apartment of his house, and Little Walter lived with him off and on until his death in 1968. Even then Muddy was still talking about taking him back into the band,

and while it is unlikely that he would have let sentiment get in the way of common sense, it's a tribute to the feeling he had for Little Walter that he even entertained the idea.

His mind seems to be a great deal on the past these days. Maybe it's because of the accident, but even before the accident he seemed pleased and gratified that audiences were discovering his old songs, his "true stuff," once more. "You know," he says, "I may not sell that many copies but the one I do sell to I want him to feel it." Most of the time when you see him he'll do his "hits," the songs with which his audience is already acquainted, things like "Hoochie Coochie Man," "Got My Mojo Working," "Tiger in Your Tank." Once in a while, though, when he's feeling good or he gets a request from an unexpected quarter, he'll send the rest of the band down from the bandstand, retune his guitar, and play the old songs in the old way. Then he will hunch over the guitar, his eyebrows knit in fierce concentration and when he finishes the song — "Rolling Stone" or "Walking Blues" or "Rolling and Tumbling" — he will glance up to the tumultuous applause, his face spread in a big grin, and he will suddenly look very pleased with himself.

VII

Muddy lives in a rough neighbourhood. The cabdriver who took me uptown said he used to live there himself. He wouldn't let his kids grow up there, though; his kids, he told me, were going to college.

Muddy stays on because he is settled and probably for the same reason that his music doesn't really change — because his roots are there. It was a good street when he bought the house fifteen or twenty years ago (Leonard Chess himself looked it over before he made the purchase), and he knows and is known by the neighbourhood. Otis Spann was living just two blocks from Muddy when he died, in April of 1970, and other musicians live and work nearby.

He wouldn't let me take the El back, though, and he probably wouldn't take a bus himself. It was a Saturday afternoon and hard to get a cab, but he kept calling one cab company after another as his wife supplied the numbers. "You see," he said with a kindly, almost apologetic smile, "they liable to give you a little bit of trouble if you standing around at the bus stop." He turned to his wife with a

worried-looking expression. "Those black boys are so damned bad."
He finally got a cab, just when we were all about to give up hope,
and supplied his address with an expression that looked something
like relief. "My name?" he said, almost as if he were incredulous that
they would ask. "This is *Muddy Waters.*"

We waited in the parlour where we could keep an eye out for
the cab through the front windows. It is a room which is kept
absolutely spotless with plastic slipcovers on the furniture, pale
watercolours on the wall, and pictures of Muddy and a young, almost
painfully innocent Little Walter that must have been taken at least
twenty years ago. There were pictures of Muddy's godchild and of a
girl in a graduation cap and gown on the mantlepiece, too, and
except for the records that were stood up in a rack beside the big
colour TV, nothing in the room gave indication that its occupant was
a blues singer or a musician of any sort.

The cleaning man was still working in the hall, and Muddy, not
yet accustomed to his crutches apparently, settled back with some
discomfort in his chair. "Where's that damn breeze coming from?"
he called out testily. "Close that damn door."

Before the man had a chance to close it, though, three small
children burst in, the eldest a girl of seven or eight, her hair done up
in pigtails and dressed like a magazine advertisement for kids. They
threw themselves on Muddy, and he shifted painfully, but his face
creased in a wide smile as they yelled, "Daddy, daddy, look what we
got." He grinned as they clambered to get his attention and showed
him a kite they had bought uptown. "Those are my grandkids," he
said as they went trooping off and the expression on his face would
have suited any proud father or grandfather.

He seemed quite content with life in general. And in spite of the
accident there is every reason that he should be. He's been successful,
he's well enough off, and he's received full recognition for his music
at last. Did he have any regrets? I asked, not really expecting any
answer. Yes, he answered matter-of-factly, without hesitation or
apology. "I'm sorry that the world didn't know me before they did.
Because I think I worked hard enough for them to know me. I
worked very, very hard to get where I am. And it just look like I was
late getting to the point where mostly the whole world knew
something about me. They could have come around a lot earlier, you
know. When I was younger and could put out more."

CHAPTER 4
JOHNNY SHINES
ON THE ROAD AGAIN

I

"I'm fifty-three years old, and I've been doing construction work all my life now. I ain't got any place doing that. I played music, and I never got no place doing that, so now I do have a chance to get somewhere. I've got a booking agent, and it seems like the world is interested in what I am doing. Music is ... you might say it almost compels me ..."

Johnny Shines is a contemporary of Muddy Waters and Robert Johnson. While Muddy is probably the most successful modern-day practitioner of the blues and Robert Johnson is acknowledged as perhaps the most accomplished and certainly the most influential of all bluesmen, Johnny Shines, who plays with all the brilliance and authority of the two men, is recognized primarily for his association with Johnson. "Robert changed everything, what you might say. Now I had Wolf's style in the beginning, and I was beginning to pick up on quite a few different guys' style as the time went along, and I ran into Robert in a place called Helena, Arkansas. And Robert and I struck up a friendship. Robert was a very friendly person, even though he was sulky at times, you know. And I hung around Robert for quite a while, and then Robert disappeared. All at once one evening he disappeared. See, he was a kind of peculiar fellow. Robert'd be standing up playing some place, you know, just playing like nobody's business. At that time it was a hustle with him as well as a pleasure. And money'd be coming from all directions. But Robert'd just pick up and walk off and leave you standing up there playing. And you wouldn't see Robert no more maybe in two or three weeks...

"So Robert and I, we begin journeying off. I was just, matter of fact I was just tagging along. Not that he wanted me along, I don't think, being a soloist, a fellow that really didn't care for nobody very much, I mean so far as running the road with him. It made it pretty tough keeping up with him, but Robert had a style that I liked, and I always felt like if you wanted something you have to get right behind it and stay with it. So that's what changed everything."

Johnson has been acknowledged as a musical genius by just about everyone with whom he came in contact, and Shines is no exception. "Robert just picked songs out of the air. You could have the radio on, and he'd be talking to you and you'd have no idea that

91

he'd be thinking of it, because he'd just go right on talking, but later he'd play that song note for note. All kinds of songs. Hillbilly, blues, and all the rest."

Today he includes a number of Johnson's songs virtually unchanged in his repertoire. In the early fifties he recorded for a number of companies, and his first commercial release was a brilliant version of Robert's "Walking Blues," retitled "Ramblin'." More recently he has put out a good number of his friend's better-known songs – "Steady Rolling Man," "Crossroads," "Sweet Home Chicago" – and certainly no one who has heard "Dynaflow Blues," his breath-taking adaptation of Robert's "Terraplane," could miss the unmistakable overtones, the slashing bottleneck guitar, the packed structure and nervous energy which characterizes the greatest of the Delta singers. At the same time, even while granting Johnson's influence, and his influence upon a whole generation of singers – Muddy, Robert Nighthawk, Baby Face Leroy, Elmore James and, through Elmore, Homesick James, Johnny Littlejohn, J.B. Hutto, and countless others – there is no cause for slighting Johnny Shines' own remarkable accomplishments as a bluesman. For Johnny Shines has over the years evolved a style that is as distinctly and creatively his own as any of his predecessors', and he stands today as probably the foremost interpreter of this rich musical tradition.

He ran with Robert for about three years. Their travels took them to Chicago, New York, Texas, Kentucky, Indiana, and even Windsor, Ontario. In 1941, after Robert's death, Johnny moved to Chicago, and after a few years of playing around professionally he settled into a fairly conventional kind of life, working a succession of steady jobs and playing music only as a sideline. Along with Muddy Waters, he was one of the first to record in the new post-war style (both recorded for Columbia in 1946 sessions that were never released), but somehow he seems not to have had the spark that Muddy had – or maybe it was just singlemindedness – and he never achieved the position of popular eminence that Muddy occupied in the development of Chicago blues.

Blues is a tough life. You work long hours for little pay, there is room for no more than a very few at the top, and the audience is always diminishing. Most working blues singers have by now gravitated to Chicago, and that seems to be the only city, with the

Clifton James/Francois Gaillard

possible exception of Houston, which will support its blues artists with club work. Even then most men hold a day job, and to keep at the music requires a determination and a stubbornness to succeed in the face of bleak facts.

There is not much of a life expectancy in the blues. Robert Johnson died before he reached the age of twenty-five, Little Walter died without making forty. Elmore is dead, Sonny Boy is dead, and among those who survive there is often a lifelessness which creeps into their music and robs it of any creative spark. Of all the singers who made it in the great Chicago era of the early fifties — when a predictable urban music was revitalized by the introduction of amplified instruments and down-home country flavour — only Muddy Waters and Howlin' Wolf, the one insulated by a phlegmatic almost indifferent manner, the other triumphing by sheer force of personality, continue to exert any influence or maintain any real popularity. The others have all drifted back to their jobs or disappeared, and while there is no question of the heights to which the competitive climate pushed the music, there is equally little question of the toll it took in human aspirations.

Johnny Shines never made it. In the sense that he was spared all the scuffling and grinding one-night stands he is lucky. Even when he was making his great sides for J.O.B. and Chess in the early fifties he never kept together a regular band. "No, it wasn't a full-time thing then. I was working out at Argo Starch when I recorded for Chess. When I recorded for J.O.B. I was doing construction work. I was probably drawing compensation or something like that, you know, to carry myself along. You understand, you're idle and you're drawing compensation and you're catching little things as you can to try to help yourself out ..."

He seems to feel a basic mistrust for the kind of life that music will often entail. While he has always been ambitious for himself he is quite clear what he will not do to further that ambition, and he speaks disparagingly of the joints and run-down bars that are often the only places to offer employment in Chicago. "It's a certain class of people," he says. "Not that there's anything wrong with them. It ain't that you're no better than those folks. It's just that there's certain places that you prefer not to go. Some people will play the taverns. Now I won't."

At one point for seven years, from 1958 to 1965, he gave up music altogether, convinced that there was no point to it. He kept up with the business anyway, though, buying a camera and taking pictures in the clubs, unable to stay away. "I'll tell you what it is, it's once you get into the night life, it's something you just don't drop all at once. I bought me some cameras and I started shooting pictures. And I got a chance to meet all the good guys and all and get autographs and things like that."

Bernardo Dennis, Leonard 'Baby Doo' Caston and Willie Dixon

Even when he was rediscovered in 1965 he was reluctant to commit himself to music, and it was four years before he appeared anywhere outside of Chicago or was willing to give himself over full-time to his new career. Mike Rowe, an English blues enthusiast, found him. "Some said I was dead, some said I was a truckdriver, some said I was doing this or doing that, you know. And finally Sunnyland or somebody gave him my address and he wrote to me. Well, after he wrote to me I didn't answer the letter, because I really wasn't interested, and then one day the doorbell rings and I open the door and who comes walking in?" Rowe didn't actually record him until 1968, but Sam Charters, on a whirlwind tour of Chicago for Vanguard Records, got him back into the studio just two weeks later. "Well, I guess before Mike got back to England Sam Charters called and asked me if I'd do another recording session. I ask him when and he says how about Thursday. And this was Friday, you know. Well, I told him, I says, I'm not ready for another recording session. Well, he say, work on it, you'll be ready by Thursday. And Thursday we cut the record. I had not had a guitar in my hands in seven years."

II

Johnny Shines is a youthful fifty-three. He is a stocky powerful-looking man whose chocolate brown skin is smooth and unlined, and he has an infectious buck-toothed grin which pushes out his upper lip. Though normally soft-spoken his voice will rise at any one of his frequent enthusiasms, and in his eagerness to make a point he will sometimes stammer a little and his voice will break. He is an easy-going man with a wide-ranging curiosity and a big booming laugh. Particularly when he is trying to explain his genuine involvement with his music he chooses his words with care, and he is always articulate and attentive in conversation.

Like most blues singers he is understandably bitter at past treatment and a little wary of the future. At the same time he possesses an almost mystical faith in the certainty of his own success. "The public don't know they want it, but they know there's something that they want from me. Otherwise they wouldn't be climbing onto me ... I know it's the next thing. I got the thing that they want. They just don't know what it is." He sees his rediscovery as the result of popular demand, and speaking of a session, at the time unreleased, that he had done for Pete Welding he said, "One of these songs in particular the public is waiting for. Which one? I really don't know. The public is going to pick this out. The public will pick it."

At the time that we talked, in early 1969, he was playing a week's date in Boston at what was to be the beginning of an international tour. The band was called The Chicago Blues All Stars, and for once the personnel really merited such a title. With Walter Horton on harp, Sunnyland Slim on piano, Willie Dixon on bass and Clifton James on drums, four of the five members of the group were soloists, and the programme they had worked out featured each one about equally. Willie Dixon did most of the talking; Johnny Shines got the adulation of the blues enthusiasts; Sunnyland Slim did his Woody Woodpecker imitations and seemed to greatly enjoy himself; Clifton James did a good workmanlike job and dredged up memories of his association with just about every blues singer who passed through Chicago; Walter Horton cadged for drinks. Everyone seemed to get along pretty well apart from the routine conflicts and bruised feelings that are endemic to any band, and they joked and reminisced about old times, shared memories, and mutual friends.

Johnny Shines seemed cheerful about going out on the road. "It's very exciting," he said, recalling his travels with Robert Johnson. "Say, for an instance, you leave here, you maybe go four or five hundred miles, and you don't know nobody, everything is new to you. It's really, I mean if a person lives in an exploratory world, then this is the best thing that ever happened to him."

All the musicians seemed pretty much in accord. They treated the engagement as a kind of adventure, exploring, meeting new people, seeing new sights. They drove around town in Willie Dixon's roomy station wagon, showing up for interviews and going out to eat, spending as little time as possible in the dingy South End hotel which all blues singers, perhaps from some vestigial memory of better times, make their stop. Now the lobby is hung with defaced No Loitering signs, the sharp-faced manager badgers guests, and the receptionist, henna-haired and exhausted, only shakes her head at this strange influx of people to see Mr. Shines. The halls smell, the plaster is peeling from the ceiling and walls, and the musicians joke about the bugs. Shit, that ain't nothing. Down home we had chinch

Robert Jr. Lockwood/Pete Lowry

bugs as big as your fist. You had to burn 'em out with lye.

Sunnyland Slim, a huge aging version of Jack Johnson — shaven-headed, mobile-faced, with a gold tooth and a flat cap — tells a long complicated story about moonshine and Mississippi that nobody understands. You mean you let them polices take that liquor away from you? Naw, man — Sunnyland gives them a pained expression. That ain't what happened at all. And he hastens to explain again in a garbled rush of words. Each offers stories of run-ins with the law. They turn from that to reminiscences of Chicago. Now, man, Chicago used to be one sweet town. Ow, man, I know it. Now you can't hardly stand on the streetcorner without some motherfucker come along, knock you on the head. Man, they done ruined the South Side. South Side sure was sweet.

Sunnyland is still trying to tell his story. I was fixing a flat, and they undressed me, man, they made me take all my clothes off. He grins a devilish grin. A famous blues singer's name is mentioned. Is he still performing? Naw, man, his old lady won't let him out at night. She got him so pussy-whipped he scared even to be seen talking with his old friends. I wouldn't have a woman, man, she gets to acting like that. You got to teach that pussy how to whistle.

All week they exchange reminiscences. They sought refuge and reassurance in familiar stories. Willie Dixon tried to get in touch with Robert Jr. Lockwood, Robert Johnson's stepson, in Cleveland. ("Robert Lockwood? I met him the same time I met Robert Johnson. Because Robert Johnson was staying at Lockwood's mother's house when we were there. He was just learning same as myself. From Robert? From anyone that came along.") Clifton James talked about a rhythm and blues singer he had been with. Chess misused

Sunnyland Slim/Val Wilmer

him? he laughed harshly. That man have misused everybody. That man have misused himself.

"You hear that?" Sunnyland Slim calls from his room. "That's me and J.B., J.B. Hutto, me and Big Daddy." Yeah? "Yeah, man, they got it on the radio. I was playing organ." WBCN, the local FM rock station, is doing a little promotion for The All Stars' appearance. They had run an interview the day before attended by everyone in the band except Willie Dixon, who stayed in the car to write a blues about Boston. Most of the questions are directed at Johnny Shines, and he answers as he has for fifteen other people. "Yes Robert had a way of playing, now on some songs you couldn't work with him. He had to work them by himself. Others I would second him on guitar ... A friend of mine carried me down to Helena, Arkansas where Robert were, he wanted me to meet Robert. Because this friend of mine thought I were good ... You know how this thing goes. There's a good guy playing at such and such a place, I'd like for you to hear him, I'd like for you to meet him. And the thing about it, what he wants you to do is to go and get your head cut. So he take me to Helena ... Robert himself never talked too much about himself. Now so many things I found out later I didn't know at the time. I found out from Walter that Robert have relatives in Memphis. And I didn't know he had relatives in Memphis, he never mentioned his people. He was a guy that didn't talk about himself whatsoever at all. And he was not a braggart. He never bragged on himself. He never said I can do this or I can do that, I'm great or I'm popular or anything like that. He just did it."

Back in the room he sits on the edge of a chair, restlessly fingering his guitar. "Rough life? Yeah, pretty rough sometimes. Sometimes we had money, sometimes we didn't, sometimes we had food, sometimes we had some place to stay, sometimes we didn't..."

Walter Horton sits perched on the edge of the bed, gaunt-faced and troubled, his long thin fingers playing nervously with each other, snuffling every now and then but otherwise absolutely silent. Earlier in the day he had seen a suit in the window of Good Will across the street and stared at it with the expression of a child, wearing his perennial black lambswool Russian hat. He had gone in and tried it on, but now he is wearing the same light gray suit that he has worn on the bandstand every night, and he, like it, has an elegant, slightly shabby look about him. He is gray-haired and dignified with a handsome sad-eyed face that stares inscrutably at Johnny Shines while Johnny talks about himself and the men they both knew.

"I started playing guitar in 1932. Started playing professionally in 1935. Howlin' Wolf at that time was my idol. He was playing at a place in Arkansas, for a guy called Will Weilers. He had something like these Saturday night fish fries, you know, good old times. And if you really wanted to enjoy yourself you'd have to go around to something like this. Well, I liked Howlin' Wolf's style, but I couldn't understand it. And I just hung around and hung around — being a youngster, you know — I just hung around until I begin to dig the guy and I really come in knowledge of what he was doing. See, I went after him. He was playing one Saturday night for Will, and he set his guitar down for a rest, as all the musicians do, you know. Well, this particular night everything changed, they started calling me Little Wolf, because when he came back I had the joint rocking. With Wolf's style, you know, and Wolf's numbers. I mean, it was just that easy this particular night. I could see what he was doing and understand it. All beforehand it was all Greek to me, but just in a few minutes time I really begin to understand what he was doing, so when he went on his break I tried it. When he came back I had the joint rocking.

"I first met Wolf, I was afraid of Wolf. Just like you would be of some kind of beast or something. Because it was an old saying, you know, people thought about magic and all such things as that, and I come along and say, a guy that played like Wolf, he'd sold his soul to the devil. And at that time Wolf had the most beautiful skin anybody ever seen in your life, look like you can just blow on it and it'd riffle. And I was kind of afraid of Wolf, I mean just to walk up and put your hand on him. Well, it wasn't his size. I mean, what he was doing, the way he was doing, I mean the sound that he was giving off. That's how great I thought Wolf was."

He reminisced about Sonny Boy and Walter Horton. "You get quite a few guys used to try to imitate Walter with these sounds and things. Now Sonny Boy had been quite exposed, that is this Rice Miller I'm speaking of. You know, Sonny Boy was probably blowing harp before Walter was born. I don't know how long he been blowing a harmonica. But he didn't know anything about this type of blowing. He met Walter when Walter was a little boy, you know, when he was playing on the streets. Walter's mother would come and run him out of the streets. So then Sonny Boy, he picks this up and he got to the place where he could get a sound out of his harp, you know, and then he'd change his harp from one side of his mouth to the other and drag it across his lower lip, *screek,* like that. In other words he made a show out of it...

"Sonny Boy had been quite exposed at that time. You see, Sonny Boy used to travel a lot by himself, just like Robert did. Sonny Boy used to wear cut-off boots, wore rubber boots, you know, like people wear to go cleaning out sewers and things. Sonny Boy used to wear those boots that he cut off and cut down on each side almost like old lady comforts or something. And that would leave this sharp part sticking up in front and sharp part sticking up behind. Sonny Boy wore those things from coast to coast. Walking and playing his harp. And he'd been quite exposed to the public, not in the real show in the limelight but I mean house to house exposure. It makes no difference how good you are, if you're not exposed to the public enough you're just dead." Walter stole off while he was talking about Sonny Boy with only a sly smile to betray that he had taken in what was being said.

By the end of the week everyone was getting a little edgy. Even Johnny Shines grew increasingly irritable. He remained polite, but he was noticeably more subdued and less eager to recall old times. He was tired of offering up his memories of Robert Johnson yet again, and seemed nettled that no one ever thought to ask about him. He was exasperated at being called upon for the tenth or twentieth time for his opinion of psychedelic music, and he seemed on edge from constantly being with strangers with whom he might or might not communicate, to whom he might or might not be no more than a phenomenon, some freak of nature which had outlived its time. You don't look old enough to have known Robert Johnson, they said. Could you play "Dust My Broom"? That just really blows my mind. "Yes, I have been hired as a showpiece, just by being black. We stopped at this place in Illinois and the guy asked us to play a piece. So Robert starts out playing and me right with him, and they tried to get us to stay there, so we stayed there a couple of nights, and the people at that time paid twenty-five cents a head to come in and see what the coloured guys looked like. And that wasn't in the South either. Well, that just shows you how unthoughtful sometimes people can be." Times had changed, but more and more he seemed to withdraw with a polite smile or a mumbled apology from the press of

Johnny Shines/Brad Barrett

attention, and often the blues fans who came to hear him do "Dynaflow" or Robert's songs were disappointed by his hanging back or, when he did sing, by the perfunctory nature of his performance.

"They had old upright pianos in those days. Half the keys would be off of them, and you'd hear a guy, and he'd scream, man, how he'd hit one of those keys on the piano, and everybody started jooking to it. I've seen the time when I'd hear a piano, heck I couldn't stay in the bed, I had to come out of it. I'm surprised somebody didn't kill me slipping through the cotton fields, trying to get to one of those jook joints. In other words the older people called them honky tonks. Sunnyland was in the honky tonk business, you know. And people knew him as a honky tonk piano player like. You understand what I mean, maybe he wouldn't say it himself, or maybe he wouldn't like the idea of me saying it. But there's nothing you can say, because he's playing back on farms and things.

"A boy called M&O was a piano player then. I knew M&O, M&O and I play together and Robert Parnell and a fellow called Piano Slim, oh quite a few different guys. I played with them, because I always fit in behind the piano, you know, just the two instruments. I could fill in and we would sound very good. Even though I wasn't. I didn't know one key from another. I barely knew one string from another. But I just had ideas and I used my ideas. And most of them were effective. So that means we could get it. And I could holler pretty good. Oh, I could scream like a panther. You think I can sing now. Christ you should have heard me back in the thirties."

III

The music that he has recorded since his rediscovery brilliantly reflects the various facets of his talents. Each record that he has made has had something different to offer, and with each there has been a conscious exploration of new territory. Inevitably it is the Robert Johnson songs which first attract attention, and for myself I doubt if anything can quite match the excitement of hearing "Dynaflow" (his adaptation of Johnson's "Terraplane" and the opening cut of the Vanguard album) for the first time. It was so dazzling, so

Walter 'Shakey' Horton/Val Wilmer

unexpected, it had all the tension, really, of a dramatic event. And it was for me like discovering Robert Johnson or seeing Skip James at Newport for the first time.

Johnny Shines is something much more than a gifted copy, however. The blues is in essence a highly conservative music, in which every artist embodies some stage in a continuing process of development, in which the individual composition achieves at best the crystallization of a tradition which goes back long before its author's birth. Even as brilliant a singer as Robert Johnson only represents a synthesis, however distinctive, of a number of different idioms, and there are any number of singers who have made a reputation on borrowings from another's style. You couldn't count all the Lightnin' Slims and B.B. Juniors and Sonny Boy and Jimmy Reed imitators. And Johnny Shines, quite apart from his haunting reconstructions of a blues style that had seemingly been dead for thirty years, is as convincing and inventive a stylist as exists within the structure of the blues.

He is, to begin with, a forceful explosive singer whose strong vibrato-laden voice possesses a range and sensitivity which is rivalled by few other bluesmen. He possesses a sensitive guitar style which always serves to complement what he is singing. On the numbers that he plays in standard tuning his guitar playing is limited and he is content simply to fill in behind the band. When he plays bottleneck, though — as on most of his recent recordings — there's room for no other soloist, and the combination of his strong soaring voice and the echoing tones of his slide guitar is overpowering in a way that recalls Muddy Waters' earliest sides or the beautiful lyrical slide of Robert Nighthawk.

"I have numbers now that I want to record with an acoustic guitar and just a bass, and this bass player just stay right with me and move when I move, I wants him to go over each song so much that he feels them himself, I want him to feel that they're a part of him. And that way I can get everything into these songs that *I* want, I wants to express myself, I mean what's in me."

"Tom Green's Farm," probably his most celebrated composition, comes as close as you can get to this ideal formulation. A beautifully written song based on traditional material and most familiar in Lightnin' Hopkins' "Tim Moore" version, it describes with chilling matter-of-fact humour the grim conditions of an

Arkansas prison farm. Despite the lyrics' ironic tone it's a serious song, and Johnny Shines does it seriously, restraining the natural exuberance of his voice and letting the guitar express whatever outward emotion he is willing to show. The slide trembling on the strings, the haunting reverberation of the notes which is only accentuated by the guitar's amplification creates a painfully sweet, almost keening effect. In a written reminiscence of Robert Johnson put together for *American Folk Music Occasional* he recalls Johnson's "talking guitar" in words that could describe his own. "He was a guy that could make a song sound good with a slide, regardless of its contents or nature. His guitar seemed to talk — repeat and say words with him like no one else in the world could ... One time in St. Louis we were playing one of the songs that Robert would like to play with someone once in a great while. "Come On in My Kitchen". He was playing very slow and passionately, and when we had quit, I noticed no one was saying anything. Then I realized they were crying — both women and men."

What is most striking about his music, though, even more than its compelling emotional surface, is the energy and enthusiasm of its performance. His voice retains a natural exhilaration and an almost strident confidence in itself which is possessed by few younger men. Listening to Johnny Shines you might think that the thirty years since Robert Johnson's death had never intervened. Not so much because the style is unchanged — the instruments are amplified after all, he is performing more in the Chicago band style, an extension of Johnson's solo slide and walking bass which Muddy popularized in the early fifties — as because he is singing with an undiminished vigour and enthusiasm. The years have not worn him down, and Johnny Shines seems to still possess an almost ingenuous enthusiasm for his music and the musical tradition in which he grew up.

He was content on his first recordings to rely on reworkings from that tradition. Since his rediscovery, however, he has revealed not only a talent for original composition but an astonishing capacity for growth and adaptation which Johnson alone seems to have shared. His blues have always depended upon irony and that special sense of paradox which is at the heart of the blues. "Well, you know that I love you, that's why you so unkind," he shouts out almost cheerfully in "Evening Sun." On "Brutal Hearted Woman" he sings, "I remember we first met one Friday in the afternoon/You said if I

JOHNNY SHINES

wanted your love, darling, I'd have to ring the silver out of the
moon." In an association of considerable complexity he goes on:

> Well, I can't live without you
>   and I'm not going to even try
> I'm afraid if you stop doing wrong
>   you won't last long
> So I'll go on and cry.

His recent recordings have shown even greater inventiveness both
lyrically and melodically. On "I Cry I Cry" he begins:

> You told me you were leaving
> Like a wounded lion I was out to kill
> But now things have changed
> All I want to do is help

And he continues:

> Now you walked out of that door
> I cried myself to sleep
> Now you're somebody else's trouble
> God knows you can't hurt me.

'I've been talking all night long, you haven't heard one word I say/
Well, you look like you been walking under ladders, take the
thirteenth for your lucky day," he sings to one woman. Of another
he remarks, "Well, my baby get contrary, she want to stop a train/
She want to hold out her hand and stop the lightning and the rain."
And in more familiar fashion he recapitulates that flat unadorned
sense of reality which is at the heart of the blues:

> I went to the graveyard, got down on my knees
> I said, Mister Gravedigger, give me back my baby please
> Gravedigger stood there, he looked me in the eye
> Said, I'm sorry man,
>   your woman has said her last goodbye.

The music only continues this singularity. I would have thought

107

his compositions a little lacking in melodic variation if it had not been for his most recent recordings. On these, however, he has shown an adventurousness in both words and melody, and he has put together elements from Skip James, hillbilly music, and traditional Delta influences in a way that I've never come across in the blues before. Admittedly his inventions do not always work. His irony is sometimes heavy-handed, and he does not always work out the sometimes startling imagery of his lyrics. But as much as any blues singer since Robert Johnson he shows a sustained and continuing creativity and an exploratory mind which finds any number of subjects suitable for his fertile imagination to play upon. "See, the question is why. The question is why and the subject is why. Why did this thing have to happen? Why did it have to happen at this particular time? Why couldn't it have been thirty years later? There's a million whys. That question why is at the beginning of every sentence. Why?"

One other thing must be mentioned in any assessment of Johnny Shines' music, and that is his remarkable partnership with Walter Horton over the years. Walter, whom he met as a boy and with whom he grew up in Memphis, has appeared on nearly every one of Johnny Shines' records, and his appearance always brightens what might otherwise be a more conventional musical performance. "I met Walter really in 1930. He — Walter — was about thirteen, and I was about fifteen, and at that time I wasn't playing anything, my father was living on a farm in Arkansas, he was trying to do farm work, in a place they call Mounds City. That was out around Marion, you know. And Walter would be sitting out on the porch, now you take a boy, an average boy, say thirteen years old, and maybe one fifteen would come along and disturb him, he would go into fisticuffs, you know, he would try to fight him or something like that. But Walter was very shy, and I used to be — he would be sitting on the porch, blowing in tin cans, you know, he'd blow tin cans and he'd get sounds out of these things. You see, this harmonica blowing is really a mark for Walter, it's not something he picked up, he was born to do it. And he's gonna do that as long as he has breath in him, he's gonna do that. I believe he'd crack tomorrow, he'd crack with a harp in his hand and he'd keep it in his hand. And probably you could never take that harp away from him. To tell somebody that Walter's probably the greatest harmonica player in the blues field, yes. But Walter could have been the greatest harmonica player in any field if he would have been attracted to the other part of music. Because right now if I want to play sweet numbers or something like that I don't have any trouble with Walter. If I play it say three minutes, I can give Walter a solo. No trouble."

Walter is everything that Johnny Shines says he is, and it is rare that you will ever hear a careless or a boring song from them as a result. Walter will coax the most incredible sounds from his harp, cupping the tiny instrument in his hands, contorting his long loose-jointed body until he squeezes out whatever effect he may be after. They complement each other perfectly. The pieces in standard tuning are opportunities, really, for Walter to solo, and on the albums that have been recorded since rediscovery and on the Van-guard set in particular he is given plenty of room.

Johnny Shines is a forceful intelligent man, very aware of the contemporary world and proud of his achievements in it. He possesses great dignity and warmth, and one can only hope that he will now at last get the success he deserves. Success is a tricky thing to define, though, and by the end of his week in Boston Johnny Shines was challenging his audiences almost openly. "Well, here's what," he said, talking about a proposed psychedelic album. "The more people tell me not to, believe it or not I didn't want to in the first place, but now everybody says don't do it. The way I feel about this psychedelic, since everybody says don't, I think I will. " He laughed good-humouredly, but there was no mistaking the bitterness of his tone.

On the last night of their engagement the nightclub was deserted, it was after one and everybody had gone home. The rest of the band wanted to quit, but Walter Horton was blowing with an endless inventiveness, an aching bittersweet sound, screwing the microphone into his throat, blowing with one nostril, and creating a dazzling variety of effects. He shifted nervously from foot to foot, his fingers fluttering, his expression lost, bent over the microphone like a cobra while the others understandingly went through the motions. Blow, blow, they shouted at him. Aw, blow your heart out, Walter. I don't want him around *my* house. He blows the socks right off it, don't he? Ain't no one here but us chickens, Willie Dixon said with a mellow chuckle. And Walter shut his eyes tight and blew for the empty room.

CHAPTER 5
SKIP JAMES
REDISCOVERED

You know I'm a good man
But I'm a poor man
You can understand.
                    —"Washington D.C. Hospital Center Blues"

I

As I first said it's a great privilege and an honour and a courtesy
at this time and at this age to be able to confront you with
something that may perhaps go down in your hearing and may be in
history after I'm gone. I hope to try to deliver and to promulgate
some things and teaching for the students and those who are very
eager and conscientious to try to learn some music and my style
especially. And I try to play it in a way some time so they can get
ideas.

Skip James thought of himself as a genius. There was little
question in his mind of the value of his music or the worth of what
he was doing. When I first met him he was adamant on the subject of
money. He had only recently been rediscovered after thirty years of
neglect, and he seemed almost scornful of my attempts to get at the
reasons for his "retirement."

"Why'd I quit? I was so disappointed. Wouldn't you be disappointed, man? I cut twenty-six sides for Paramount in Grafton,
Wisconsin. I didn't get paid but forty dollars. That's not doing very
good. Wouldn't you be disappointed?

"No more contracts. I don't sign no more contracts unless they
come up with the money first. If they're good for the money that's
one thing. Otherwise — *otherwise* Skipper'll just have to be a drifting
man."

Certainly Skip James came to terms easily enough with his new
celebrity. Although he was thrust without warning into a world
whose existence he could not even have suspected, he never pre-
tended a false humility or a gratitude that he didn't feel. "Well, I
suppose you want to know about my background," he said. "I was
born in Bentonia, Mississippi in 1903. Seems like I had a natural
talent for music. We used to have a well, and every time I'd go to the

*The material quoted in this chapter is based on separate interviews by Peter Guralnick and
Bruce Jackson. The Jackson material is used with permission.

Skip James at Newport, 1964/Dick Waterman

well for water I'd beat a tune on the pail. My mother saw that I was musically inclined. Well, I always have been very apt, I guess I must have been gened to that effect. I wasn't no more than eight or nine then. Just a kid. So I want to Yazoo City High School. There I met Miss Alma Williams, I never will forget her. She gave me lessons — one lesson, that was piano, not guitar. She taught me the rudiments, what you call the fundamentals, nothing fancy. After that I was on my own."

He played in Wheeler and in North Nicholas outside of Memphis. He worked in the sawmills and learned boogie woogie from Will Crabtree and Clarence Williams. Guitar he picked up from Rich Griffith and Henry Stuckey. "But I don't play guitar like nobody else," he said. "If there is someone, I have never heard of him. All my music is my own, I don't pattern after anyone or either copycat. Even when I sing a song you might have heard someone else do I rearrange it to suit myself. It's all original."

All through the thirties and into the forties he travelled with a gospel group both on his own and with his father, the Reverend Eddie James, to whom he seems to have been exceptionally close. When he was rediscovered in 1964 he had not played music actively in twenty years. "There were lots of companies eager to sign me. But I wasn't going to sing for nothing." Instead he worked a succession of jobs around Memphis and Birmingham, was ordained in both his father's and mother's churches, and returned to Mississippi to do farmwork some time in the fifties. Bill Barth, Henry Vestine, and John Fahey found him there in the Tunica County Hospital in June of 1964, and in July he appeared at Newport, still weak from his illness but with a song he had written in the hospital called "Sickbed Blues."

For anyone who was at Newport in 1964 it was an unforgettable experience. After an afternoon of legendary blues performers — Sleepy John Estes, Robert Pete Williams, Mississippi John Hurt, and the Reverend Robert Wilkins — Skip James appeared, looking gaunt and a little hesitant, his eyes unfocused and wearing a black suit and a wide-brimmed flat-topped preacher's hat that gave him as unearthly an appearance as his records had led us to suspect he would have. There seemed some doubt about whether or not he would actually perform, but then he was introduced and after some fumbling and retuning of his guitar he launched into what must be considered his greatest composition and one of the most affecting blues ever recorded, "Devil Got My Woman."

> *I'd rather be the devil*
> *than be that woman's man*
> *Cause nothing but the devil*
> *changed my baby's mi-i-nd.*

Paramount found me through H.C. Speir in Jackson. I played just about two verses of the "Devil" for him. Of course I didn't play the "Devil" like I play it now, since then I put in a little addition to it. But anyway, I played about two minutes and he stopped me and beckoned for me and said to me, Skip, he says, you made a terrific hit!

As the first notes floated across the field, as the voice soared over us, the piercing falsetto set against the harsh cross-tuning of the guitar, there was a note of almost breathless expectation in the air. It seemed inappropriate somehow that this strange haunting sound which had existed till now only as a barely audible dub from a scratched 78 should be reclaimed so casually on an overcast summer's day at Newport. As the song came to an end and Skip, who had gradually been gaining confidence while he played, peered out at his new audience, the field exploded with cheers and whistles and some of the awful tension was dissipated.

II

"That was the highpoint of the man's career," says Dick Waterman, who managed Skip, Son House, Mississippi John Hurt and just about every other country blues singer who was rediscovered at that time. "He came and conquered. It was high drama. That was exactly what it was. And in the true sense of the word 'dramatic.' If he had come, played, conquered and quit right there, there could have been no greater legend in this entire world than Skip James."

Skip James did not, of course, quit just after Newport or disappear altogether from sight. At the time that I spoke with him he was just ending his association with Bullfrog, the company which his co-discoverers had formed to exploit his rediscovery. In the year that he had been with them ("I wouldn't sign for more than a year") he had seen no records and little money or evidence of good faith. He was, naturally enough, upset and a little distraught from the strain of the break. "I don't care if I never record again," he said at one point, and undoubtedly a great number of his references all through the conversation were directed at Barth, who was serving as his road manager at his expense and to his express displeasure at that time. But two days later he signed with Waterman; he got a good recording contract with Vanguard shortly thereafter, and he was looking forward to a bright future. He had every reason to be confident that he could make a living, and a good one, too, at his new career.

It didn't work out that way. His personality for one thing was not suited to rediscovery. A proud almost haughty man who took great pride in his background and education ("My father was one of those you call DDDs, I think that stands for Doctor in Divinity, something like that. Well anyway, he pastored one of the largest churches in the city of Birmingham at one time, and he was the president of Selma College there for twelve or fifteen years. And

then quite naturally he was
pretty well called super-annuated.
Because he was eighty-six years
old."), he by no means fitted the
stereotype of the primitive
country blues singer. He was a
stiff unyielding man whose mind
seemed to run along abstract
lines which were helped not at
all by his relentless attempts at
explanation. He had no real
interest in his audience, and unlike Mississippi John Hurt, with
whom he was locked in a curious juxtaposition of outlooks
and styles and with whom he often
travelled and appeared, he had no
particular charm for them either.

Mississippi John Hurt/Dick Waterman

"He knew that his good friend John Hurt's music was much
more widely accepted," says Waterman, "that John played to wider
and larger audiences, that John was an artist in demand, that John
made more money. That, however, did not under any circumstances
alter his appraisal of John's music. Which was that it was play-party,
ball-less, pleasant music, good music for dances and country reels
but not to be taken seriously as great blues."

And Hurt? "A genius, he thought of Skip as a genius. Well, John
thought very little of his own music, it was just a whole bunch of
songs that everyone had been doing at home, and he thought of
himself as just a no-talented little picker by comparison to Skip.
Skip he regarded as being a man of awesome talent, of awesome
genius."

His music, too, was complex and not at all simple to understand. It struck a very precise balance between delicacy and orna-
mentation and depended for its effect upon a conscious artistic
approach virtually unique in the blues. His piano was absolutely
unique. He learned it, he said, in the barrelhouses from Will Crabtree. Later he came under the influence of more sophisticated
pianists like Clarence Williams and Little Brother Montgomery, from
whom he picked up "Special Rider," a piece he adapted for guitar.

Skip learned from them no doubt, and apparently he picked up a great deal from Crabtree.

"At his rest periods I'd get right on the stool behind him," he told Bruce Jackson. "Somehow he taken a liking to me because he seed that I was very interested and egotistical about trying to learn music, which you might say conscientious. And of course I was reared up to be kind of malleable in respect to old people. So when he'd get ready to take his rest, go off and get him a drink or sandwich or gamble (he was a great gambler, you know), he'd turn it over to me and I would entertain as long as I could keep some of his versions of sounds. And after I got strong enough then he'd be paying more mind to his sport."

If he patterned himself after anyone, though, it certainly didn't show up in the records he made in 1931 which resemble nothing so much as a bravura display of anarchic impulses, combining blues, barrelhouse and private inspiration in a blend which threatens at times to destroy any semblance of order which may have been established. It is a style characterized by nervous rhythms, inexplicable pauses, and tumbling cascades of notes, and if Will Crabtree played anything like this then our picture of what the barrelhouses must have been like will have to be radically altered.

His guitar for years seemed equally unique. Slightly more sedate in character it possessed an intangible quality which led its admirers to reach out for bizarre musical explanations. Occidental vocals set against oriental scales. A unique, specially manufactured and long since discontinued guitar which alone could produce the hollow doomy tones of Skip's 1931 recordings. An imperfect recording process. None of these descriptive attempts turned out to be true. Not much more prosaically it turned out that Skip played most of his pieces in open D minor tuning tuned down two frets, a feature which had appeared in the musical approach of no other recorded blues singer and gave his songs their unique hollow tonality. For that reason in his appearance at Newport he was immediately able to recapture the very qualities which made his work appear to be so remote and far removed in time.

What would have been even more unlikely to anticipate was that his playing should be representative of a whole school of musicians, that Skip James in effect was the product of a unique and very specialized local strain which found its parallel in no other

116

recorded style of blues. Of course he did always credit Rich Griffith and Henry Stuckey, even going so far as to assign specific credit for particular songs. In his recollection, though, they "rapped" on the guitar, and it is his intricate three-finger picking which is the distinctive feature of his style. It is impossible at this point to determine exactly what the whole truth is (it may even have been that Skip James was the dominant influence in this so-called Bentonia school and that it was he who first broke away from the less sophisticated frailing technique), but it seems evident now that the story is at least a little more tangled than Skip would have had us believe.

Around Bentonia Skip and Henry Stuckey are remembered as brothers, and whether this is true or not Skip was obviously extremely close to the older man. Arthur "Big Boy" Spires, a Chicago blues singer who grew up in Yazoo City, remembers seeing them together at picnics and country frolics, Stuckey on guitar and Skip playing piano. All through the twenties and thirties they played together off and on, and though Skip travelled a good deal ("I used to move around a good deal in my younger days. I reckon that's why

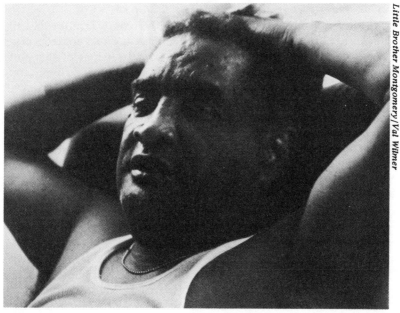

Little Brother Montgomery/Val Wilmer

they called me Skip.") they seem to have gotten together frequently whenever Skip was in the Jackson region. From the first they took an attitude which was more analytic than most bluesmen because, as Stuckey recalled in Jacques Roche's study, "when the first country blues records came out they 'studied' some of Blind Lemon Jefferson's pieces but only for the purpose of 'playing them better'."

They couldn't have been very popular outside the region, though, as Skip was influential only through his records (Johnny Temple and Joe McCoy recorded his songs and Robert Johnson did a version of Skip's "22-20", which was itself an adaptation of Roosevelt Sykes' "44") and neither figured very prominently in the recollections of other bluesmen. There was in fact none of the interchange which characterized the blues of the Delta, where Charley Patton and Son House are legend, their presence looming over artists even of the present day, or the blues tradition in general which prizes its recollections of Blind Lemon Jefferson in South Carolina, Virginia, and other places equally far flung from his native Texas. It is indeed something of a wonder that the Bentonia style was preserved at all, and we can only put it down to chance, really, and to Skip's own manifest ambition.

He was living in Jackson in 1930 with Johnny Temple, the only blues singer of any note with whom he had any real contact, when he tried out for Paramount. There are several versions of the story. In one Skip merely went down to Speir's music store to apply for a job as help. Sometimes it was Temple's idea, other times it was his own. In any case there was a roomful of singers auditioning, Skip recalled, and of them all he was the only one to pass. Two days later he was in Grafton.

He thought of himself at that point as a professional musician. By 1932, though, he had given up blues and put together a gospel group to accompany his father in his preaching. With The Dallas Texas Jubilee Singers he toured Kansas, Texas, Oklahoma, and Arkansas and when his father moved to Alabama to head schools in Tuscaloosa and Selma, he took a job in a Birmingham iron strip mine and drifted away from his music.

His pieces are still played in Bentonia today. Jack Owens, a contemporary of Skip's who not only grew up with him but at one point was married to a former wife, plays his "Devil Got My Woman" as a kind of spirited buck dance and Cornelius Bright,

Jack Owens/Val Wilmer

about twenty years younger, employs the same cross-tuning and falsetto voice in singing both Skip's and songs of his own. It's a style which seems to have grown up out of all contact with the outside world and it remains preserved as a little pocket of history untouched by time, carrying the image of Skip and Henry Stuckey in living memory just a little while longer.

III

I saw Skip James a great many times after Newport. He appeared at the Gaslight and the Second Fret and Toronto's Riverboat and the Club 47. He was always careful in conversation to make clear the distinction between these *coffee* houses and the barrelhouses in which his music had grown up, and while there was not, of course, the drama inherent in that first occasion at Newport, he maintained a standard of creativity and performance which never wavered.

Like a good many other blues singers Skip seems originally to have left his musical vocation with very few regrets. He was clearly bitter over his recording experience, and no doubt he felt a calling for the church. It seemed extraordinary to me in talking to him that he had not touched a guitar in all those years. It was even more extraordinary that, once recalled from a life in which his curious dignity must have seemed very much out of place, he continued to create and, removed altogether from the world out of which his music had sprung, he continued to write new songs and rework old ones.

His music was as adventurous in its way as Charlie Parker's or Thelonius Monk's, and when he was first rediscovered he seemed to take it as an opportunity to make up for lost time. It was touching in the beginning to see his eagerness to perform, the zest and enthusiasm with which he threw himself into the music. When he appeared at the Unicorn shortly after Newport with Mississippi John Hurt he seemed barely able to contain himself he was so full of energy, and during the breaks he would be up among the audience or fooling around on piano with his nervous rhythms and crashing chaotic runs. They did everything that week, blues and spirituals and Jimmie Rodgers yodels and even an improvised solo on "Silent Night" which sounded closer to Monk than to any blues piano I've

Cornelius Bright/Val Wilmer

heard on record. He had been practising since Newport (he was embarrassed, he told me, by the recordings that had been made, though those recordings were hailed as the most exciting blues to have emerged in thirty years), he was eager to show off new runs, and there would be moments of sheer exhilaration as he raced through his familiar repertoire, throwing in unexpected fillips like "Lazybones" and "Girl of My Dreams."

He didn't work much the last few years of his life. He was sick a lot, and the folk boom collapsed. And, too, he never attracted the audience which Son House and Mississippi John Hurt and other rediscovered blues singers gained for themselves, so that when he did play it was never before audiences of more than thirty or forty. Sometimes there would be as few as fifteen people in the house, and Skip would occasionally appear listless and dispirited. Sometimes he would seem merely to want to get the performance over with. But more often he would take a patient, almost fatherly attitude towards his young audience and try to explain his music to them as he played...

Now you know sometimes it seem like to me that my music seem to be complicated to some of my listeners. But the one thing that seem to be complicated to me, and that is that they can't catch the ideas. Because one thing is certain fact, and that is you must be musically inclined to get anywhere. Now I have had some students that are very very apt — they can catch ideas very quick — and other children you cannot instill it in them I don't care no matter how hard they tried. Well, there are some people they just don't have a calling for it. Now I might have wanted to do some things I've seen other people do and are prosperous at it and I would like to take it up myself. But it just wouldn't fit into my life, it wasn't for me. So the thing that a person should do seemingly while they're young is to seek for your talent where ever it is at, and then when you find where it is most fit to put it in execution, do that. Well, for myself I been out travelling ever since I quit school. I've had quite an experience at different ages and different times. And that's the best teacher I found. That's something they cannot take away from you. Personal experience.

All of his songs, he insisted, came from personal experience. "Little Cow and Little Calf Is Going To Die Blues" came from a time when "I used to handle horses and cows." "Crow Jane" was about "the contrariest woman I ever did know. She thought she was so good she didn't have to die." And when he came to "Hard Time Killing Floor" he was very careful to explain just what hard times were to a generation which had had no experience of the Depression.

> *People all drifting from door to door*
> *Can't find no heaven, I don't care where they go.*

He was very conscious of the gulf between himself and his audience, and while there were occasional snickers at a malapropism or the elaborate formality of his speech (everyone was referred to as his "predecessor"; girls became "damsels"; he apologized frequently for "vulgarities"), he retained a courtliness and an overall dignity at which it was impossible to laugh.

Skip James died in November of 1969. His death was marked by a notice in the *New York Times* and by a fanciful tribute in *Rolling Stone.* His funeral was attended by his wife, a few white friends, and blacks from the Philadelphia neighbourhood in which he had passed his last few years unheralded and unrecognized as an artist of any sort, much less a great one. Undoubtedly the greatest celebrity he ever achieved derived from Cream's recording of his "little tiny song," "I'm So Glad." This netted him $6000, enough to pay the funeral and hospital expenses anyway.

He could have been bitter, but he wasn't. The irony of his rediscovery must have occurred to him at times, but if it did it seemed no less surprising that he should have been neglected all these years than that he should have been sought out and found after so long a time. And if he was destined to be ignored in his second coming, if it seemed sometimes that he had been snatched from obscurity only to be returned to an obscurity just as profound, that, he was confident, was something which history would remedy. He seemed to possess a serene faith that this, too, would pass. He was above all a man with a sense of his own worth. "He was a man," as Dick Waterman said, "of intense pride in his ability. He was a genius and he knew it. I recall one occasion when a fan came into the dressing room, picked up Skip's guitar and played a Skip James guitar run. He then asked Skip if he'd ever be able to play the guitar as he did. Skip looked at him for a long moment and slowly replied, 'Skip has been and gone from places that you will never get to'."

CHAPTER 6
ROBERT PETE WILLIAMS
FREE AGAIN

I

"In this world no man, no woman knows what trouble really is. In this world. Now you take this. You setting here in this house, but you don't know what kind of trouble you run into before you get back home. Ain't that right, man? Ain't that the truth? And I'll tell you something, this the troublest world. But it's not the world, it's the peoples in it. It's the peoples in the world now today. You got your radio, you got your TV, every time you pick up your news, every time you turn on your radio or your TV, there's something happening, ain't that right? There's trouble all over the world. See, now if they could just study and look back — I'm dumb, what you may say dumb, I never been to school a day in my life, that child over there [his wife Hattie] she haven't never been to school. Which we trying to school our children now, we trying to school 'em every chance we get. But I hope that they don't grow up and get in all this racket. I hope they don't. Because if I could move back to where I thought it wouldn't be this humbug today — like it is now — if there was just some way I could move back I would move back, I really would."

Robert Pete Williams sits under a colour picture of Martin Luther King and the two Kennedys. He's drinking the afternoon away and seems upset that we won't join him. At the back of the house his wife is fixing a dinner which he insists that we share. There are three bedrooms partitioned off by curtains and two refrigerators whose contents he points out as proof that he was preparing for our visit. He was intending that we stay at least the night and like a number of other blues singers I have met seems proud that he has visitors who have come such a distance to talk with him. The other residents of his street give us curious stares, and the next day one of his neighbours stops by to look us silently over. It is an unpaved dirt street, certainly rural and made up of rather misshapen jerry-built structures like Robert Pete Williams' and ranch houses with middleclass aspirations. The neighbourhood is entirely black, but it is not as poor as many areas just adjacent and Robert Pete Williams complains bitterly of the "educated fools" who will not even say hello to him and pass him by as if he is beneath their notice. There is a Mustang parked next door, and telephone lines will be coming in next month. Robert Pete himself owns a TV and a stereo console. He lives in relatively comfortable surroundings, and while he still operates a scrap metal truck at this point he could probably begin to live on his earnings from music alone. Perhaps for this reason he directs most of his resentment not at the whites who have kept him in virtual servitude nearly all his life but at the young, black as well as white, who by upsetting the system he sees as trying to take away the gains that he has made. There has been a boycott up in Maringouin, and he views it more as a personal affront than as a measure of political or economic self-determination. He thinks integrated schools might work up north, but here in rural Louisiana they just mean trouble. His connection to the greater world exists only in the most tenuous of terms and except for his blues would be without any relevance at all. He is a very religious person, a sad gentle man who feels he missed his vocation when he did not take up the Lord's call many years ago, and his songs, like his judgments, are tinged with a fundamentalist, almost holy fervour that has little to do with politics or political realities.

> *So much is happening in this old wicked world, Lord*
> *Every time you pick up a paper, listen to the news*
> *So much is happening in this old wicked world.*

> *I was reading*
> *In the news*
> *The other day*
> *Where one of them great mighty jets*
> *Had trouble in the air*
> *31 passengers got killed*
> *Oh Lord, Oh Lord, I wonder who was in 'em*
> *Was it childs of God?*
> *Lord, I hope to sail in God's kingdom*
> *Have mercy on me*
> *Man I could just feel when they was falling through the air*
> *Lord have mercy on the poor people's souls.*

There was an old man on a horse to mark our arrival in Rosedale. He was wearing a white cowboy hat and holding the reins loosely in his gnarled black hands as he talked with the white filling station attendant. He remained there motionless as we slowed up, then warily circled the town, coming back each time to the central crossroads — filling station, grocery store, post office, another grocery store — which makes up Rosedale's business district. It was as if he were set there purposely to underline the strangeness of the commonplace, the foreignness of the world that we were about to enter.

Rosedale itself is no different than any number of other small hamlets in the surrounding community. It is made up of blacks and whites in both impoverished and comfortable circumstances. Tar-paper shacks stand side by side with prosperous suburban homes. Out beyond the consolidated school there are antebellum mansions which might have served as a faithfully recreated movie set, and the pretty rolling farmland is dotted with horses and cows. Robert Pete Williams, it turned out, lived over closer to Livonia in Maringouin, but his post office address was in Rosedale so we slowly cruised within its township limits, looking for a Negro who might lead us to him or for some secret sign of his presence.

The first black people we approached regarded us with dull-eyed stares of incredulity which gave way to muted hostility only after we repeated our question several times. Robert Pete Williams? No, they had never heard of him. Eddie Williams or maybe George Williams. What did you say his name was again? We would repeat it patiently at first and then with mounting despair as the awareness grew upon us increasingly that it was impossible to make clear either our intentions or our good will.

Some teenagers led us eventually to the postmaster's house where the postmaster, Mister Gene, was spending a quiet Memorial Day at home. We approached the door with some trepidation, especially when we noted the sheriff's car next door, but Mister Gene was perfectly friendly and explained that while he didn't really know where Robert Pete Williams lived he thought it was out the West Oak Road. We thanked him, followed his directions out through town, and looked in the rear view mirror only once or twice to make sure that the sheriff's car was not following us. The old Negro was still sitting on his horse at the crossroads.

We drove past the white neighbourhoods and out away from town, but there were no names on the mailboxes, or numbers even, and we were unable to find any clue to Robert Pete Williams' presence. After driving for several miles we saw a black man ploughing a field with his son. I climbed across a ditch and waited for him to reach the end of his row. Did he know of a blues singer named Robert Pete Williams out this way? The postmaster had sent us out. He looked at me a little puzzled, and his boy seemed frightened as the tractor sputtered, coughed, sputtered again and died. Well, he said with an almost friendly grin, he didn't know this Robert Williams, but the fellows out at Romig's Service Station knew just about every musician in the area. Why didn't we go over there? He was sure they'd be able to help us out.

Romig's is run by a white man but staffed entirely by blacks. The white man was standing out in front by the pumps. Was this Robert Williams white or coloured? Coloured? Ask one of the boys in there. Inside the garage a number of black men were sitting around talking and trading stories. The owner came in behind us and announced that we were looking for someone. He stood behind us as we explained our mission, and almost before we could finish talking there was a profusion of denials. No, there was no such person living in the area. They knew every musician who lived anywhere nearby here. What did you say his name was again? Maybe you mean Robert Patterson. Yeah, that must be it. He mean Robert Patterson. You remember Robert Patterson. Oh yeah. He don't live here no more. He live over in Baton Rouge. Haven't lived here for years.

Had he been in prison? my friend asked. Yeah, that's right. He spent some time in Angola. Did he have a lot of kids? Well, I don't know if he got a lot of kids now. Yeah, it's Robert Patterson you looking for. You won't find him here. And if it ain't Robert Patterson it's probably Robert Jenkins. He never did no time in Angola, but he sing a lot of blues. More rock 'n' roll like, but he's a good blues singer. The white man nodded approval, and there was animated debate among the mechanics and hangers-on as to whether this Robert Jenkins had ever lived in Rosedale or in Scotlandville. No, I growed up with him in Baton Rouge. I lived next door to him all my life, one man insisted. We thanked him politely and drove back toward town.

Just before the bridge where you turn to go back down West Oak Road there were some old people sitting out in front of their houses drinking and fanning themselves. One old man was beating on an upside down bottle of Seagram's Seven, about five times normal size. I approached him, and he told me his name was Eddie Williams,

his father's name had been Henry Williams, his grandfather's name....
Meanwhile my friend had gone inside the run-down coloured cafe
which stood beside these ramshackle houses and without any hope
of getting an answer asked the same question we had been putting to
every other black resident of the area repeatedly all afternoon.
C'mere kid, I was addressed by a toothless old lady, who sat on her
porch rocking and spitting tobacco. The old man next door beat out
the same monotonous tune on his bottle of Seagram's, humming
along with the rhythm. I tried to explain to the lady why we were
looking for this man, but neither of us was able to understand much
of what the other was saying. My friend emerged from the grocery-
bar. There's someone in the bar who knows what I'm talking about,
he said excitedly.

Inside a youngish Negro sipping beer repeated what he had
already said. Oh, he's the cat that been overseas. He drives a
scrap-iron truck. You can just look for his truck. He live over by the
railroad. It was hot inside, and over in the corner was a jukebox with
records by Lightnin' Hopkins and John Lee Hooker as well as
popular soul tunes of the day. He drew us a map on the back of an
old paper bag and asked us if we could follow it. We were still a little
mistrustful, I think, but we went over the directions once
more and got back in the car. I tried to repress my mounting sense of
excitement, but it was hard not to feel that we might have hit on
something at last.

The map bore out, the directions worked fine, and except for
one or two false turns we found everything just as it was indicated
on the paper bag. We passed Romig's without slowing down, drove
further out into the country, crossed some railroad tracks and turned
onto a dirt-paved street. As we drove past one of the houses
we heard a whistle and turned to see a man come running out of the
doorway with a big smile on his face. We turned around and almost
bounded out of the car, shaking hands and introducing ourselves all
around. Robert Pete seemed genuinely glad to see us and a little
puzzled that we had had so much trouble finding him. He had left
word at the gas station, he said, and he had parked his pick-up truck
so we could spot it from the road. He had even had his little girl
write his name on it. We looked, and sure enough there it was.
Written in chalk in small letters it said Mr. Robert P. Williams on the
side of the cab. With great goodwill he showed us in.

II

Lord, I feel so bad sometimes,
*   seems like I'm weakening' every day*
You know, I begin to get gray since I got here
Well, a whole lot of worryin' causin' that...
One foot in the grave look like
And the other 'un out
Sometime I feel like my best day gotta be my last day...
Lord, my worry sho' is carrying me down
Lord, my worry sho's is carrying me down
Sometimes I feel like, baby, committin' suicide
Oh, sometime I feel, feel like committin' suicide
I got the nerve if I just had anything to do it with...
"Prisoner's Talking Blues"

It's difficult to approve the banalities of most blues singers after listening to Robert Pete Williams. More than anyone else he shatters the conventions of the form and refuses to rely upon any of the cliches, either of music or of lyric, which bluesman after bluesman will invoke. Instead he sings blues which reflect a unique and personal vision; he makes each song unmistakably his own. And while at times his genius may seem perverse in its oddness, when he succeeds and each odd element comes together he suggests a metaphysical dimension to the commonplace as he recounts the day-to-day experience of his life in almost painful detail.

I got up this morning, and I put on my shoes
I strung my shoes, then I washed my face
I walked to the mirror for to comb my hair
I made a move, didn't know what to do
I stepped way forward, started to break and run
Oh baby, oh baby, baby it just ain't me
I done got so ugly, I don't even know myself.

Robert Pete Williams was born in 1914 in Zachary just outside of Baton Rouge. When he was fourteen his family moved to Scotlandville, and he has lived in and around that area all his life. He comes from a large family, six girls and three boys, eight of whom

130

are still living, and grew up doing mostly farm work. "I started out
when I was a youngster thirteen years old. I used to skin cows, sell
the hide. Sell the bones, I used to sell the bones for fertilizer. I
worked at a dairy, I get up at two o'clock in the morning to go to
work. Milk that man's cows, then I go out and hustle on the side.
Well, you see, I couldn't draw that money like the youngsters
drawing their money today. If I work for you you pay me fifty
cents a day, which was twelve dollars a month. And my mother
sent my sister to pick up that money every week. Cause she took
care of us, she brought us all up right through till we was raised.
Well I come up the straight way, I likes to work. And I been like
that all my days."

> *I tell you one thing —*
> *I was sorry that I ever was born a man,*
> *I wisht I was born a woman.*
> *·Work out in the hayfield until sun go down*
> *And you know what I got to do when I come in?*
> *Got three or four cows to milk, man...*
> *Some day I swear to God*
> *I sure look to get away from this place*
> *I be so tired sometimes, I ask my old lady*
> *I say, Look-a-here, gal,*
> *If you was able I would ask you to go*
> *Get somebody to go to bed with you*
> *That's how tired I am, gal.*
> *She say, you shouldn't work so hard.*
> *How in the world can I help that?*
> *Tell the man that you tired, she say.*
> *I say, I telled him that, but he don't pay me no mind.*
> *He hear me blowin', he say, What's the matter?*
> *I say, Man, I tired and hot.*
> *He say, Let's get it, boy.*

Robert Pete Williams takes great pride in his reputation as a
hard worker. Even during the Depression, he recalls, he always
managed to keep some kind of job, and he has vivid memories of
sleeping in barns, subsisting off pepper grass and raw potatoes, trying
to keep his family together. He has a kind of nostalgia for those

Robert Pete Williams/Terry Pattison

times, too, when for three dollars he could buy all the groceries he needed and distinctions were clearer and more sharply drawn.

"Yeah, I seen better days then than I see now. At fifty cents a day. You know what I'm talking about? Okay, the money. I could take about three or four dollars, go to the store to make groceries and, you know, flour was thirty-five cents a sack, flour, meal, you'd have so many groceries you couldn't pack it back. You'd have to have a wagon or a buggy or something to bring it back. Now today — I just can't see where the money's going to. I might give my wife fifty dollars to go to the GI store, you could go to the store to make your groceries and you could pack it back. And the way the world running today, it got me all sick. Cause I didn't come up that way. I never been to school a day in my life. Cause I come up the straight way. And everywhere I put my head, into any white man's door, I knock on his door, walk in, he say, Come in. See, that's Pete. I'm welcome. I can't read, I can't write. I never been to school in my life. I never studied no rascality, nothing like that. So that make me have a good record all over the world. Up until 1955. That's when I got in trouble. I guess you all know I been in trouble."

> Well, on my way a-goin' along, I got no success at all
> I go to my bossman's house, walkin' in,
>   forget to reach for my hat
> When I forget leave it on my head
> Cause he likely to get him a club an' knock it off my head.
> Yassuh and nosuh, all over there's no good place
> Oh, Yassuh and nosuh, an' all over this earth
>   there's no place
> He may be young, he don't have to be
>   more than sixteen or seventeen years
> You got to honour him at the groun'.

The trouble he got into had nothing to do with race. It was, like so many other episodes of his life, a misunderstanding. "See, I didn't get into trouble on my own. I got in trouble by a smart guy that taken me for the wrong man. And I say this from my own life. You setting here in my house, ain't you? You's a long way from home. But it don't make no difference how far you is from home, if I get bullheaded and try to take your life you kill me right here in my house. Simply keep your life. Ain't that right, man?" His voice rises, and all the while, flushed and excited by the story he is telling, he is holding a gun and waving it in our faces. It is only later that my friend tells me it was a toy gun. "Here. Give me your hand. Well, I wouldn't misuse you, but ain't that right, man?

"Cause this fella, Jackie Lee, come up to me and ask me where I come from. Well, I tell him, I come from Zachary. Now he got mad at this, he cursed me, because he thought I was being a wise guy. See, he taken me for the wrong man. And I say, well I wouldn't curse you. But he come up to where we was sitting, my sister and brother and me, and he cursed at me. And when I went to walking out he grabbed me. Well, I tore loose from him, I told him don't come no closer, but there was no way I could get out of that place. And I saw that he meant to kill me. So the first time I shot him in the stomach. He kept coming, and the next shot hit him in the heart. So I just beat him up to the draw. And that's how I was misused. Cause I was sent to prison all for the sake of that one I referred to was paid to go against me.

"I was sent there for natural life. I got out in 1959. The captains up there said, Robert Williams. Yes, sir. Said, Come here and bring that guitar. I want it tuned up. I say, Yassuh, Captain, it's tuned. Says, Get over here, I'm gonna dial the telephone and let the family at the house listen. And the wives they would listen and think they was having a party. And they tell me, they say, You see you? I say, Yes, sir, Captain. Say, you ain't got no business here. They say, We like you to pick them blues, them ole lonesome blues on the guitar. Now let me tell you something. They say, We used to be able to get a man away from Angola, but we can't do that any more. We used to carry him away so he could be working our farm or working our yard, something like that. A good Negro like you. Well, we can't do that now, they stop us from doing that. But we gonna see that you get on away from here. And they got me away from there in 1959.

"I was carried away in 1956, April 6, 1956. When I come in they put the stripes on me. Big stripes. Iron ball. Before the guard. Looking up in the gun barrel. They pulled the stripes off me, pulled 'em off, put me in khakis, made a guard of me. Put me over the big stripes, got them big stripes all sitting around. And this captain riding a horse, to every guard, when he got me, he say, Robert, you got that gun loaded? I say, Yes, sir, Captain. I got it loaded. He say,

Someone cross that line, you kill him? I say, Captain, I said, I don't have to kill him. I say if he break that line, you know I can stop him. Well, he didn't like that, but then I explain to him what I mean. If he break that line I can bring him down, I can shoot him in the legs, I can stop him without killing him.

"Well, I stayed there doing that for a little while. Then the captain tell me, We gonna send you down to the dairy farm. It's a mean man down there. If he do you any harm you just raise your hand, let us know you coming in. Well, I went down to this dairy farm, they had cows you couldn't put the machine on, they was too low to the ground. So I get to milking and this man, he standing over me, and I wonder if I'm not milking 'em right or something. But when I'm finished he shake his head and say. Who learned you how to milk? Cause I seen many a milker but I never seen anyone could outmilk you. Well, he never raised a hand or foot at me. Said, Robert, you look like a good old darkie. He say, I got some dogs here, want you to help me with them, they's bloodhounds, you know. Said, I want you to help me train these dogs, will you do that? I said , Yes, sir. I do that. So I do that, I run the dogs for that man. And one day I was running those dogs, I run into a bush, I got struck in the eye. Well, Mister Olsen up there in the yard, he took a look at me and he said, What's the matter with Robert's eye? He thought someone had jumped on me. Ain't nobody jumped on him, said Mister Bilodeaux. He was just running the dogs and he got struck in the eye. Nobody jumped on him, uh uh, he say. Well, say, you see him? said Mister Olsen. I don't want nobody laying a hand on him down there. Cause Robert is a good Negro.

"Well, I knowed I wasn't going to stay there long. I used to tell people, I ain't gonna be here long. I say, I got a man gonna help me, and that man is Jesus Christ. They'd laugh at me, but I'd tell 'em all the time I'm gonna leave you all here fightin' and carryin' on. So, you know, one day I was in the post, I was settin' there one day with the gun across my lap, someone come in there and patted me, said, Don't worry. You'll be home with your family before Christmas. Well, I got up, I looked all around, cause I knowed that no one could get in to the post, I couldn't close my eyes cause I had to look for the line walker, to flash him back. But I fell down on my knees and prayed. And it was just like that voice said. If you carry yourself clean you gonna get along all right no matter where you be. I obeyed orders, I did my work right, I prayed. And I was home in December 1959, just three and a half years. And I had a natural lifer."

"The amazing thing," says Richard Allen who along with Harry Oster recorded Robert Pete in prison and was instrumental in getting him released, "is that the other prisoners believed him. Every one of them claimed to have been framed, they each had their own story, but they somehow recognized that he was different from the rest. They believed him. Of course they had all heard of Leadbelly. Everyone in Angola knew that he had gotten a governor's pardon for his music. So they were all naturally anxious to record for us. We didn't have any difficulty finding singers to record. But Robert stood out very definitely from all the rest."

"A man from Denham Springs that I hadn't never saw, Mister Eastley, come and got me. Hadn't never saw me, until Mister Harry Oster come in there and said to make up a sad blues about my family. Well, I told him I didn't know, but he gave me a twelve-string guitar for me to pick and I made up a sad talking blues about my family. You all might have heard that. It was that 'Prisoner's Talking Blues.' I didn't know what I was going to say or anything. But it was sad, you know. Some of the prisoners there, they couldn't stand it and so I had to cut off. All them prisoners, standing around crying, thinking about their homes. They made me stop singing."

> Sometime I feel like I never see
>   my little ole kids anymore
> But I don't never see 'em no more,
>   leave 'em in the hands of God...
> In a way I was glad my poor mother had 'ceased
>   because she suffered with heart trouble
> And trouble behind me sho' woulda went hard with her
> But if she were living I would call on her sometimes
> But my old father dead, too
> That'd make me motherless and fatherless
> Family done got small, looks like they're dying out fast
> I don't know, but God been good to us in a way
> Cause old death have stayed away a long time.

On the record you hear the catch in his voice and wonder if it is a sob, you hear the chirping of birds in the background and muted

accompaniment of the twelve-string guitar. In the privacy of your
room on your hi-fi you listen to a man's naked suffering.

"One morning I was laying across the bed, somebody come and
touch me. There's somebody want to see you at the office. Okay, I
go over to the warden's office, there's a big white man sitting up

Robert Pete Williams/ Parker Dinkins

over there. I say, Good evening, bossman. I didn't say boss, because there was more than one of them. They say, You ain't no gal-boy, is you, Robert? I say, No, sir. You all know what a gal-boy is? They use the boys at Angola for jailbirds. Youngsters. I say, no, sir, I said, Look, I'm in prison, if someone try to use me for a gal-boy, I say, you better get ready, either they die or I die. Cause I'm going down to my grave. Well, he say, good. Are you ready to go home? Yassuh. I'm ready to get away from this place. He said, Well, I'm the man to get you away. Say, You heard of me? I say, No, sir. I heard talk of you. You Mister Eastley. He say, I'm Mister Eastley, I used to be warden here. Said, I heard talk. Well, I'm gonna get you away from here. I ain't carryin' you with me today, but I be back. And two days later he come back and got me. He come in an airplane and took me away. That's where I met my wife. The other ones that I had, when I got in trouble they all went the other way. It's a funny thing to say — in this world no man, no woman knows what trouble really is. In this world."

Even parole was not particularly easy for Robert Williams. In fact he was kept in virtual bondage until 1964 when after five years of diligent efforts by Harry Oster and Richard Allen he finally obtained a full pardon. In the meantime he was not permitted to travel, he was forced to turn down invitations from Newport and other folk festivals, and he worked under conditions which amounted to near-slavery.

> You know, I walk along, talk to myself
> I wonder,
> Is everybody have the same mind that I got?
> Sometimes I have a mind to leave this place
> I tell my people that sometimes
> But they say, You know you doing time.
> Yes, I do know I'm doing time
> But I thinks about my brothers then
> All of them is well, and I'm the onliest one
>   hanging around here
> I take that real bad sometimes.

Many of the songs which he recorded for Harry Oster continued to reflect the bitter conditions of his daily life, and in addition to

"Death Blues" there was the earlier poignant reflection, "Pardon Denied Again."

> *Lord, I carried myself on the pardon board*
> *You know, I got denied again*
> *Been on the board three times*
> *Each time I was denied.*
> *They tell me the governor was on the board*
> *All around the board, a-looking at them people's case*
> *Lord, they must have passed mine right in*
> *Because they denied me again.*
> *I got, I got a big family on my hands*
> *They's out there in that free world*
> *Waiting on me to reappear*
> *Oh Lord, they want me to return again*
> *Back to my home.*

Eventually he did return to his home. In 1964 he went back to Scotlandville where he did some farming and then got a job in a lumberyard for $1.40 an hour, the highest salary he has ever earned. Two years ago he built his own house in Maringouin outside of Rosedale ("I built it according to the old country way," he told us proudly, pointing to the reinforced bolsters at every beam) and with his brother-in-law wired it himself. He is today a much more settled person and perhaps his blues suffer for it. But he seems happy with his young wife, Hattie, and if he does not show the same fierce exuberance which he displayed in 1964 at Newport (at his first major appearance outside the state) he seems a much more contented and peaceful man. The rush of emotion which was evident then has modulated itself a little.

> *Well, I told my wife, don't look for me back home soon*
> *When I get to balling, swinging out*
> *   with a little old teenage gal*
> *I'm gonna have myself a ball*
> *I'm a balling man, and I don't care what you men say.*
> > "Free Again"

"I'm strictly a one-woman man," he told us with a beautiful smile.

"I'll tell you the truth, I'm slow. I didn't know what a woman was until I was twenty years old. That's right. I didn't even know what a woman was."

III

Robert Pete Williams has been playing music since 1934. It was then that he got his first guitar. "Music been following me all my days. It just come to me. I started out beating on a bucket. I left that bucket, and I made me a guitar. Then I got myself a guitar for a dollar and a half, the strings was raised up so high you had to mash down on them. I was just banging around, trying to learn something on it, you know.

"Until one of my friends was working for a white lady, she say, Pete, you so interested in getting yourself a guitar, why don't you go to my boss madam house, she got a guitar and she may sell it to you. She bought it for her boy to learn on, and he ain't got no interest in that guitar, he don't even pick it up. So I went down there, knock on the porch, she come to the door, say, What you want? Can I help you? I say, Yes, ma'am. I heard you had a guitar down here that I'd like to get from you. That you bought for your son to learn, but he didn't have no interest in it. She say, Yesss. She say, I got a hundred and seventy-five dollar guitar sitting back in there now, I want it out of my house. She say, You got any money on you? I say, Four dollars. She give me that guitar for four dollars. And that was a hundred and seventy-five dollar guitar.

"Well, back in those days I used to play dances, Saturday night parties, fish fries, all that kind of stuff, you know. And they all used to call me Peetie Wheatstraw. Play the blues, Peetie Wheatstraw, they say. Cause I could holler pretty good and raise my voice, sing that false stuff, that was before my throat begin to bother me. But my wife didn't like for me to play at these parties and such — this was my first wife, y'understand — she'd get jealous and she'd grab at me. And this woman'd be pulling on me, you know, so I can't play my music. People paying me to play here, I tell her. It may not be more than fifty cents for the whole night, but they paying me just the same. Well, okay. One Saturday night, I had my shoes all shined, they was setting out on the porch all ready for me to play. All of a sudden the shoes disappeared. I say Ella, where my shoes at? She say, I don't know. I say, Okay, I'm gonna go up on the corner, stay up there for a while. Here come Eloise's cousin. Say, Pete, ain't you gonna play tonight? I say, Yes I am. No, you ain't, man. Eloise done burned your guitar up. Ain't nothing left but the strings. And that was a hundred and seventy-five dollar guitar, that was a wonderful guitar. I ain't never had one like that since."

The music that he was playing at these Saturday night fish fries and all-night parties and country balls was in a much more conventional style than the blues that he will play today. He was influenced first of all by the records of Peetie Wheetstraw and, much more evidently, Blind Lemon Jefferson. He was also strongly influenced by local musicians like Henry Gaines, Frank and Robert Meddy, Silas Hogan, his uncle Simon Carney, and Lacey Collins whose songs he will still do today. Interestingly enough, Collins's style sounds very much like a cross between Lightnin' Hopkins and Skip James, and the one song he did for us in that style, although more conventional in imagery, was every bit as distinctive as Robert Pete's own singular resolution. Of the others Silas Hogan alone recorded (and then only in the fifties style of amplified blues which Excello, a Crowley, Louisiana company, developed) although Simon Carney played in the same style of knife accompaniment which Robert Pete used on his recorded versions of "Rolling Stone" and "Poor Boy (Long Ways From Home)."

It was some time in the forties, though, that he developed the style by which we know him today, an arresting, absolutely unique blend without apparent influence or precedent. In a definitive monograph which he wrote originally for the *Little Sandy Review*, Al Wilson describes the basic change which took place in his musical approach.

> Robert Pete demonstrated this change in graphic terms to David Evans in an interview which I missed. Evans had asked Pete if he had ever changed his style, and the answer was "Yes." Asked to explain Robert Pete instructed him to pay attention as he played two songs. The first, in E minor (standard tuning), sounding much like "A Thousand Miles From Nowhere" (on Prestige Bluesville No. 1026). It had a heavier bass than usual for him and, while using a fairly intricate right hand, he did not venture up the neck past the third fret with his left. However, in the second number, in A minor

(standard tuning), his left hand was everywhere, based primarily in the fifth to eighth fret area, but going as high as the thirteenth fret, and with frequent quick glides on the bass strings. Then he explained as follows:

"This here [indicating the song he had just completed] that carries so many notes to it, you see. I'm picking from the box back down to the key, and then I wasn't doing it a while ago – I was just from here [plays note on the third fret] – but now I'm picking from the box back down to the key, and then I can stay up at the box and pick, too, you know, which a lot of people can't do.

"Some people pick up a guitar, they'll stay right down there at the key and that's far as they can go, but if you're going to pick a guitar go ahead on, learn what you can on, play from the box on back down to the key, you see. I plays like that."

At this point Evans asked when he had changed his style. Pete replied:

"Well, I changed my style when I see where I could find more notes on a guitar. I was a grown man when I changed my style then – I say I was about twenty-eight years old then.

Now Evans asked what Pete felt was responsible for a change resulting after playing another way for ten years. Pete answered:

"The sound of the atmosphere, the weather changed my style. But I could hear, since me being an air-music man. The air came in different, with a different sound of music. Well, the atmosphere, when the wind blowing carries music along. I don't know if it affect you or not, but it's a sounding that's in the air, you see? And I don't know where it comes from – it could come from the airplanes, or the moaning of automobiles, but anyhow it leaves an air current in the air, you see. That gets in the wind, makes a sounding you know? And that sounding works up to a blues."

His admiration for Blind Lemon inspired Williams to become an extremely facile guitarist: fortunately he did not also adopt Lemon's harmonic scheme. Like most other later blues guitarists with exceptional facility, Lemon played not in the modal framework but within a chordal one. These "sophisticated" guitarists inevitably adopted the only harmonic language they heard about them: the supreme blandness of I-IV-V progressions of American pop music, or worse still, that old favourite, the ever-so-happy ragtime progression (in the key of C, A-D-G-C), brought to bear on the country blues idiom for the first time (on record) by the same Blind Lemon Jefferson. Fortunately Robert Pete's left-hand technique is based not on a chordal language, but on a thorough knowledge of the blues modal scale in all areas of most keys, facilitating extensive melodic improvisation on nearly any piece, plus a small number of effective chords (usually partial ones) for spice.

Ninety per cent of his songs are done in the five keys in which he can, and does, improvise guitar solos and fill-ins at will in any area of the fingerboard. These keys are E, A and D in standard tuning, and G and D in Spanish. He often maintains the A-A-B framework of the standard blues structure, but there is almost never a reliance on the standard metrical structure of 2-2-2-2-2-2 (underlined numerals indicate vocal units) measures. Instead the units (particularly the guitar portions) are extended, often greatly, to accommodate the spontaneous improvisation which is the cornerstone of his style. Such people as Lightnin' Hopkins, John Lee Hooker and Big Joe Williams do this also, but their extensions aren't as prolonged, their figures tend to be cliches (each has about eight) which recur from song to song, and they don't know nearly as many keys. Thus Robert Pete fulfills a unique condition in blues, one which the others merely hint at; a musical style in which improvisation plays nearly as important a role as pre-determined factors.

Robert Pete's harmonic conception is a feature even more unique than his combination of technical finesse and primitive approach or his emphasis on improvisation. His three favourite keys are E, A and D (standard tuning), and in the first two he plays in the minor (actually Dorian mode, usually) mode on nearly all selections. In the third, D, his main chord has no third at all; such modality as can be ascertained results from the fleeting notes up the neck, usually minor but in some pieces major, which linger in the memory when the third-less root position chord is being played ... His conception is nearly always of the modal (one chord) nature, whether the mode (chord) be major or minor in a given piece.

Almost all blues by the other artists fall into the major-key category, in which minor thirds are plentiful but are dissonances which never appear in the cadential chord. Thus Robert Pete's use of the major in the keys of open G, open D (actually Mixolydian mode, usually), and C and G (standard) is quite typical in this regard. Nearly all of the small remainder of blues by other artists left fall into the intriguing "hollow" tonality described above, a tonality employed by Robert Pete in D (standard) and in open G tuning played in D. The other chief exponent of this tonality is Skip James, whose avoidance of the third in his cadential chords in D minor tuning was responsible for the eerie, mystical quality so often commented on blues lovers, and often misinterpreted as an "oriental" or "minor" mode. Much of Robert Pete's very finest work is in this tonality, and ranks with Skip's 1931 Paramounts at or near the top of the entire blues heap in general excellence.

Along with D (standard) his two favourite keys, as noted above, are E and A, in which he invariably employs the minor triad in nearly all songs. This is his most unique feature; Robert Pete, alone in the history of recorded blues, plays in minor keys extensively, using this tonality over 50% of the time.*

Robert Pete is still working on new techniques today. Just before we arrived he had bought himself a rack harmonica, and he was anxious that we hear him play slide, because, he said, he had been practising the last few months. The blues he sang for us were certainly just as imaginative, and just as intense, too, as the blues that he has put on record. And yet, as he himself admits, "Sometimes I got the blues so bad I just got to play. Other times I just don't feel it. Just the other day my wife asked me if I could play a blues for her. But I couldn't do it. I just didn't have that feeling." Lately there are more and more of these days, and, prompted no doubt by the same sense of ambivalence which has pursued him all his life, he has foresworn the blues altogether several times in the past few years. At one point he asked us, "Would you like me to make up a blues for you?" and the song he sang for us was a brilliant, imaginative fantasy of a train trip he had taken recently between Peoria and San Jose. But he shook his head sadly at the end and complained that he didn't really have the feeling even that day and that the song itself was unsatisfactory to him.

It may perhaps be necessary, then, to look on the prison blues as the product of a unique combination of genius and circumstances which, one would certainly hope, is not about to be repeated. For Robert Pete Williams there is no difficulty in adjustment. He has never regarded himself as a professional musician; until recently he never made any money from music at all, and it may have been our describing him as a blues singer as much as anything else that made it so difficult for us to find him. Certainly his neighbours know him better as a scrap-iron collector and he thinks of himself more as a man who has worked hard all his life than as a bluesman like Lightnin' Hopkins or Slim Harpo or Lightnin' Slim, all of whom he

*Alan Wilson, "Robert Pete Williams: His Life and Music," *Little Sandy Review,* 1966.

has met more as a fan than as a professional colleague since his release from prison.

He dates his career as a musician, if he thinks about it at all, to 1964 when he was first allowed to travel. He plays very little around Baton Rouge, not because the opportunity does not arise (the night we were there some men came over and wanted him to play at a local jook joint with a three-piece band) but because "I'm too old to fight. And some of the people don't know nothing else. They gets to drinking, and right away they start pulling out knives." He is acutely conscious, too, of the way in which he got into trouble and makes a point of avoiding any situation which might jeopardize his freedom. A few weeks before he had played at the local high school with a fiddle player who lives just a few miles away. It had not been particularly successful, he said (his guitar drowned out the fiddle, which had no amplification). And the great majority of his bookings come from college festivals anyway, further away than can be gauged in distance or even imagined in rural Louisiana.

He cuts a strange figure at these festivals. He fulfills few of the expectations which an audience raised on the dramatic manner of a Son House or B.B. King has come to expect. He is uncomfortable and plainly detached from his surroundings, he is without any kind of an act, and while he plays a newly purchased amplified Gibson of which he is very proud, neither the songs nor the style are the least bit familiar.

His musical uniqueness is surely the most difficult and striking aspect of his art. It comes as a shock, after all the familiar blues figures, to hear this jagged music, the rapidly picked notes and eccentric rhythms, the start-and-stop-and-start-again of its energies, the brilliant flights of improvisation, and the denial of melodic resolution. Robert Pete continually invents and reinvents a music which is free to the point of occasional anarchy, and listening to it can hardly be a passive experience. I can recall my own bewilderment at first hearing him on *Angola Prison Spirituals* among other, unsurprising singers; he challenged all the assumptions I had picked up from the blues — the conventional melodic scheme, the regularly accented beat, the rhymed lyrics, the traditional verses taken at random and passing for personal statement. Undoubtedly Robert Pete Williams is as exploratory in his way as John Coltrane or Gerard

Manley Hopkins, and for the listener who is not prepared to give up his preconceptions certainly he is just as difficult. He can be, as well, equally rewarding.

IV

As the afternoon wore on and he kept on drinking Robert Pete grew more and more expansive and his stories somehow all began to blend into one another. They all shared a common theme and a common protagonist: an innocent, rather woebegone Robert Pete Williams either put upon by circumstances or taken advantage of by scoundrels but always victimized because he does not know the ways of the world. Memories of his recent trip to California blend in with recollections of prison, and each experience is recalled with a mute sorrowfulness that might be taken for self-pity if it were not evident that Robert Pete Williams feels sorry not just for himself but for the human condition, that it is not merely his own story that he is relating with so heavy a heart but the entire human experience which he views with profound sadness.

He is obviously at a disadvantage in any case in a world with whose terms he is only fitfully conversant. His illiteracy, his "dumbness" is a constantly reiterated theme, and one of the things for which he is most grateful to his wife is that she has taken over their finances and even managed to put aside a little money from his music. This last tour was probably his most successful, and he was able to send home more than $3000 with which, he boasted proudly, Hattie had opened an account at the bank. Even so he intends to keep up the scrap-metal business - he had just gotten $67 worth of goods free from a local farmer because, he said, the man knew he was a good Negro — and he has nothing but contempt for the slicks and cheats who are chiselling welfare. He cannot understand in fact why everyone does not adopt the same attitudes that he has. They read almost like a Boy Scout motto: be honest, be straight, work hard, carry yourself right and everything will work out for you.

Perhaps because he has lived in a world in which things have not always worked out for him there is a curious duality running all through his life. He would like to consider himself a good Negro and a good Christian, but he turned his back on preaching to go on singing the blues, and though he conducted himself in exemplary fashion by the curious terms of a white South he was sent up to prison for three and a half years and ended up serving nearly ten for an act which could at most be called a minor infraction of Southern justice.

> *That old judge musta been mad*
> *First time I got in trouble*
> *Whoa, Lord, he throwed the book at me*

This duality comes out in various ways. In his music. In his philosophy. In his permanent and deep-seated distrust of the world. In his view of himself as an innocent cast abroad in a world he doesn't understand. Like many people who have been permanently scarred by life his response has been to withdraw into a rigid and formulaic code whose terms do not really reflect the diversity of his point of view.

"I'll tell you something true," he said at one point, leaning foward and speaking confidentially, as he flicked the ashes from his cigar on a pale sickly-looking plant. "I think different things about myself. Sometimes I get out there and be full of this thing, all feeling good, you know, just jump right into the blues. Other times I can't hardly pick at all. What's wrong? Well, it look like to me blues is evil, God is warning me, I got to get myself straight. And yet still and all I don't know, something hits me sometimes and I feel peculiar, I might be riding along, say now you get in your car and ride, well the ideas just come to me out of the air. Why is that? What made me think of that?

"You know, I'm a whiskey-headed man, I'm a whiskey-headed man, sure that's right, you know I likes to drink. But I'm not like some of these people, cause I knows how to drink. And I can drink right here at home and don't bother nobody. Ain't that right, Hattie?" His wife, still labouring over the stove, clucked sympathetically as the tan kept up its steady racket and kids kept drifting in from the yard to their father's express annoyance. "You know, when I'm on the road I don't hardly eat at all. Mister Chris, he got worried about me. He say, Robert Pete, you ain't eating enough. But I takes whiskey for my breakfast, the whiskey's good for you if you drink it right. Four drinks a day, it keeps you feeling good."

By the end of the afternoon he had polished off a fifth by himself and his eyes were red-rimmed and a little glassy. But it was a Saturday, a holiday, too, and he wasn't working anyway, not, as he was quick to point out, because he was not industrious but because he was waiting for copper to go up to forty cents a pound again. On Sunday when we came back he would be perfectly sober in any case and though he had promised to play us some more music he never picked up his guitar but spoke instead about God and reincarnation.

"Hattie!" he said at last when we had long since forgotten his previous invitation. "I want these fellas to eat." We protested that we weren't really that hungry, that we had just eaten, that we couldn't eat by ourselves, but no other member of the family would sit at the table with us and Robert Pete himself kept on drinking, spooning himself a portion of creamed potatoes every so often just to keep us company. He noticed that one of the dishes was dirty and angrily insisted that his wife replace it. "You know, you can ask all over the world," he said, as if to reassure us, "if I had the phone numbers you could call up these people right now — cause I been travelling since 1964 — and they will tell you Robert Pete Williams never made a crooked move." Around the room were mementoes of his travels. A picture of him in a beret taken abroad. Snapshots on a beach in California with one or another of his collector friends. A clipping or two, the records he has made. We asked if we could take some pictures of him ourselves and Robert Pete clamped a hat down on his head and stood out in front of the house with an arm around his wife, who though she is quite a pretty young woman, was reluctant to have her picture taken at all. We left in a hurry so that the kids could have what was left of the meal while it was still warm, and as we sat in the car Robert Pete Williams gave us advice about directions, warned us to be careful driving, warned us again, beamed proudly as we shook hands all around and told us — as if that had been the point of our whole visit — that now we could tell our friends back home that we had had a real country supper.

I

Don't laugh at me, baby, please don't laugh at me
Don't laugh at me, baby, please don't make fun of me
Bear in mind, baby, there's a time for everything...
Didn't make myself, baby, Lord I didn't make myself
Didn't make myself, baby, I didn't make myself
Bear it in mind, there's a time for everything.
                Chester Burnett (The Original Howlin' Wolf)

Howlin' Wolf was feeling sorry for himself. "How are you, Wolf?" asked the pretty girl from the Chess publicity department. "I ain't nobody," came the response in a sorrowful whisper. We brought him ice cream, matches, and with some misgiving a bottle of Harvey's Bristol Cream. Are you sure we ought to bring him anything to drink in the hospital? He said he wanted sherry, repeated Loren, the Chess publicist, who treated Wolf and all his requests with the same blank incredulity. Wolf opened up the package and inspected its contents approvingly. His look of satisfaction vanished, though, as he took the sherry from its brown paper bag. "Quick! Get this thing out of sight before the nurse catch you," he said. "But I thought you wanted sherry, Wolf," said Loren. No, no, he shook his head, genuinely agitated now and speaking in that hoarse growl that serves him for a voice. "Cherry chewing tobacco – that's what I really wanted." And, as if to remind us that he was a man who always abided by the rules, the growl dropped to a whisper and he said, "They don't *allow* no alcohol in here."

It is misunderstandings just such as these that plague the Howlin' Wolf's life. He is suspicious to an almost crippling degree, and he trusts nobody. Not the government or women or the Europeans ("We don't live like those people over there. I don't like their way of living.") or Chess Records. Not the white or the coloured or his fellow musicians. You might almost say his distrust borders on a state of paranoia except that it is a product as much of real factors in his life as of any inner fantasies. He is virtually illiterate in a world that has no place for its less fortunate citizens. He is out after a buck in a system ("Ain't no place better than the U.S. This is a free enterprise system. You can get whatever you want in the U.S.") that has mercilessly exploited even those who are its natural children.

151

He has been let down time and time again by unscrupulous promoters and clubs and management firms. He swears he will never leave Chicago again, but at sixty he hasn't got the money or the inclination or temperament to change.

He looks shrunken in his hospital bed. He has lost, he volunteers, about sixty pounds and is now down to two hundred and ten. "All that grease was blocking my heart and stopping the blood from circulating," he explains. "I want to get back up to around two hundred and twenty, but I had to do something." He is still a huge man in any case, and his face in repose takes on a kind of nobility and gives him the look not of "some fierce beast" (as he has been described by a fellow blues singer) but of a warrior-king. There is a squareness of line and a delicacy of feature which seems somehow out of place in the seamed map of his face.

This is his third time in the hospital in less than six months, and it is rumoured around Chicago that Wolf will kill himself before the year is out by this endless compulsion to work. He started singing and went back on the road before he was fully recovered from the first heart attack. Then in Toronto he had a second, and, convinced that he was going to die, he snuck out of the hospital in the middle of the night in an orderly's pants and bare feet. It was only at the insistence of his band that he was returned to the hospital, but even so he has little faith in doctors or medicine. Since then he has been recuperating in Chicago, sitting in at the clubs and performing against doctor's orders. This time he is back in the Illinois Central Hospital for a throat condition about which he seems to be only mildly concerned. What really concerns him is the human condition, the unpredictable vicissitudes of life. "I wished it could have been better," he says, summing up his career in that sorrowful tone which he uses to convey an infinite weariness with the world and its burdens. "Somehow or other, though, it just wasn't for me to have the breaks that other people had."

The other occupants of the room — three middle-aged white men, one of whom has a hacking cough that frequently interrupts our conversation — watch this spectacle in mild disbelief as their roommate, a coloured man of indeterminate age, speaks softly into the tape recorder microphone for two young whites. "That's right," says Wolf. "I just do my best. I don't say nothing about nobody. Except me. Stay in my place. Speak when spoken to. That's just about it."

II

I'm the wolf that howls, trying to be satisfied

Howlin' Wolf was born Chester Arthur Burnett in West Point near Aberdeen, Mississippi June 10, 1910. He grew up on the Young and Mara Plantation, and with the exception of the war years which he spent in the Army in Seattle, Washington ("No, I didn't like the Army. They drill us so hard it just naturally give me a nervous breakdown.") he spent nearly all his adult life until 1948 doing farm work. It was not, in fact, until his father's death that he really went out on his own, and he still speaks of his father with unreserved admiration and respect. "He died somewhere about '49, no he didn't ever get to see my success. He wasn't no blues singer, but he was a great ballplayer. Country ballplayer. Nobody ever gave him any trouble, he was just so nice to everybody."

His father bought him his first guitar. "I played in the South ever since 1928, the fifteenth day of January, that was when he got it for me. Guitar and mouth organ both, cause that's what had me interested. The first piece I ever played in my life was by Charley Patton, was a tune about hook up my pony and saddle up my black mare. From there I got with Dick Banks and Jim Holloway from Drew, Mississippi. Then I got with another guy, his name was, can't call his name now, but he was a Banks, too, and we run around the plantation on a Saturday night and play that stuff. Charley Patton? Charley Patton was more Indian than he was Negro. He was the foundation of 'Spoonful.' He was the first man I have heard sing that, and 'Red Rooster,' too. And I don't know, I just naturally liked the way he played."

Wolf at this time was playing harmonica and guitar together and already billing himself as the Howlin' Wolf, a name which seems to have grown out of his childhood and which, while previously taken up by at least one older singer, was singularly adapted to his size and demeanour. He is remembered playing on the streets of Drew and Cleveland in the thirties and, of course, there were always "the hop joints and all out on the plantations. It was kinda like Jimmy Reed way back then. Oh sure, I was playing the blues, but I didn't really know how to play either one."

It was Sonny Boy Williamson (Rice Miller) who taught him how to play the harmonica. "See, Sonny Boy married my stepsister, Mary. Maybe by my being around so much they didn't stay together long, but anyhow I was over all the time pestering at him to show me how to play that mouth organ. Sometimes I think he'd show me something just to get me out of the way. Cause he would give me something, and then I would go off by myself and practise it. Oh, Sonny Boy at that time was a wild guy. We'd play together sometimes out on the plantations, but then he would take the money and drink it right up. I just had to cut out, I wasn't making no money with him, so I had to put him down."

He knew Johnny Shines at that time, too. "He'd come to Hughes just about every weekend." "Wolf? He was my idol," says Shines today, and he recalls in the most vivid terms the forcefulness of Wolf's music and personality. When he speaks of Wolf it is with real awe as if the older man must have possessed some supernatural force or power. Wolf laughs off any suggestions of that sort. "I'm just an entertainer. When I go out, I sing for the people. Before I became an entertainer I sang for myself."

He spent the thirties and forties mostly farming around Mississippi and Arkansas. In 1948 he moved to West Memphis. "Was it a change? Sure, it was a big change. It was more money. That was the biggest change of all.

"Well, you see, that's where I got my break. Back in the country the people weren't able to pay you too much. Sometimes you'd work all night for a fish sandwich, glad to get it, too. In Memphis I started to really get somewhere."

In Memphis he no longer played solo either. He got together a little band with Willie Johnson and M.T. Murphy on guitars, Junior Parker and later James Cotton on harp, Willie Steele on drums, and a piano player named Destruction. Wolf himself would alternate between harmonica and guitar, but for the most part he would concentrate on his singing and selling spots for the fifteen-minute planters' broadcast he had gotten himself on station KWEM in West Memphis. It was this more than anything else that landed him a recording contract, for like B.B. King and Sonny Boy Williamson at that time he had gone about as far as he could go on word-of-mouth reputation. Their broadcasts catapulted all three into the public eye.

"What started me recording, Ike Turner carried me over to Memphis to Sam Phillips. Chess had some kind of thing in it at that

time. But after Chess turned him loose he named it, I think, the Sun label. Well, first record I cut he had to send it to Chess for him to push it. No, I don't remember which one it was exactly. But anyway Ike Turner and Sam Phillips fell out some kind of way, and Ike turned around and started sending my records over to this fellow Bihari in Beverly Hills. I didn't know what was happening. I was just a country boy glad to get some sounds on wax. Well, all right. Chess sent a man down to Memphis to straighten me out. He signed me to a contract, took me up North, put me in the union, and when I got back to West Memphis I was working a job there."

Muddy Waters got him his first job in Chicago. Muddy Waters? you say in some incredulity. "Well yeah," says Wolf apologetically. "I got in touch with him because I didn't know nobody here. He carried me around to the clubs and helped me get started." This is something of a revelation, because the rivalry between Wolf and Muddy is legend, even extending as far as the 1969 festival at Ann Arbor, where Wolf stalled and stretched out his set in an attempt to prevent Muddy from getting on at all. What he goes on to say is more characteristic of the ambivalence of their relationship and the grudging admiration they apparently share for each other. "Oh sure, I heard about Muddy and Little Walter going around and cutting heads at that time. They cut heads, but when they got to me they'd back up, cause I was too heavy for them. See, Muddy never did play in West Memphis much, because I was living there. And right here in Chicago Sylvio'd hire him once in a while to come work with me." Wolf pauses, shakes his head. "People'd never give them too much of applause. Well, you see, they always is been shy of me. Seems like they always had a cold side towards me. But I never did quit trying to be friends, I never let on that I knowed..."

Humility doesn't sit well on him either, though, and in a minute he's back to telling you of all the times he's been cheated. By Chess, too. The Chess man winces. "That's right," says Wolf, lapsing into his characterization of aggrieved innocence. "Well, you see, I don't hate him, cause it wasn't his fault. I been with Chess since 1948, I spent the biggest part of my life with them, and if they taken advantage of me I don't worry about it, I just go on with what's going on, say nothing, cause once you start out with a person as a fool you have to end up with him as a fool. One time you let people know how much sense you got, right away they quit having anything to do with you. Of course," he adds finally in a typically magnanimous gesture, "I don't *blame* them. I don't blame nobody."

III

The first time I saw Howlin' Wolf he was appearing at the Club 47 in Cambridge, a small basement coffeehouse which was only then beginning to make the transition from strict folk to Chicago blues and amplified music. Wolf practically forced the change all by himself. With his extravagant act, the overpowering force of his voice, above all that gargantuan presence he very nearly overwhelmed the club, and when he returned a year later I did a piece on him for a local newspaper. The first night I came to see him he seemed to be taking it easy, sitting down at the front of the stage and letting the band do most of the work. It was a slow night and somehow or other through his guitarist, Hubert Sumlin, we were introduced. I was the guy who had done the newspaper story on them, Sumlin explained. "Oh yeah?" said Wolf, interrupting an account of how he had been stomped on in Alabama ("They acted like heathens down there, stomping all over my breast.") for a dozen wide-eyed listeners. "Well, sit down." He laid a meaty hand on my shoulder. "Sit down, boy." He wanted to see the article, he said.

Glancing over it, he apologized that he didn't have his reading glasses. Could someone read it to him?

> Howlin' Wolf is bigger than life. He eclipses lesser performers with his size and the gusto of his performance. A bluesman like Junior Wells or James Cotton will try on different styles, will jive his audience in a shuffling attempt to ingratiate himself. Wolf rolls on the floor, he passes a broom obscenely between his legs, he appears in his farmboy's overalls — yet somehow nothing Wolf does is jive, no matter how often you've seen it before or how familiar the gesture is. The Wolf is always himself. Like James Brown his vulgarity carries with it its own conviction.

The kid who is reading looks up at me. Vulgarity? James Brown? Its own conviction? Wolf's fans are appalled, I want to sink through the floor in embarrassment, but Wolf is enjoying it, unbelievably a slow smile of appreciation creases his face. "That's good," he growls. "Where'd you get that from?"

> He imitates no one, and as he prowls the stage, suddenly lurching heavily forward, leaning on a post waiting out the instrumental break, impatiently biding his time, the self-created public personality becomes the man. The mighty Wolf, he shouts, "making his midnight creep/Hunters they can't find him/Stealing chicks wherever he goes/ Then dragging his tail behind him." He turns his back on the audience and his massive hips begin to shake. "I'm a tail dragger..."

"That's the truth," he murmurs wonderingly, explaining to his admirers in that rasping whisper. "Chicks all dig the Wolf. They *all* dig the Wolf. Because he is mighty Wolf, he's a mountain Wolf, he wipes out his tracks," to their impatient nods. They want to know if he knew Robert Johnson or if he could reprise "Dust My Broom" for the second set.

> His dance is awkward and ungainly, his voice overpowers with a fierce rasping force, he proclaims himself. "I am/A backdoor man/ Well, the men don't know/But the little girls, they understand." His glance quizzically suggests evil. There are elements both of self-mockery and genuine self-esteem when he sings, "Take me, baby, for your little boy/I'm three hundred pounds of heavenly joy."

"Three hundred pounds of heavenly joy," he repeats approvingly,

Howlin' Wolf at Club 47, 1966/Michael Aradi

savouring the phrase. "Where'd you get that from, boy? You make it up all out of your own head?"

> It doesn't matter that off-stage he is a genial soft-spoken man, drawing on his pipe, near-sighted and blinking. It is irrelevant that off-stage his name is Chester Burnett. Onstage he is the Wolf. His legend has become himself, and when he howls it is a real howl, of frustration, of bitterness, of rage.
>
> Howlin' Wolf is nearly sixty years old. He sings of events which may have occurred forty years ago in the rough traditional style of the Mississippi Delta. Yet he is modern enough to have appeared with The Rolling Stones on *Shindig* a couple of years ago when they had a hit with his "Little Red Rooster." The Stones and the *Shindig* dancers sat reverentially at his feet as the camera came in for close-ups of his great sweating face, seamed and unshaven, while he did his elephantine dance and waggled his hips at the nationwide audience and leapt ponderously up and down two or three times, and looked as if he were about to swallow the microphone as he blew his harp into it ...

Elephantine? The kid hesitated on the word and glared meaningfully at me. When he is finished sweat is pouring down my face, and I try to think of some way to make apology, but Wolf apparently thinks nothing of it, in fact he is visibly pleased. At the end he pumps my hand several times and once again expresses wonderment at my sources. More revealing, though, is his reaction when he goes back up on stage.

It had been up till then a desultory evening at best, and Wolf certainly wasn't working very hard. The first thing he did on returning to the stage was to get rid of the chair. He next got out his harp and then proceeded to give a performance that not only equalled but actually surpassed any claims I had made for him. He leapt in the air, he rolled on the floor, he cradled the microphone between his legs, he pounded at the posts with a frightening ferocity, and at the end of the evening he lay on his back roaring into the mike and struggling to get to his feet again and again. Each time he would raise himself to a sitting position and then fall back and the whole stage would shudder, until at last he leapt up and towered over us in the front row and announced, "The Wolf don't jive. His friends know that." The next night, I heard, he was completely exhausted, and when I saw him later in the week he was still worn out from his exertions. But he had had to live up to his notices.

There is no question that he is, like Jerry Lee Lewis and James Brown in other fields, a compulsive performer. "I sing for the people," he has said. "If there wasn't any people listening there wouldn't be no Wolf." Almost alone among blues singers he has an act which can be separated from his music, and he works very hard to please his audience. He does sacrifice in the process the enormous dignity of someone like Muddy Waters, but he achieves at the same time an engagement with his material that often eludes Muddy today. Rather than present the same set repertoire which other singers offer night after night, Wolf in person will draw upon the most surprising sources. He will dredge up from a musical memory, which apparently goes back forty or fifty years unimpaired, snatches of songs by Tommy Johnson and Charley Patton and singers even before their time. On a given night he may do "Hellhound on My Trail," his own familiar "Spoonful," songs he never recorded, and adaptations of contemporary material that has just taken his fancy. For "Smokestack Lightnin'" he will act out the whole drama, sight the train and hop on board, and in "Going Down Slow" he mimes physical decrepitude with considerable skill. These are not gross enactments either — Wolf could have been a great actor — though his act sometimes does give rise to serious lapses in taste. It's all part of his involvement with the moment, however, and that, more than anything else, is his mark as a great entertainer.

Even more striking is the impact of the music itself. Technically limited and for the most part restricted to the same three-chord progression, there is nothing really prepossessing about it, with the exception of Wolf himself. He is very much aware, though, of his strengths as well as his limitations. "I'm not much on execution," he is quick to admit. "I just play my patterns, that's all." He makes sure at the same time that the music always remains focused on his presence, on the force of his personality, his voice, the savage thrust of his delivery; he never ventures into territory with which he is unfamiliar, and perhaps as a result of all the blues singers popular since the war Wolf alone has managed to retain not only the style but the vigour and the flavour of his early recordings as well.

To some this is a sign of the built-in limitations of his art. The people at Chess call it stubbornness when they feel like being polite. "Well, you see, Muddy is the kind of person you can give any kind of

Howlin' Wolf with Hubert Sumlin

lyric, he's what you call a quick study," says Willie Dixon admiringly. "Wolf, you can't give him too many words, because he gets 'em all jumbled up. And if he gets 'em right, he still ain't gonna get the right meaning." "I can do my own songs better," says Wolf, "but, you see, they won't let me. They'll let Dixon give me songs to do, that's to keep me out of being the writer." "You've got to understand," says Malcolm Chisholm, Chess's chief engineer, "blues is a music of bare competence. And that's what these musicians are. Barely competent." Wolf sees it almost as a matter of self-preservation. "I don't play anything but the blues," he told Bruce Iglauer, "but now I never could make no money on nothin' but the blues. That's why I wasn't interested in nothin' else, you know."

Whatever the reason (and it may be guile or stubbornness or simply, as Chess suggests, the inability to adapt), this singlemindedness has had demonstrably good results. There have been no girl choruses, there has been no "Howlin' Wolf Twist," and with the exception of a single abortive excursion into psychedelics (which Wolf, dismissing it with typical aplomb as "birdshit," denies having had anything to do with and Chess with equal vehemence claims was initiated at Wolf's insistence after the success of Muddy Waters' *Electric Mud*), his entire output since the fifties has shown a remarkable consistency of achievement and design. Wolf has always done just what he is good at and only that, making up in integrity what he lacks in musical variety and evoking in the most vivid terms a traditional style which might otherwise have all but passed out of existence.

That style is itself an amalgam of several quite separate strands — Charley Patton's rough vocal tone, Tommy Johnson's lyrical falsetto, and the overamplified Memphis boogie beat of the fifties — which come together uniquely and quite unexpectedly in the person of Howlin' Wolf. Shaped to begin with by the singular properties of his voice, a harsh rasping instrument which immediately recalls Patton, it is modified by a delicate approach to phrasing if not intonation which is best exemplified by the falsetto "howl." This Wolf claims he got from Jimmie Rodgers, the Singing Brakeman, though it sounds closer to Johnson than to Rodgers' yodel. One's sense of musical paradox is further borne out by the crude approach to instrumentation carried over from his Memphis days. For Wolf, unlike Muddy or Sonny Boy, failed to change his style even when he came to Chicago and his back-up today still has the same slapdash quality and the same uninhibited energy that it did in the early fifties. Some time ago for a short while Wolf's harp — a very rough though serviceable approximation of his brother-in-law, Sonny Boy's — was pushed into the background, but today it is back once again, and Wolf is even taking music lessons in a fruitless attempt to improve his guitar playing.

His greatest strength, apart from the raw power of his voice, lies undoubtedly in his sense of dynamics. Here, too, he proves a walking contradiction — far from overpowering a song, as he is clearly quite capable of doing, he frequently shows the most acute sensitivity to the sound of the music and to the contrasts in his voice. He does not, it is true, seem particularly concerned with the words. He will sometimes in person repeat a verse over and over, chewing on a line until he has extracted every last level of feeling from it but without much regard for meaning. What he seems more interested in is the possibility for different readings, the range of moods he may explore, and in this regard he is the most experimental of bluesmen, closer to a jazz orientation than the more stolid singers like Muddy or the less thoughtful ones like Buddy Guy.

If all this gives the impression that his music is thrown together or accidental, nothing could be further from the truth. Nobody works harder at his music or his arrangements than Howlin' Wolf; no one takes himself or his art more seriously. Undoubtedly this is part of the problem. "That's why a lot of people laugh at me," he complains. "Because I stand out for what I think is right. Any time you stand out for right, you know, peoples gonna laugh at you. Cause you're doing something. Now if I wasn't doing nothin', wouldn't nobody be saying nothin' about me."

IV

It's one o'clock in the afternoon and Wolf has been rehearsing his band steadily for three hours. Everyone else is tired and getting stale, but Wolf is in no mood to take a break. He has been out of the hospital for about four weeks. He will be going back on the road in another month or so, but now he is working up material (which he has written with his music teacher Cash McCall) for a new album. In the Chess rehearsal studio with him are L.V. on bass, W. Williams his drummer, a studio guitarist, and Hubert Sumlin. A young black couple is watching. The boy plays rock 'n' roll and would like Wolf to teach him the blues. "You can't play no blues," says Wolf irately, "unless you have some hard times. Young people today, I don't care whether they're black or white, they didn't come up like Muddy and me, they come up too easy."

The band listens patiently. They seem amused as he explores one of his favourite themes to the boy's acute discomfiture, though the girl seems slightly scornful. She has, it would appear, little use for the blues or for this cantankerous old man. Her Afro proclaims her to be one of the new breed.

Wolf sits turned around in a fold-up metal chair, looking studious and slightly puzzled in his big horn-rimmed black glasses.

164

His shirt is open at the neck and he cradles a beat-up old guitar
(acoustic, not amplified) in his arms. In front of him are the
words and chord changes to the song scrawled out in big letters, and
he tries to show the guitars where they are going wrong. He has had
Sumlin playing rhythm and the studio man playing lead, but now
after a number of fruitless attempts to show the studio man what he
wants he goes through the changes once again with Sumlin and
switches their parts. It sounds better that way. "That's right, that's
right," says Wolf, listening attentively. "I want you playing against
each other, the two parts playing against each other." The studio
man, a reading musician, is still not sure he understands. Wolf
demonstrates again clumsily on his own guitar. They run through it
once again, and this time the studio man thinks he has it right. W.
Williams and L.V. the bass, a huge man bigger even than Wolf, wait
patiently. They seem to accept Wolf's idiosyncrasies with a kind of
bemused tolerance. Or maybe it is just the whiskey that they are
passing back and forth among each other. Sumlin, who has been with
Wolf the longest, wears a perpetual and lop-sided grin on his face.

You give me a heart attack

sings Wolf, the words mirthlessly echoing real life;

You make my love come down on me.

This time the guitars get it right, and Wolf turns up the volume of
his mike. "You give me a heart attack..." Over and over again he
sings it, adjusting a word here, changing his phrasing there, trying
different keys, until at last the musicians are exhausted. Okay, says
Wolf. We'll take a half-hour break. Someone goes out for sandwiches, to be consumed in a disconsolate silence as Wolf launches
into one, then another of his familiar diatribes — about Europe
("They don't pay you no money, them Europeans. You got to pay
one hundred dollars just for eating and sleeping. Shit, I do better
staying in Chicago."); Chess; his rivals ("Some folks are jealous and
conniving-hearted."); and business conditions in general. Someone
mentions that Willie Dixon is in the building. "That big fuck," says
Wolf. Shall I tell him you're here? Wolf makes a fist. Later Dixon,
who is supervising a dub-down on the new Albert King LP, hears

that Wolf is rehearsing. "Oh yeah?" he expresses mild interest, but he avoids a meeting. They regard each other warily with mutual respect, but neither is anxious to test the other.

"The first time I seen Wolf," says Hubert Sumlin when Wolf is out of the room and the others have wandered off, "was way back when I was fourteen years old. The next time it was 1948, he was playing at a place called Silkhairs down in Mississippi. I was seventeen years old then, see they didn't allow no kids in a place like that. Well, I was sitting in a car outside and I saw this big old guy. And I said, I'll be goddamned, is this Wolf?

"Well, see, you know how it is on the plantations, crop harvesting, all that kind of stuff. We was averaging about eighteen dollars a week back then, but my mother, I got interested in music, she bought me a ten dollar guitar just like the kind Wolf has here, a round hole guitar, just like that. Well, I loved to play that guitar so well I took it with me into the field. The man caught me, she-it, it was me and his son, he broke it right across the tractor wheel. Well, after that he bought me a twenty dollar guitar. And just about that time, man, Wolf came out and played for us out on the plantation there, Clark Plantation. That's why I was surprised. Cause here he was playing at a big club, Silkhairs was a real big club.

"So I stacked me some Coca-Cola cartons up in back, I musta stacked me about fifteen or twenty. Man, I'm up there on top of them Coca Cola cartons peeping through the window when them crates start to slipping. Well, then the man come around and he say, Get on out of here. Well, the next thing I did, there was a big line of people waiting at the door, I got down on my hands and knees and I creeped through their legs. I made it just about all the way through, but he had me put out again. Well, then I went and got my oldest brother, and he went and told the man I was all right. And he talked to Wolf about it, and this time Wolf made sure that I wasn't going to get put out. And I went and played every night. And then I got hired. It took me two months to get hired. But I kept going every night. And I been with him ever since..."

Sumlin breaks off in embarrassment as the others file back in. I'm reminded, though, of Wolf telling me years ago of how he had "come in possession of Hubert in West Memphis. I partly raised him from a kid. See, by my playing around the country he fell in love with me and he wanted to stay with me so I just kept him." It's an

Howlin' Wolf at Club 47 / Michael Aradi

odd relationship to say the least. Sumlin is a peculiarly vulnerable sort of man, and Wolf, despite his pious disclaimers, has never had a good reputation with musicians. He is said to have knocked out Sumlin's front teeth and Sumlin, if it can be credited, is said to have knocked out one of Wolf's in return. Nevertheless it is his single enduring musical relationship (no one else in the band has been with him more than a year, and it is unlikely — given the unpredictability of his temperament and his legendary tightness with money — that any will be with him a year from now), and despite Sumlin's occasional attempts to break away they appear locked forever in a love-hate, affection-spite, typical father and son relationship.

Wolf lumbers back into the room, and Sumlin gets the other musicians set up while he fumbles at his pipe. The young man who had asked him for instruction earlier has been patiently waiting all this time, and when he brings up the subject again Wolf finally relents. This time he is gracious about it, he gives the boy his address, he admonishes him to practise, he has a slow-breaking kindly smile for the girl. She is not charmed, but Wolf fails to take notice. It's time to get back to work. This time Wolf decides to sing in a higher key. "B natural," he says. "Ain't nobody can sing in B natural except Sonny Boy. There ain't nobody else." He pulls the microphone towards him, adjusting it wearily, and starts out once again, his voice straining this time and gaining in conviction as he employs it marvellously like some worn familiar instrument. It floats out across the room, the guitar lies forgotten at his feet, and for once the hard work and banality of the lyrics seem put aside. At four o'clock they finally get it right and move on to the next song.

V

Shortly after I left Chicago there was a publicity item to commemorate a session that had taken place in London involving Wolf and some British pop stars — Beatles, Eric Clapton, Rolling Stones. Intended as a kind of follow-up to Muddy's *Fathers and Sons* it was something that Marshall Chess had been particularly anxious to arrange. It was going to be Howlin' Wolf's last big payday.

Sadly all the numbers that were done were remakes of old

songs, and even without hearing the album it's pretty easy to imagine its excesses and shortcomings. It seems at this point unlikely that Wolf will ever get to record one-tenth of his fabulous repertoire, and as a result we will lose yet another part of a priceless heritage. It's something that no one is going to get very upset about right now. In ten or twenty years maybe it will be a matter of some concern, but then, characteristically, it will be too late.

The people at Chess have a genuine liking for Wolf. Phil Chess in particular spoke highly of him and his music. He feels that the heart attacks will slow Wolf down ("He'll probably be thinking of the old ticker," he says, thumping his own chest) and cut into his uninhibited style of performing. Knowing Wolf, you wonder. Wolf is not exactly sparing of himself, but in another sense Chess may be right. There really is very little place in the world for Howlin' Wolf today. He was not meant to be patronized, and he was not meant to be preserved as a curiosity. Unlike Muddy Waters he's never had much success with a wider audience, but then he doesn't really seem to want it either. He's too forceful a personality to curry favour and too inflexible apparently to change.

And he is a mass of contradictions, too, which sometimes threaten to cancel each other out. A big man whose delicacy of face and feature often escape the eye. A member of the rather raffish blues community who is fiercely domestic in his outlook and attitudes ("You can't get your rocks off in Europe," was one of his many complaints about touring, and he is supposed to be devoted to his wife). A black man whose pride in race, far ahead of its time, has led to a frustration with his people and his position within his own community. A crude self-taught musician whose music relies upon an extraordinary sensitivity to dynamics and voicing. A man with an enormous zest for living who spends the greater part of his life complaining and feeling sorry for himself.

"Well, I just may go back to working by myself like I used to. Sometimes it seem like it get so hard I just can't go on. Well, I'll tell you one thing. I know that as long as there's a Chess in the business they'll remember me. If I get to the place where I can't help myself they'll always hold me up." He paused a moment to let it sink in. Then he brightened up a little. "You see, I done got too old to get a job," he said with the flash of a gold-toothed smile. "Now I really got to stay with the music."

CHAPTER 8
**BOPPIN'
THE
BLUES**
SAM PHILLIPS
& THE SUN SOUND

Sun Records in Memphis. The bright yellow label with its eleven Sun beams. Jerry Lee Lewis and His Pumping Piano. Carl Perkins the Rocking Guitar Man. Rufus "Bear Cat" Thomas. And, of course, Elvis Presley, the original Hillbilly Cat. That's the way the credits read, and it all sounds curiously old-fashioned now. But if the origin of a music can be traced to any one source, for rock 'n' roll that source would be Sun. And if there is one man without whom the revolution which took place in American popular music seems difficult to imagine, that man is Sam Phillips.

Phillips, an ex-radio engineer from Florence, Alabama, first got into music in the late forties "when Negro artists in the South who wanted to make a record just had no place to go. Rhythm and blues record men like Jules and Saul Bihari would come down South into Tennessee from the West Coast with a tape recorder and set up a studio in a garage to record the Negro blues singers of the South. So I set up a studio in 1950 just to make records with some of those great Negro artists."

It sounds a little disarming, but Phillips in fact recorded Howlin' Wolf, Walter Horton, Bobby Bland, Little Junior Parker, and B.B. King, all at the very beginning of their careers. Memphis, of course, was a hotbed of blues activity at the time; in addition to Howlin' Wolf, B.B. King, Rufus Thomas, and Joe Hill Louis all had their own radio shows, and there was a relaxed social and musical inter-change which was reflected in the music. Phillips leased all his sides to the Biharis, and they appeared on the Modern and RPM labels, until he met Leonard Chess, who was just then starting out on his 5000-mile promotion and recording swings through the South cutting artists in the field and selling records out of the back of his car. Phillips started supplying Chess with material, too, and it was from the fall-out that resulted from this arrangement that Howlin' Wolf eventually ended up on both the Chess and RPM labels at the same time. This led to a considerable amount of ill feeling, as well as a lawsuit, with the Biharis signing Ike Turner, just out of his teens but already appearing as house pianist on many of the Memphis sessions, as talent scout and producer. Chess Records spirited Howlin' Wolf off to Chicago and then concentrated on consolidating their holdings there. Sam Phillips went on to found Sun Records.

Sun Records was, in the beginning, almost exclusively a blues label. It featured local artists like James Cotton, Willie Nix, Dr. Ross, and Harmonica Frank, the Great Medical Menagerist. Phillips kept up a steady stream of blues releases until 1954 when Sun No. 209 featured a nineteen-year-old white singer doing an easy fluid version of Arthur "Big Boy" Crudup's "That's All Right" backed, appropriately enough, by a Bill Monroe bluegrass tune. "He's the new rage," a Louisiana disc jockey said of him at the time. "Sings hillbilly in r&b time. Can you figure that out? He wears pink pants and a black coat and owns a Cadillac painted pink with a black top. He's going terrific, and if he doesn't suffer too much popularity he'll be all right."

That was Elvis Presley, of course, and of the ten sides that he cut for Sun five were blues, five were country, and taken together they established a whole new mode in music. It was a synthesis that a lot of people had been groping toward for some time. Bill Haley had already had a couple of hits on what were essentially white covers of black material. Johnnie Ray crossed over a little bit going the other way. It was a natural enough connection, especially after the fact, but Sam Phillips was the only man to sense the nature of that connection and, perhaps because of his extensive background in blues and "race" music, the only man to exploit it to its fullest.

"Over and over," says Marion Keisker, Phillips' secretary, "I remember Sam saying, 'If I could find a white man who had the Negro sound and the Negro feel, I could make a billion dollars.'" With Elvis, Phillips apparently found the key, because following Elvis's success he had a succession of rockabillies who did just that. All of his major artists were poor whites who had not only lived in constant contact with black people all their lives but had obviously absorbed a great deal of their culture. "The man who taught me guitar was an old coloured man," said Carl Perkins, the son of a sharecropper himself, who grew up working side by side with blacks every day. "See, I was raised on a plantation in the flatlands of Lake County, Tennessee, and we were the only white people on it. White music, I liked Bill Monroe, his fast stuff; for coloured I liked John Lee Hooker, Muddy Waters, their electric stuff. Even back then I liked to do Hooker songs Bill Monroe-style, blues with a country beat." For Charlie Rich it was just something he picked up in the fields, and Jerry Lee Lewis remembers sneaking off to Haney's Big House to see B.B. King, Sunnyland Slim, and all the honky tonk pianists. Elvis himself recalled for a British interviewer:: "I'd play along with the radio or phonograph. We were a religious family going around to sing together at camp meetings and revivals, and I'd take my guitar with us when I could. I also dug the real low-down Mississippi singers, mostly Big Bill Broonzy and Big Boy Crudup, although they would scold me at home for listening to them. 'Sinful music,' the townsfolk in Memphis said it was. Which never bothered me, I guess."

It all seems prosaic enough in retrospect, but at the time even Sam Phillips must have had his doubts. Elvis hung around the studio for nearly a year before Phillips actually recorded him, and when he did it was not a blues but a sentimental ballad that they initially went into the studio to record. According to legend "That's All Right" was worked out during a break in the follow-up session, and that's the way it sounds: easy, unforced, with all the raw vitality and exuberance of some musicians who got together to make music for themselves and their own amusement. And once they got past the problem of a B-side (in this case "Blue Moon of Kentucky," Bill Monroe's classic blue-grass tune, which they approached with equal irreverence), they were home free. Sam Phillips brought the acetate down to the very popular Memphis DJ Dewey Phillips (no relation), who played it over and over on his *Red Hot and Blue* show, which was listened to by black and white Memphians alike. With the response that the record got, there was nothing for it but to get "the man of the hour" down to the radio studio for an interview. Elvis was so self-conscious that he hid out in a neighborhood movie theater, the Suzore No. 2, but his parents retrieved him and sent him down to the station, where Dewey elicited that it was all-white Humes High School from which he had graduated ("I wanted to get that out," said Dewey, "because a lot of people listening had thought he was coloured").

The confusion continued well past the point that the record had achieved widespread local success. "I recall one [rhythm and blues] disc jockey telling me that Elvis [Presley] was so country he shouldn't be played after 5 A.M.," said Sam Phillips, "and the country jocks said he was too black for them." But Phillips, and Elvis, persevered in what amounted to a sustained campaign to democratize American popular culture. At the same time Sam Phillips, for all of his business acumen, seems to have decided that Elvis had cornered whatever market there was for this strange new music, at least for the moment. When Carl Perkins came in to audition about a month after the record's release ("I still couldn't get over hearing [it]," he told

Michael Lydon), Phillips told him, "'No, boy, I'm not taking nobody.' I said, 'Just ten minutes.' I did some fast things, and he said that was too much like Elvis, but he liked the country material." It was not until he sold Elvis's contract to RCA (another miscalculation of some small proportions, although the $35,000 he received was helpful in setting up a financial base for the company) that he allowed Perkins to record the kind of music he had been playing around his home town of Jackson for the last couple of years. The result was "Blue Suede Shoes," and it was one of the biggest sellers of all time.

There followed a period of remarkable activity and accomplishment. Carl Perkins, Johnny Cash, Charlie Rich, Jerry Lee Lewis, all achieved national stature while other artists like Sonny Burgess, Billy Riley, Onie Wheeler, and Warren Smith each enjoyed good local success. In Jerry Lee Lewis's case Phillips was once again the reluctant discoverer, and Lewis, who had sold all the eggs from his father's farm to make the trip to Memphis, had to threaten to camp out on the Sun doorstep before getting an audition. Whatever his receptivity, though, Phillips' instincts were always good. He always seems to have gotten the best out of his artists, and they in turn would seem to have fed off of each other's talents. Jerry Lee Lewis, for example, made the bigger hit out of a brilliant adaptation of Elvis's "Mean Woman Blues," which Roy Orbison, another Sun alumnus, was to take almost note for note in a highly popular 1963 version. Elvis covered Carl Perkins' "Blue Suede Shoes" shortly after his switch to RCA; Jerry Lee did a great version of Perkins' "Matchbox," on which he had originally played; and Johnny Cash joined Perkins to write two of Perkins' early hits, "All Mama's Children" and "That's Right." All in all it was a period of extraordinary creativity, on the part of both artists and producer, and I think all these interrelationships can be taken as evidence of the peculiar symbiosis which even today continues to exist among Phillips' widely scattered Memphis artists.

His production methods were instinctive and almost always appropriate. Like Leonard Chess he was one of the first to go for a heavy echo effect, but the overall sound was crisp, clean, and full of life. Also like Leonard Chess, the primary focus was on the artist, and it was in his handling of their diverse talents that Phillips excelled. He sensed not only their particular gift but their potential as well, a potential which in some cases the artist himself did not see.

"I had written 'I Walk the Line'," said Johnny Cash for the twenty-four-hour radio History of Rock 'n' Roll, "I meant it for a very slow mournful-sounding ballad, and we got into the session, Sam Phillips kept having us pick up the tempo until – I didn't like it at all, the tempo we recorded it at. First time I heard it on the radio, I called him and begged him to not send out any more, to not release it, I didn't like it at all. And he said, Well, let's go ahead and give it a chance. And so we did, and it was the biggest thing I've ever had."

This period of artistic and commercial success was short-lived. Rock 'n' roll died, killed off by the moneymen's need to control the product and the consequent payola scandals; the bigger artists were lured off by the major companies, the rest went their separate ways. Some got into studio work; others disappeared from sight, never to be heard from again. Jack Clement, Phillips' assistant, is a successful Nashville producer. Carl Perkins, after years of alcoholism and semi-obscurity, joined Johnny Cash's troupe, which also employs his old drummer, W.S. "Fluke" Holland as a member of The Tennessee (once Two) Three. Jerry Lee Lewis, of course, was brought down by scandal and then resurrected in the country field. And Elvis remained prisoner to the end, insulated by a retinue of personal retainers and a wall of privacy which was all but impenetrable.

Sam Phillips went on to greater things. He is a man of diversified financial interests and one of the original investors in the Holiday Inn chain. He maintained Sun Records until the mid-sixties, mostly out of nostalgia, it would seem, and out of loyalty to the few artists who had stayed on with him. His interest had gone out of it, though, and while he has never really gotten out of music altogether, it seems clear that he will never again be as involved as he was when Sun Records was in its heyday. He has left in any case a remarkable legacy, both of black blues and the white adaptation of it which became rock 'n' roll. He has written in fact one of the most astonishing chapters in the history of American popular music, and for this we can only be grateful.

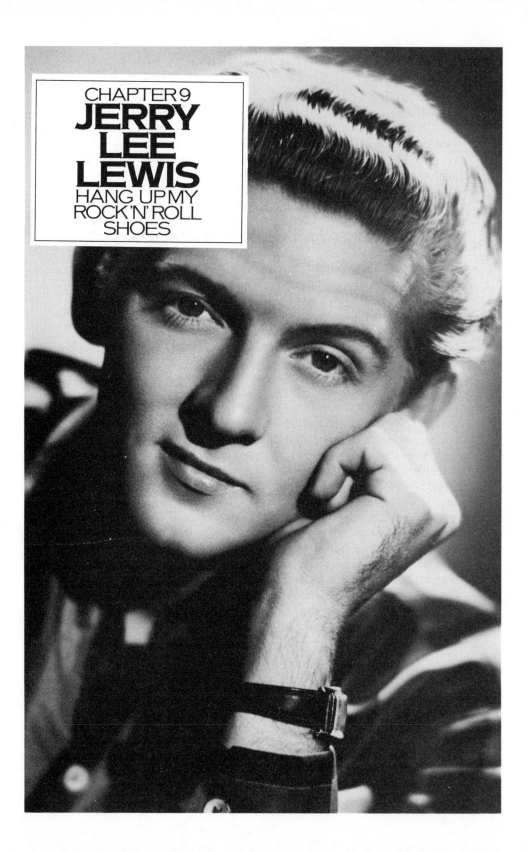

CHAPTER 9
JERRY
LEE
LEWIS
HANG UP MY
ROCK 'N' ROLL
SHOES

I don't wanna
I ain't gonna
Hang up my rock 'n' roll shoes
                    Jerry Lee Lewis *ca.* 1961

I

"Oh, I coulda been a great songwriter," Jerry Lee Lewis admits with no reluctance at all. "I reckon I coulda been one of the greatest. I still write some, I just don't record any of them. Because I prefer to concentrate on my entertaining instead."

It's the kind of statement you'd expect from Jerry Lee Lewis, self-proclaiming, boastful, spoken with a theatrical flourish and a certain wry amusement. There is an arrogance in his demeanour which is familiar from his act, and indeed offstage as well as on he is the same unlikely mixture of brash egotism and bubbling irrepressible charm. You can like it or loathe it, it's all the same to Jerry Lee, because Jerry Lee Lewis is going to change for no man. There is one difference, though. For this interview Jerry Lee Lewis is nervous, bored, this man who commands a stage as if it were his private domain is, in his own home, restless and apprehensive as he submits to what he considers the tyranny of more irrelevant scrutiny, more useless questions. He slouches opposite me, wearing cut-off shorts and a gaudy Hawaiian shirt, looking jaded and a little paunchy around the middle. There he is, my idol, Jerry Lee Lewis, drumming his fingers and offering something less than candour in his responses.

"Well, I can't really see as how anyone influenced me. God, man, I just got with it, you know, I created my own style." He leans forward, waiting for the next question, and his eyes squint past the vibrating machine which sits in the middle of the room, past the four gold records on the wall, to the breakfast bar where his wife Myra is fixing him a lemonade ("Put a little vodka in it?" he says half joking, because Myra does not allow drinking in the house). "I just started playing back in Louisiana when I was growing up. My folks bought me a piano when I was a kid and I been working at it, playing piano and entertaining, oh Lord, since I was eight years old... Oh yeah, I love it, man. I still get a kick out of entertaining people. Last few years we tried to cool it a little, we gotten it down to fifteen, twenty days a month, but it's still just go go all the time, you know, man, I'm never at home."

The house is set up along these lines. It's a long low single-story ranch house which consists of a functional row of bedrooms to accommodate whatever part of the Lewis entourage may be present at any given time. There are in addition to Myra and Jerry Lee, their daughter Phoebe; Cecil Harrelson, Jerry's road manager, ex-brother-in-law and boyhood friend; his sister, singer Linda Gail Lewis, and her present husband, Kenneth Lovelace, who plays guitar and fiddle in the group; Dick West, the equipment man and another long-time personal friend; Jerry Lee Jr., his mop-haired fifteen-and-a-half-year-old son by an earlier marriage and presently a member of the troupe; assorted children, pets and babies; and whoever else happens to be around and just feels like dropping in. Today Cecil and some of the band members are going off to fish in the lake which is the feature attraction of the residential estate on which Jerry Lee lives forty-five minutes outside of Memphis. Jerry Lee Jr. is working on his motorcycle and keeps coming in to ask his father – who has just had a new one delivered today – if he can borrow his. "Shoot, you'd tear it up just like you done your own," says the father. "I'd pay for it," mumbles the son petulantly. It remains a running source of battle with them, and one is reminded once again that happy families are all alike.

The only other rooms in the house are the den in which we are sitting, fitted out with comfortable leather-upholstered furniture, a dining room set off from the kitchen by a counter partition, the music room in which a piano sits, eerily illuminated, on a slightly raised platform, and Myra's ceramics room which leads from the house to the garage. Out back there is a swimming pool whose tiles are supposed to be designed in the shape of piano keys, but though I hear splashes and every now and then get a glimpse of one of the swimmers I don't get a chance to examine the pool first-hand. 'I'll tell you the truth," says Jerry Lee. "I'm gonna do just what I want to do, no matter what anyone says. You know, I mix and mingle with people pretty good. And if I want to get out and shoot a game of pool I'm gonna do it. People can stare if they want to, but I'm gonna do it."

As he loosens up a little and expands upon the nature of his genius and accomplishments his wife attempts to exert a restraining influence. She is a slim, very pretty and tastefully gotten out young matron, and it's hard to remember after all the scandal of their marriage thirteen years ago that she is actually only the same age as myself. He has done a great many benefits, she ventures to put in. "Shoot yes," agrees Jerry Lee. "I done Danny Thomas benefits, benefit for the PTA, charity, I done just about everything in fact except benefit myself." Myra looks displeased at the turn the conversation has taken, but all through the interview she defers to her husband in all matters, putting in a mild qualifier or demurral but on the whole seemingly just as mesmerized as I am myself by the spell of this arrogant, complex and mercurial man.

"Well, you see, I always liked Moon Mullican, Merrill Moore, a lot of them old boogie woogie piano players, I never knew who half of them were. All those old records I used to listen to — 'Drinkin' Wine Spo-dee-o-dee,' 'House of Blue Lights,' 'Hey Ba-Ba-Re-Bop'—you know, all them kind of sounds I used to hear back home in Louisiana when I was growing up. And I used to hear people like B.B. King, too, blues singers, I never did know their names. Well, anyway a lot of them songs must have been recorded before I was born. When I heard it it sure sounded good, though.

"I started to play when I was eight years old. I played a lot in church, you know, listened to a lot of things. Well, that was the Holiness Church, Assembly of God, and I went to Southwestern Bible School near Dallas in Waxahatchie (don't ask me to spell that). I wasn't really studying to be a preacher, but I was in the church for quite a while. Yeah, I used to sing, and we travelled around quite a bit, I done some preaching. We sang it with a beat, yeah we always sang it with a beat. Oh sure, I was performing on the stage way back then, I had my act then, of course it was not quite as polished then as it is now, it was just more naturally good. I hadn't had the chance to really polish it up at that time."

The first piano he played, a Starck upright, has been preserved for posterity, holes in the keyboard and all. His father, Elmo, who himself played guitar and encouraged his son in his musical career, tells the story that Jerry Lee was as good within six months of the time he started playing as he would ever get, a story which says something for his natural genius and indicates somewhat the nature of that genius. For his playing evidently found its own resolution even at an early age and quickly fell into the same patterns which

179

Jerry Lee Lewis/Michael Ochs Archives

dominate his style today — a brilliant explosive and altogether distinctive mix of country and barrelhouse blues which has changed not at all since his first recordings some fifteen years ago.

"Well, I used to hang around Haney's Big House, that was a coloured establishment where they had dances and such. Oh Lord, that burned down, I don't know how many years it's been gone. But anyway Haney was this little coloured fellow, and we was just kids, we wasn't allowed in. So we'd slip around to the back and sneak in whenever we could. I saw a lot of 'em there, all those blues players. No, it wasn't such a big deal like it is today. Somebody wanted to go down, it wasn't no big thing just because it was a coloured place. Of course we was about the only ones down there. Me and my cousin, Jimmy Lee Swaggart.

"Anyway, I'd go down there, sometimes I'd go alone and I'd hear them, catch a riff that I liked and go home and do a little picking myself. Yeah, I was playing guitar, violin and drums in addition to my piano back then. Sure, I still pick 'em up sometimes, just for a little variety.

"I started working, well, my first record didn't come out until 1956, that was when I first started making it really big, so to speak. But I'd been playing before that at the Wagon Wheel in Natchez, Mississippi for about six years, ever since I was fifteen years old. Oh, we played all kinds of music. Pop, I guess you'd call it, yeah pop. I worked with some people I knew from back home, Mr. Paul Whitehead, a blind fellow, he played piano, trumpet and accordion. And I played drums at the time. Or on the weekends I'd switch to piano and he'd play accordion, 'cause we had a man named Johnny Littlejohn who'd come in and play the drums. It was just a regular night club, you know, it wasn't no exclusive place, it wasn't plush, just a regular place. Oh, we had a few knock-down drag-outs every once in a while, but it never did bother me. I was raised up on that.

"Well, you see, that's where I got 'Whole Lotta Shakin'. I picked it up from Johnny Littlejohn, heard him doing it one night and then I started doing it. But it was never done like that before. I think originally it was done by Big Mama Thornton.* She done it before she done 'Hound Dog.' I inquired on it over at Hill and Range because there was some dispute over the writers' royalties. If I'd

*It was done, in fact, in 1955 by Big Maybelle in a version derived from that of its composer, Nashville boogie woogie pianist Roy Hall, but bearing little resemblance to Jerry Lee's.

known that at the time I would have gotten some of it for myself. Because actually I wrote quite a bit of it myself. At least I thought I did.

"Well, how I come to Sun, I was just a kid trying to get a start. I'd been to all the other record companies and I'd been turned down. I'd been to Shreveport, to the Louisiana Hayride, and I was turned down. So I came to Sam and Sam, he started out, he had B.B. King at one time, all them cats. When I auditioned I sang everything from Muddy Waters blues to 'Silent Night.' The first thing I had recorded was a little tune I had written long before called 'End of the Road.' And, of course, that old Ray Price tune, that was the A side. There was just drums and piano on that record."

The first song, "Crazy Arms," was a minor hit that showed off all the familiar Sun production techniques. It had built-in echo, solid musicianship, real feeling for the music, and a finely controlled frenzy. On the label it read Jerry Lee Lewis and His Pumping Piano, a designation that would stick right through to the end. The first record indicated that Jerry Lee Lewis was going somewhere, but it was the second, recorded by Jack Clement in a single take at the tail end of a session, that established him overnight as chief claimant to Elvis Presley's throne and that was to become his trademark. "We came in and recorded the song, and we ran through it once just to get the level on it," he recalled for the twenty-four hour radio History of Rock 'n' Roll. "Jack Clement was handling the controls. We took one take on it, and that was the take that we released on the record." "Whole Lotta Shakin' Going On" went to the top of the pop, r&b, and c&w charts, like "Blue Suede Shoes" and "Don't Be Cruel" before it and nothing since. "They're the onliest ones that did it," muses Jerry Lee today. "For a while I thought that woman was like to do it with 'Ode to Billy Joe,' but she didn't." It is one of the achievements of which he is proudest, and one which he always mentions to interviewers.

"Whole Lotta Shakin'"" went on to sell six or seven million copies, and Jerry Lee was thrust into the national limelight with appearances on Ed Sullivan and Steve Allen and rock 'n' roll tours which he headlined. He insists that he was not unprepared for this, that his act was as explosive then as it is today. Others remember it a little differently, however. "Jerry, when he started he was people-shy," Carl Perkins told Michael Lydon, recalling their first tour

*together. "Johnny Cash and I were on tour with him in Canada, his
'Crazy Arms' was just out, and he'd sit at the piano with just one
corner of his face showing and play Hank Williams tunes. He came
off one night in Calgary, moaning, 'This business ain't for me, people
don't like me,' and John and I told him, 'Turn around so they can
see you, make a fuss.' So the next night he carried on, stood up,
kicked the stool back and a new Jerry Lee Lewis was born. And we
regretted it because he damn near stole the show. Four nights later
he was top of the bill." And an observer who was present at his first
Memphis appearance, a Mayor's Charity Day concert at Ellis Audi-
torium which featured Onie Wheeler, Warren Smith, Carl Perkins,
and Billy Riley, claims that Jerry Lee was the low point of the show.
"Well, you know, it was just pitiful. I don't know whether it was his
long blond hair or the way he talked or what, but we all thought he
was a queer or something, he just looked like a sissy. Why, he just
about got booed off the stage."*

"I first came to Memphis, I'd do just about anything. I even cut
a session with Carl Perkins. I'd just finished up a session myself, and
he was coming in to cut some stuff, so I just played on one or two of
his numbers. I got paid fifteen dollars, and I don't even remember
the name of the song. ("'Your True Love'," interjects Myra: "And
they flat know who's playing on it.")

"Oh yeah, we're all good buddies still. Carl's a good fella. I done
my first tour with Carl and Johnny Cash. No, Elvis had just left Sun.
When I come to Sun he was already giant. I don't know, we were all
doing our thing, it was all friendly enough, but everyone did his own
thing. I see these guys quite often every now and then. Last time I
saw Elvis I was fooling round with him at the International Hotel in
Las Vegas about a year ago. Oh, we was singing and cutting up. You
know, Elvis has kept himself pretty isolated, though. Too much if
you ask me. Me, I like to get out and hunt and fish with the boys,
I'm going to do just what I damn please. And you know, I make just
as much money as any of those guys. I can guarantee you that.

"Me and Elvis? For a long time, you know, we were just
matching each other, record for record, price for price, show for
show. The newspapers made a big deal about it, I never paid that
much attention, but one time, I don't know what magazine it was
– *Look,* I think – they had a full page on me and a full page on
Elvis right opposite each other. For a long time it was pretty hard to

figure just who'd be number one, we was matching each other like that, tit for tat.

"Well, I had a whole string of hits. After 'Whole Lotta Shakin'' there was 'Great Balls of Fire' and 'Breathless' and then me and another fellow wrote 'High School Confidential.' Then we had, oh let me see, 'Break-Up' and then that Ray Charles thing and then I got in the country field of music. And I just keep rockin' on. Now we got twelve Number One records in a row, and you just better believe it."

II

That, of course, does not exactly tell the whole story. Between the "Ray Charles thing" ("What'd I Say?") and the country music there was a lapse of eight years. And even before "What'd I Say?," his last big hit for Sun, pickings had gotten pretty slim. Some critics have contended that it was lack of material, but Jerry Lee has always shown a fine eye for material and anyway he had Otis Blackwell — a prolific composer ("Breathless," "Don't Be Cruel," "All Shook Up") whom Jerry Lee refers to as "a little coloured fellow in a derby hat" — writing for him. To repeat a story that has become stale already from too much repetition: in 1958 Jerry Lee Lewis married his thirteen-year-old second cousin, Myra Brown, and, when the news broke just prior to his first English tour, took his young bride to England and flaunted her, seemingly without a second thought, in front of his British fans. The result was predictable enough. The papers had a field day, the tour was unceremoniously cancelled, and Jerry Lee Lewis was washed up as a rock 'n' roll star. Three years later, it's true, he did have that hit, but he was blacklisted for all intents and purposes for the next ten years.

"I don't think it was my marriage," he contends even today. "I don't blame the people. I blame the record company. Well, you see, that was Sam Phillips, man, he had some thing with the record distributors. Other companies, you get a hit record, they really market the product. Sam was always in some kind of fight with his distributors. You see, people wanted to buy 'em, they just couldn't get 'em. Cause it's a proven fact, man, I couldn't never sell any records on Sun Records. Even before my sales were dropping off. Oh, sure, the marriage may have affected twenty-five to thirty-five

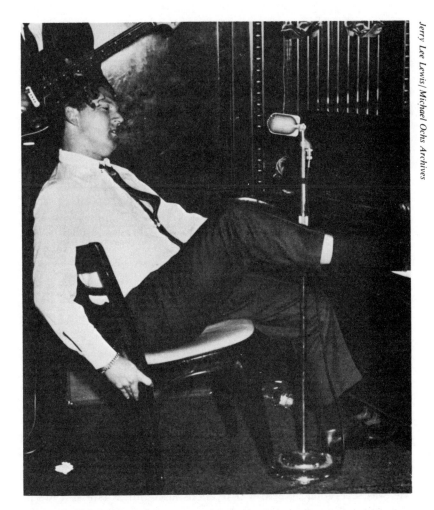

percent. But it didn't have no one hundred percent effect."

His response in any case was predictable enough. The first record released after his English debacle, "The Return of Jerry Lee," consisted of snippets of songs introduced by interview questions which not only referred to his marriage but actually harped on the subject. "How did you propose to your wife, Jerry?" asked the interviewer, George Klein, formerly president of Elvis Presley's class at Humes High School. "Open up, honey, it's your lover boy, me, that's a-knockin'" came the classic opener of "High School Confidential." The flip side, "Lewis Boogie," was no less strident in its tone.

My name is Jerry Lee Lewis, I'm from Lou-isiana
I'm gonna do ya a little boogie on this here piano

it began with typical modesty.

"I think," a friend of his suggested to a Memphis interviewer, "he felt like he had to thumb his nose at the whole world. To some extent he's still doing it today. But back in those days, man, he was wild." Certainly as late as 1961 when he finally got some airplay with "What'd I Say?", the follow-up, "It Won't Happen with Me," was brashly proclaiming the demise of Elvis Presley, Ricky Nelson and Fabian while maintaining:

It wouldn't happen to me,
  it wouldn't happen to me,
  it wouldn't happen to me
Oh no, not me.

Even today he remains fully as self-absorbed, and he will still interject his name into a song at every available opportunity, not so much to boast as to put his signature on it, to make sure that you know exactly who it is, as if there could be any mistake.

He enjoyed something of a vogue in the middle sixties when Jack Good signed him to a multiple appearance contract with *Shindig,* a network show with good popularity. It was Good, too, who put on the rock 'n' roll version of *Othello, Catch My Soul,* which starred William Marshall, The Blossoms, and Jerry Lee Lewis. He was, everyone agreed, a marvellous Iago, but as late as 1968 he was still casting about for a viable re-entry into the pop music world. Then suddenly he stumbled across something that by his own admission should have been obvious from the beginning.

"It was, uh, I wanted to, uh, do something different. I knew that we had to make a move, it was right there under my nose the whole time. I been singing this kind of music ever since I was a kid, I just got hung up on rock and it seemed like a big thing to do. It seemed like such a natural thing, and here I'd been sweating my brains out the whole time. It's like a farmer sitting out on a three hundred acre farm, and all the time oil's flowing under him and he ain't got enough sense to get at it. Well, one day he finally hit, and then he's a smart man. I knew something had to be done. So I went in and cut myself a country song. Then I had to go on out there and play it. And that song just took off. The company [Smash Records, a division of Mercury] was all shook up, they didn't know what to think. I had to come right back in and cut me an album."

It's hard to say how he feels exactly after this ten-year odyssey in search of his audience. He's not bitter, he insists, and if you ask him he stubbornly refuses to admit that his confidence might ever have wavered. But when you wonder, especially in the light of the recent rock 'n' roll revival, if he might ever go back to singing for the rock market he just shakes his head and says no, the country fans have stuck with him and he guesses he'll stick with them now. "I'm singing real country music the way I remember it. I think it is the best thing for me, the best thing for country music, the best thing for everyone concerned ... I sing the way I sing because I feel that way."

III

"I really love my country stuff. Of course I brought a lot into country. If you want to call my records country. Cause I don't think the same person who listens to my records listens to Roy Acuff. Merle Haggard? No, I don't go in for that kind of stuff too much. It's all right, but I just sing my pretty love songs and drinking songs and leave it at that."

Jerry Lee Lewis has never been exactly an introverted performer. His greatest strengths have always stemmed from his exuberant style, and his approach to a song — in its single-minded insistence on draining all possible levels of energy from that song — has varied little over the years. Even in country and western, a field not exactly noted for its dramatic or pyrotechnic displays, Jerry Lee Lewis has retained his theatrical flair. He is always the showman who, far from being content with a mere rendition of his latest hit, must always act it out in the broadest possible style.

His first sessions for Sun pretty well established the breadth of

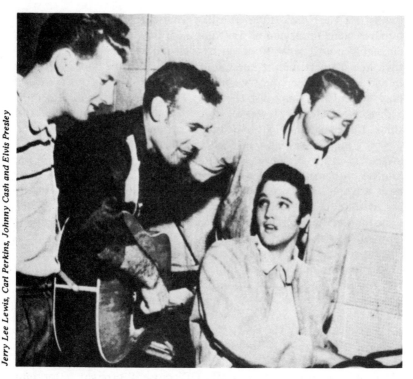

Jerry Lee Lewis, Carl Perkins, Johnny Cash and Elvis Presley

his talents, and he has throughout his career recorded everything from blues and country to "The Crawdad Song" and "Old Black Joe." Aside from his very first record he has written little of his own material — "Lewis Boogie," "High School Confidential," "Lincoln Limousine," a lugubrious account of the assassination of President Kennedy which he insists is not political ("Shoot, that's just telling the truth, man, it's just history on a man who got killed. It's like singing about mama. Or Casey Jones."). But he has put his individual stamp so unmistakably on everything he has ever recorded that there has never been a successful cover of any of his songs while he has himself covered and cut the hits of artists as diverse as Chuck Berry, Fats Domino, Little Richard and his erstwhile rival, Elvis Presley. What makes his approach to a song so unique is this singular ability to galvanize even the most unlikely material (he once used a *Shindig*-inspired duet with Neil Sedaka on "Take Me Out to the Ballgame" for a typical display of rock pyrotechnics) and turn it into a prime vehicle for his talents. You get the impression sometimes that like the proverbial actor reading the telephone book Jerry Lee Lewis could hold an audience spellbound with his version of "Tea for Two" or, as he did in his Sun audition, with "Stardust" or "My Blue Heaven."

The element that stands out the most, however, both in his music and in his in-person act, is his constant experimentation and the seemingly limitless energy he will impart to a performance. His style, it is true, may have been formed at an early age, and certainly his piano, while always exciting, is no virtuoso accomplishment. Within the technical limits of voice and instrument, however, he shows an almost endless inventiveness and a willingness to reach for effects which will occasionally misfire to the detriment of the song itself. He will not sing a song the same way twice ("I musta done 'Whole Lotta Shakin',' oh Lord, ten thousand times, and I done it different every time."), and for anyone who has seen him more than once or twice in person it becomes quickly apparent that this is not an idle boast. Most of the songs he records, he insists, he doesn't even get to see until ten or fifteen minutes before the session, and as a result a great many of his numbers improve in performance. His music carries a unique, almost swaggering assurance and whatever the field — blues, country, or rock — a vaudevillian flair which he attributes to Al Jolson. Al Jolson? "Sure," he said to my evident disbelief. "I loved Al Jolson, I still got all of his records. Even back when I was a kid I listened to him all the time." All right then, Al Jolson. In Jerry Lee Lewis musical strands as diverse as Hank Williams, Jimmie Rodgers, Bing Crosby and Sunnyland Slim all meet without apparent quarrel or difference.

He is in addition, of course, a highly visual act. Like Little Richard, Chuck Berry, Elvis, all the old-time rock 'n' rollers, he perfected the art not only of deliberate outrageousness but of creating a distance between himself and that outrageousness which permits him to be extravagant and to make commentary on the proceedings all at the same time. He wraps his legs around the microphone, he entertains effortlessly with a wiggle of the finger and a quizzical grin, he regards his audience with a certain curiosity and an appetite which has yet to be satisfied. Then, in a finish which has become his trademark, he kicks back the piano stool, shakes his blond hair forward, hitches up his pants and with a studied laziness begins a slow grind. He may play a couple of notes with his foot or he may sit down on the piano; his hands hover high above the keyboard, then, swooping down, race up and down the keys performing tricks, while he is endlessly entertained by the audience's enjoyment of him. At the finale the guitarist is on his amplifier, the drummer is perched precariously on the drums, and Jerry Lee Lewis roars from on top of the piano in a climax that creates an instant of pure theatre which could never be fully anticipated or exactly recreated. It's a combination of showmanship and calculated hysteria which is somehow saved from the realm of the ridiculous by Jerry Lee's whole-hearted commitment to the moment. For, while there is an element of self-parody implicit in the act, Jerry Lee Lewis always takes himself seriously enough to insist upon absolute attendance. I've seen him shush a blonde ("Honey, will you kindly quit your yakking? There's lots of our loud numbers where you can do all the talking you want. But this here's a real sad song and you ought to listen.") and stop a couple from dancing with the admonition, "I'm the show." Because he is, and he knows he is, a condition which is essential to the born entertainer.

Like The Rolling Stones, he was in his time the bad boy of rock, and he remains to this day a perennial reminder of a certain type of adolescent rebellion. When he appears on the *Ed Sullivan Show* he has his hair tousled by Ed; he shows up at the Country Music Awards in tuxedo and sneakers; and when Tom Jones, a long-time fan, gives him some national exposure he returns the favour by throwing a well-intended duet on a medley of his hits into total disarray. There is a puckish grin on his face as he perversely alters the familiar rhythms of "Whole Lotta Shakin'," leaving Jones looking foolish and confused. "I cut his ass," he proclaimed proudly to John Grissim of *Rolling Stone*. "And he knows it, cuz I taught him what he knows. Love him like a brother. But I don't want him to forget who the old master is."

IV

Lake Charles, Fort Smith, Tulsa, Oklahoma City, Sulpha Oklahoma, Pascagoula, Denham Springs, Conroe Texas, OFF. A few years ago that's the way Jerry Lee Lewis's schedule read. An endless string of one-nighters hopscotching across the heartland of America. Today it isn't all that different, except the one-nighters have lengthened to week-long engagements, there are occasional dates like the ones at the International, and there's a little more time off. Even so, Jerry Lee Lewis keeps busy. At the time I saw him he was just in from Las Vegas on a ten-day break, during the course of which he'd get down to Ferriday to see his folks and kin, relax around the house a little, and fly into Nashville for a recording session. It's a grueling pace, but for all his talk of tapering off it's hard to imagine Jerry Lee Lewis really cutting down. Among white musicians he has the same reputation as James Brown has among blacks: the hardest working man in show business. And, like Brown, he seems equally mesmerized by the trappings of success, drawn not only by the acclaim but by a real need to perform. "I'll never get tired of playing this music," he said once when he was in Boston. "I'm never going to stop playing it. I'll go on playing just as long as there are people to listen."

There is little question, however, that fifteen years on the road have taken their toll and it's understandable that, after having driven himself and his musicians all that time, he and his band have gotten the reputation around Memphis of being a little "squirrelly." He frankly acknowledges it; he seems to look on it as an advantage in a business and in a world that is more than slightly nutty itself. "Sam?" he said, speaking of Sam Phillips to John Grissim. "He's just like me. He ain't got no sense. Me and him and Jack Clement. Birds of a feather flock together. It took all of us to get together to screw up the world. We've done it. Now I went on to greater fame, and I'm screwin' them up worse than ever."

In one sense musicians are not at all like real people anyway. Even among musicians, though, Jerry Lee Lewis stands out as an eccentric. Musicians who have toured with him point out that he has to be treated with a deference bordering on outright worship. "He's the king of rock 'n' roll," says Charlie Freeman, now a member of Miami's Dixie Flyers. "Just ask him, he'll tell you." "Lord, I never seen one yet you could call normal," says the wife of a well-known Memphis artist. "But Jerry Lee, he really takes the cake. Of course he's grown up a lot in the last couple of years. I think Myra's had a lot to do with that. He used to be a real wildman. Him and his father-in-law, he played bass in the band, you know, they were a real wild bunch of fellows. But I do believe he is finally growing up."

Her assessment in many ways seems pretty close to the truth. Jerry Lee Lewis is growing up. He's happy to have finally reclaimed some of his old popularity, and he is probably more comfortable with his country music fans than with the young kids. They in turn have acclaimed him as something like the prodigal son come home, a sentiment with which Jerry Lee would probably concur since he has seen himself as just another good ole boy right along. In attitude and belief he is not all that different from the more prosaic citizen who has sowed his wild oats. And, as the years go by, there seems little doubt that his attitudes will mellow, his views of society will grow increasingly more conventional, and his religious beliefs, always just beneath the surface, will assert themselves more strongly.

He does not differ from other musicians either, black or white, in his avoidance of political statements of any sort. He admires Merle Haggard, he says, but doesn't approve of injecting politics into song. Was rock 'n' roll a kind of integrating force? I ask him. "Well, I got along fine with Richard — Little Richard and Chuck Berry, never did have any problem. We done tours across the country with different coloured acts." He thinks hard. "No, man, if it done anything it look like to me it got to be a problem after that, if it done anything I believe it caused some problems —" He breaks off. Myra shoots him a warning look, perhaps his own better sense silences him, but at any rate we leave it at that.

His relaxations, his aspirations and professional ambitions are not all that different from the average guy. He likes to hunt and fish. He'd still like to make a movie. At one time it was a Bible movie, but now he's more serious about it. It would have to be the right kind of vehicle. Not this Glen Campbell-Elvis Presley type of movie. "I'd want the right producer, the right director, the right writer," he muses aloud. "I don't want to do any of these beach party productions." There's still a possibility that they might do a film version of *Catch My Soul,** Jack Good was on the phone about it just the other day and he's very enthusiastic about that.

And his music? Well, he figures he'll just keep on the way he has. As long as the public doesn't get tired of him it'll still be rockin'

---

*The movie was eventually made with Jerry's imitator (and Elvis' stand-in) Lance Le Gault, in the role of Iago.

Jerry Lee and his Pumping Piano. "You know, if I could just find another like 'Whole Lotta Shakin'," he muses wistfully. "Some records just got that certain something. But I ain't gonna find another. Just like I was born once into this world and I ain't gonna be born again. Just the same I sure would like to run up against another one like that."

Even so his records still sell 250,000 on release and half a million on anything resembling a hit. He continues to pack them in with his country and western show and — perhaps because this audience is more discriminating than his rock fans, perhaps because it is not as fickle — seems proudest in fact of his achievements in this field. One thing that continues to nettle him is *Billboard's* failure to list his first top c&w record, "What Made Milwaukee Famous (Has Made a Loser Out of Me)," at Number One. "It was Number One. *Cashbox* had it Number One. I don't know why they did that." Jerry Lee Lewis looks really annoyed for the first time in the interview. They printed a correction the next week, it turns out, but the memory still rankles.

"You know," says Jerry Lee Lewis in a reflective mood, "a lot of people think if you can make a lot of money, that's what this life is all about. Well, that can't be what life is all about, you know? If I can just play my piano and sing ... you know, the proudest I ever was in my life was when I got my first record out. When I heard it on the radio for the first time that really done something for me. I guess that's about the biggest thrill I ever had in the business. Disappointments? I been — the good Lord been pretty good to me. I've lived and breathed and taken care of my wife and seen my kids growing up. Well, life is just a vapour," he winked at me, as if I, too, should recognize this vaguely Shakespearean allusion. "You breathe it in and what the heck, it's gone."

V

"Is that it? You got it all down?" With the interview over Jerry Lee Lewis suddenly brightened up. All through the questioning he had sat slumped in his seat, his legs sprawled over the arm of the chair and his face assuming that look of slit-eyed indifference which has become so familiar from his stage performance. It was not that

Jerry Lee Lewis with child bride Myra, 1958

he was bored exactly. It wasn't even the inconvenience of the interview — though there was clearly that, too — so much as its irrelevancy in the scheme of Jerry Lee Lewis's life. For Jerry Lee is a man who lives in the present exclusively. He has little use for or interest in the past, and it was only when he was freed from this barrage of meaningless questions that he ever really grew animated. Would I like to see the house? he asked. Here were Myra's ceramics, and here was the legendary Starck ("To show you how much I played it I made holes in the keys. And nobody played it but me. I used to play that thing, oh five, six hours a day. One of these days I'm gonna have it restored. Not too much, you understand. Just so's it looks right."). You ought to give it to the Country Music Hall of Fame, I suggested. "Yeah, that's right," he mused, weighing no doubt some obscure advantage in his mind. "Well, they already asked me for it. But I don't know yet if I'm going to give it to them. I haven't made up my mind yet."

Out in the driveway amid the chromium assortment of Cadillacs, Lincoln Continentals, convertibles, and motorcycles Jerry Lee Jr. was still working on his motorcycle. "You ain't got that fixed up yet?" said his father. The boy hung his head sullenly. Jerry Lee just shook his head. "Well, Peter my boy, I thank you. I appreciate your coming out to see us. Now don't you take no wooden nickels or no silver dollars neither along the way. If I ever get up to Boston I expect I'll see you up there. And if you're ever in Memphis again, you be sure to look me up, buddy, you hear?" We parted on the best of terms, and with great good feeling Jerry Lee went back to working on his motorcycle.

POSTSCRIPT

"Jerry Lee Lewis and Myra Brown, whom he married in 1958 when she was just fourteen, have been divorced in Memphis after testimony from Myra that their marriage had 'become a nightmare.' Lewis threw it all away twelve years ago when he married his young first cousin and has been making a comeback in recent years through country music. Now, he's under court injunction 'not to threaten, molest, or intimidate' his twenty-six-year-old wife..."

Rolling Stone,
December 7, 1970

CHAPTER 10
CHARLIE RICH
LONELY WEEKENDS

I

"You remember him, honey," Charlie Rich says to his wife Margaret Ann. She shakes her head and squints after the man whose offer to buy her husband a drink she has just politely declined. She's left her glasses at home tonight and looks very pretty and pleased that someone is at last going to do a story on Charlie. "You remember," he says again with a sorrowful insistence that expects no response. "We were in the high school band together, God it seems like eight million years ago."

Charlie Rich was born in Colt, Arkansas, a little town across the river from Memphis just outside of Forrest City, thirty-seven years ago in 1932. He started out with Sun like Elvis and Jerry Lee Lewis and Carl Perkins, and he and his wife remember when Johnny Cash used to put chewing gum between his teeth to keep himself from whistling through the gap. He speaks of Cash and the others with a mixture of admiration and regret. Surprisingly there is no bitterness, but Margaret Ann is quick to tell me that Charlie can't get on Cash's TV show and she hints with a certain ambivalence that John has forgotten his old friends.

Charlie Rich looks older than his thirty-seven years. He is a big distinguished-looking man whose hair started to gray when he was in his early twenties and is now completely white. He has a handsome beefy face, but there is something vulnerable about it, and even with friends, while he always bestows a polite measure of attention, he seems more reticent than not. Occasionally, too, his attention will wander, his gaze will drift out of focus, and a look of pain will come into his eyes. Except in his music he seems to find it difficult to express what he is feeling, and in these moments the carefully maintained facade of casual non-concern seems to crumble, and he looks for a moment like a soul who is going through hell.

"Every gray hair he has on his head, he earned it," says Margaret Ann, a talented composer herself and Charlie's principal booster for the last eighteen years. "You see, his people are Missionary Baptist, his mother still plays organ for the church today. It's a real small fundamentalist type church, a bit basic, very narrow in their thinking. I don't mean to speak harshly of it, but that's the way they are. There's no in-between with them. It's all yes or no, right or wrong, black or white. Now you take a country boy from a poor

197

Charlie Rich/Michael Ochs Archives

family, throw him into a business like this, it just isn't easy. I imagine he feels guilty all the time.

"When he was a little boy he wanted to be a preacher. His mother and father used to have a gospel quartet, and he would hear them practising, his mother told me he used to hear them practising and he'd go in the bedroom and cry. I don't know why. That's just the way he would react.

"He's got two sisters, both of them are in the church, one of them's married to a Missionary Baptist preacher. His mother — I don't know how to explain it — she's worried so much about his drinking she doesn't even think about the music life anymore. You see, his father was an alcoholic before he reformed. I only knew him after he reformed, and then he was the best man who ever lived. He was a real homebody, he had a real musical talent himself. At least, he was musically inclined, but he was too shy to ever be a performer. You see, church was their whole way of life, it was their social life, it was their politics and morality, it was everything. I wish he could learn to compromise. He's just not prepared for this. I'm not a city girl myself, but I lived a little closer to town. But it's the only way he knows to make a living. I hate it."

Margaret Ann says all this not at all as if she were making some personal revelation but almost with an air of casual conversation. She is devoted to Charlie, but at the same time she is very ambitious for him and apparently anxious that his story get told. Charlie, of course, has long since excused himself from the conversation, and is conferring with the club manager or having his picture taken with a friend just back from Vietnam. He has a habit of withdrawing whenever the talk gets around to him, and perhaps in his quietness or, more likely, from the deep brooding melancholy which seems to haunt him, he gives the impression of some fierce latent power held in check. When I spoke with her over the phone in the afternoon Margaret Ann was particularly anxious that I come out to see Charlie that night, not only because I would get a chance to see him perform but also because she would be there.

"I can tell you more about Charlie than he's ever going to tell you," she admitted quite openly. And, too, of course, the Vapors was a pretty good club. "Not like some of the places he plays. Oh, some of those places are real dives. You just about have to get stoned to play in them."

It *is* a nice enough club, a dining room and a panoramic dance floor, with a three dollar cover charge and jacket and necktie required for gentlemen. There are two other acts on the bill — Narvel Felts and Ace Cannon and his honky-tonk sax — and every day there is a tea dance from three to six. The MC keeps things moving so there are four hours of continuous entertainment, and even though there is no place for the musicians to relax and talk quietly back-stage the atmosphere is convivial enough so that it doesn't much matter. Old friends stop by the bandstand, or else it's friends of old friends. Everyone knows everyone else, it seems, and Charlie Rich engages in the expected bantering in a courtly diffident way. "Of course I remember you," he says almost convincingly, "Sure howya doing?"

Margaret Ann stands out among all the bouffant hairdos and lacquered nails with her quiet presence and delicate beauty. Although she is herself a small-town girl who graduated with Charlie

from the Consolidated High School in Forrest City some twenty years ago, she looks in her Pucci-styled pantsuit like some exotic species set among the back-slapping middle-aged couples and gawky young marrieds who frequent the Vapors. Indeed there is no question, without her ever coming out and saying so, that she finds her surroundings dull, her neighbours provincial and that from the time she first wrote away and subscribed to *downbeat* in high school she has always considered herself different. Charlie Rich is no less different. "Back in high school," says Margaret Ann, "they used to call him Charlie Kenton, he loved Stan Kenton that much. That was his idol. I can remember one time, they had a concert with June Christie (that was my idol) and Stan Kenton both. Oh, that was great. Well, you know, they're trying to call Charlie a country singer now, but he isn't really. I would say he borders on being a jazz performer primarily. That's what he listens to. Brubeck, Miles Davis, Count Basie — you know, that sort of thing. I think in a way that's one of the reasons he's had such a difficult time of it. They just don't know where to place him, they don't know where he fits in."

Up on stage the MC bounds to the microphone and joins in a scattering of applause for Ace Cannon, who has just finished a loud uninspiring set. Charlie Rich's ears hurt (they have been bothering him for several months now), he is tired from a flight in from Dallas just that afternoon, and he suffers, he says, from emphysema from smoking too much. He sighs as the MC announces his name and wearily makes his way up to the stage as Narvel Felts' band — kids who might just as well be playing rock 'n' roll, dressed up in tuxedoes — gets set up to play. All the musicians know each other apparently, and the crowd knows Charlie from appearing for so many years around Memphis. So he gets a nice round of applause and sitting behind the big grand piano — pushed into a corner, almost hidden from sight — he strikes the familiar opening chords of "Lonely Weekends," the song by which he has come to be known, his first and biggest hit.

Charlie Rich cut "Lonely Weekends" for Phillips, a Sun subsidiary, at the tail end of 1959, following Jerry Lee Lewis's fall from grace, long after Elvis Presley, Carl Perkins, Johnny Cash and Roy Orbison had left the company. He had played piano on sides by Cash and Ray Smith and even Jerry Lee, whose own pumping piano wasn't able to make the adjustment to Charlie's composition. "I'll Make It All Up to You." In addition to what he wrote for Jerry Lee, he provided songs for a number of Sun artists and generally served as a house musician and composer for Phillips' rapidly diminishing stable until "Lonely Weekends" established him as a performer in his own right. Of all his discoveries, Sam Phillips said at one time, Charlie Rich alone had the raw talent to rival Elvis. The statement may well be true, but it is one of the few instances in which Phillips' aesthetic judgment differed radically from commercial reality.

Charlie Rich never made it anywhere near as big as his fellow Sun artists. He was a victim for one thing of Phillips' increasing indifference to the record business. After 1958 Sun Records seems to have become little more than a hobby among Phillips' diversified financial interests, and there is no question that artists like Charlie Rich suffered from lack of promotion. There seems to have been a certain reluctance on Charlie's part, too, though, which contributed as much as anything else to his lack of striking success. He got out of the Air Force in 1955 after serving three years in Enid, Oklahoma, where he had a small jazz group that played local dances, officers' and enlisted men's clubs, and had a weekly TV spot. He came back

to Arkansas after his discharge and for a couple of years tried
working his uncle's farm in West Memphis ("As a farmer," says
Margaret Ann, "he made a pretty good piano player."), and he kept
up his music on weekends, picking up ten dollars at the Sharecropper
Club where he worked off and on for more than four years. He did
a little singing, too, but it was mostly, he says, quartet stuff, scat
singing with the band. It was not his idea to go to Sun. It was
Margaret Ann, working almost surreptitiously, who approached
Bill Justis, then serving as an A&R man for Sam Phillips.

"I knew, at least I thought I knew, that he'd be happier doing
this. So I called the Sun Record Company, and I talked with Bill
Justis (I'd met Bill one time before at a party), and he was his usual
cool hip self. He said, What are you calling me for if you're already
Rich? Well, I almost never talked that man into going over there.
First I took some tapes in, and Bill was interested. Then Sam signed
him, he did give Charlie a contract, I guess I can thank him for that."

Charlie stayed with Sun until 1962 when the company virtually
folded. He went to RCA next and then to Smash, where with his first
release he achieved a second national hit in "Mohair Sam." He looks
back on his stay at Smash as one of the happiest periods in his
musical life (both he and his wife regard Jerry Kennedy, his producer
and Jerry Lee's current doyen, as a "ray of sunshine in a den of
iniquity"), and he emphasizes that this was the only time in his
musical career that he was allowed to do what he really wanted to
do. After "Mohair Sam," though, the records didn't sell, bookings —
which have never been plentiful — fell off, and after two years he
signed with Hi, an independent Memphis label, and finally with
Epic, a subdivision of Columbia, where he is at present and for whom
he has had a mild string of hits in the country market.

> *I got loaded last night on a bottle of gin*
> *And I had a fight with my best girl friend*
> *But when I'm drinkin'*
> *I am nobody's friend*
> *But, please, baby, wait for me until*
>   *they let me out again.*

If you weren't familiar with the song the words would probably
be lost, with Charlie hidden behind the big piano, Narvel Felts'

band a little loud, and the voice mike lost in the instruments' amplification. Charlie isn't very engaged in his performance anyway. Mostly he runs through songs both he and the audience are going to be familiar with. By the end of the evening he will have done "Lonely Weekends" and "Mohair Sam" three times each, he sings his wife's "Field of Yellow Daisies" which, she says, Tom Jones has recorded, though she doesn't seem to think much of his version. "Life's Little Ups and Downs," she tells me proudly, has been covered by artists as diverse as Wayne Cochran, Brook Benton, and Jerry Lee Lewis, and she refers throughout our conversation to the publishing company which she started with Charlie's manager's wife ("It's called Makamillion" she says, making a face. "Don't you dare print that, it's so awful.").

> *I spend a whole lot of time*
> *Sittin' and thinkin'*
> *Sittin' and just thinkin' about you*
> *Well, if I didn't spend so much time*
> *Sittin' and drinkin'*
> *We'd still have the love that we once knew.*

"I hate that song," Margaret Ann bursts out suddenly, turning away from the stage. "I can't stand it. You know, it really hits home. That's Charlie Rich, that's his life. That's the real Charlie sure as life." It's a beautiful song, I say, moved both by the song and the revelation, but Margaret Ann shakes her head as if to say that for her it's not just a song. "Well, it's tough on Charlie being on the road. He's a natural-born loner, he's getting older, too, and it's hard on him. Because it's rough, it's abnormal to have to get out and show yourself, to relate to people you've never met. You know, I think if every musician were exactly honest they'd tell you nobody can live like that. I never met a musician that wasn't a little bit odd, that didn't use a crutch of some kind. You just about have to have something. The life they lead is bizarre."

> *I know the same thing has happened before*
> *And every time it does I hate it more and more*
> *But when I'm drinkin'*
> *I am nobody's friend*

So, please, baby, wait for me until
they let me out again.

In the course of the evening people continually stop by our table — men and women whom Charlie has known for a long time or just fans who would like to speak with him or get an autograph. Charlie greets them all with the same gracious deference, he is never rude or abrupt with any of them, but at the same time he is never enthusiastic either. "You know my wife, Margaret Ann," he says to Narvel Felts, an overweight tired looking man with a strained booster's manner, whom Margaret Ann has denied knowing all evening. They exchange some trade gossip. Both were just in Texas, and they talk about fishing in Texarkana. The MC waves to him from the stage and announces jovially, "I'll see you later." "I can't wait," says Charlie glumly. The kids in Narvel Felts' band stop by towards the end of the evening. "One more set," Charlie tells them. "Just fifteen minutes." They groan, and Charlie, too, seems to be shouldering a burden that he never meant to undertake.

The Vietnam veteran at his table is getting drunker and drunker. He has the coloured boy taking photographs snap one picture after another of him and Charlie Rich. "You really ought to do something with that 'Lonely Weekends'," he says over and over half jokingly. "I think you really got something there, boy." Charlie smiles obligingly every time, but just what their relationship is is not clear.

Everyone offers to buy him a drink, but Margaret Ann firmly limits him to beer, and he is not even drinking much of that. A lady at the table — sitting there with an older woman who might be her mother — asks me if I might do a story on a group she manages; they sing countrypolitan with a lot of original material, and if I'll only stay in town until Friday I'll get a chance to see and talk with them. She looks disappointed when I tell her I'm leaving next morning, but she doesn't say another word for the rest of the evening. A husky crewcut comes up and asks me if she is with anyone — she is a big striking-looking girl with petticoats which flare out her striped dress — but I don't know and he's too drunk to really listen. By the end of the night Charlie is really distressed at the constant flow of people and the continual demands from every quarter. He remains gracious, but every question I ask is interrupted by a drinking buddy or autograph seeker and at last he breaks away with a cry of pain. "I

204

gotta get out of here. These people are driving me nuts." I'm finished with the interview and I start to gather up my material. "I don't mean you, man," Charlie offers half apologetically. "It's just — *all these people.*" I nod at him, I don't know what to say, but I appreciate his consideration.

II

"Piano players have a helluva rough life," says Charlie Rich with wry detachment. He is annoyed when he comes off stage after the first set because the piano, although it is, surprisingly enough, in tune, cannot be moved towards the front of the stage. He goes and speaks to the manager and arranges to have an electric piano substituted. At his wife's urging he sits down next to me, and we shout back and forth over Narvel Felts' tired pastiche of country hits and double entendre novelty songs and Ace Cannon's yacketty sax. Margaret Ann is right about his reserve, although it seems as if it is not so much that he is shy, perhaps, as that he finds it inappropriate to speculate on his musical talents. The story he tells is virtually the same as Margaret Ann's, only it omits the psychological terms and for that reason, while it loses a great deal of colour, it gains considerably in complexity.

"I was raised up as a churchgoer. Of course I don't swing with that anymore cause for one thing you're working all night Saturday night, you're working such odd hours, really, you don't have time for that sort of thing. My mother and father, though, they used to be in a quartet. When I was a little bitty kid just coming on up I used to hear 'em around the house all the time. My mother gave me piano lessons, I guess the whole family was musical, myself and two sisters, it was pretty much of a musical family.

"I started playing with a group when I was around fourteen or fifteen. Just local stuff around my hometown, in Colt and Forrest City, like that. I did a lot of jazz things while I was in the service — Brubeck, Oscar Peterson, things like that. After I got out I came back here and picked up more of a blues feel. See, I was raised up on a farm, plantation, what have you. Naturally we had a lot of coloured people working for us, and naturally they sang their music — blues, so to speak — in the cottonfields. I'm not prejudiced, never

Charlie Rich with Billy Sherill

have been, I think in a way musicians are the least prejudiced people around because they appreciate each other for their talent, not their colour. Well, I don't really know how to explain it. I understand it, but it's hard to explain. It was the music we heard. I think I just feel it, man, because blues is a feel.

"Well anyway I came back here and I farmed a couple of years over in West Memphis. I was playing clubs over here, mostly weekends. I was doing some solo stuff, piano-bar type of material, and I was playing with a five-piece group, still playing my jazz. We had one guy in the group, Sid Manker — he was the guitar player on 'Raunchy' — he really dug that music, he was a great jazz buff. And we used to play at a place called the Rivermont Club, at the Sharecropper, too, oh for a number of years.

"At the time that Elvis came out I was still interested in my jazz favourites. Oh hell, he influenced a helluva lot of people. He was the guy who really got the ball rolling, who got people interested in rock 'n' roll, in the good type stuff. As a matter of fact, 'Lonely Weekends' reminded a lot of people of Elvis. Which is good if he done it, but not especially good if it's someone else trying to sound like him.

"I came to Sun, actually my wife took some tapes over to Bill Justis — you've heard of him? — he liked 'em pretty good, he asked me to come in and I actually started off as a writer and session man. Sam? Well, you see, Sam knew what he liked. Sam, you might say, yeah, he changed me from so much of a jazz feel to a feel of rock 'n' roll. It was due to the type of material we did and the type of writing that he wanted at that time. That was the reason why I switched from playing primarily jazz to going into the rock field.

"No, we never actually made a tour. We played some of the package shows, we played some of the shows on certain tours, but we didn't actually make a tour ourself. I played all over Memphis, we used the same group out of Memphis, but I never got a regular group, because to do that you got to be working all the time, and I don't want to work all the time.

"It's funny, you work a twenty-five or thirty-minute thing in a dance type situation, believe it or not I have trouble remembering my own songs. People come up to me and ask me to play this or that, and I'll give it a try, but a lot of the time I just won't remember the thing. I don't want to make a list, 'cause if I do I won't follow it. I don't like being in a set pattern of doing things. I don't write like that either. I don't really go in with a programme to write about. I may get a melody, and that's what's the toughest. After I get a nice melody the words come along pretty much by themselves. I don't try to write like a computer. I have to feel it and think it. I don't write with a message in mind, I just try to tell a good story.

"I think the stuff we did on Smash, I think I was probably more satisfied with the way those things came out, the type of music we did, I mean as far as the overall production was concerned. We worked with Jerry Kennedy and a whole groovy bunch of people who could get the feel I want. You don't always get that kind of scene. Most of the time you've got to suit yourself to them. Now, see, I don't like to be rushed, but I'm going into Nashville and I've got to do a whole album in two days. I wanted to do it last month when I didn't have anything on, but somehow these things never work out. That last record we made, I was set up way in the back in Studio B at Columbia. We had the horns blowing in through a wall. The drummer was way off at a distance. It was a beautiful idea, man, I thought it was a beautiful idea at the time. But I wasn't satisfied with the way it worked out.

"Oh, there's so many things involved in getting a hit. There's the producer, there's the musicians, you need the right song. It's overwhelming, really, the odds that you face. And even if you have a real great song it still may not hit for ten years."

He said this last with a finality born of resignation. "You see how bashful he is," said Margaret Ann, when she saw that he wasn't talking anymore. "He won't tell you anything." "What do you mean?" said Charlie indignantly. "I've been talking my head off." He glanced up at the stage and stood up wearily. "Well, I guess I better go see if I can tame this electronic monster." He gave us a wry smile. "That's the reason I say piano players go through hell."

Charlie Rich doesn't seem to have the temperament to be a star. Whether it's lack of ambition or his drinking or some other more arcane reason he has never achieved the success which he deserves or fulfilled in any but an artistic way the promise which Sam Phillips saw in 1958. Margaret Ann thinks it's the diversity of his talents, and certainly of all the rock 'n' roll stars — more than Elvis or Jerry Lee or Carl Perkins or Little Richard or Chuck Berry — he shows a breadth and musical enterprise which does not admit categorization. He is being packaged today as a country singer, but while it seems to be working out pretty well commercially it would be wrong, as Margaret Ann points out, to limit him to a field in which he is no more at home than blues or pop or jazz or even gospel. He is a musician in fact of extraordinary eclecticism, someone in whom a variety of elements have fused to create an artist who functions with all the necessity of a country or blues performer but with considerably greater musical complexity.

He has a voice of remarkable range and feeling which he uses to great emotional effect. The material he does is very much his own personal brand of soul, encompassing almost the entire spectrum of American popular music. He has written distinctive compositions in every mode, and in fact his most successful songs cannot be confined to any one category but run the gamut from country "weepers" like "Sittin' and Thinkin'" to rock standards like "Lonely Weekends" and adaptations of material by Little Esther and Joe Tex. On his first records, it's true, he sounded very much like Elvis Presley, but if anyone fulfilled the artistic promise which Elvis originally showed it is probably Charlie Rich. The music that he does, his approach to the music, his ability to make each song a unique and personal vehicle for individual expression is something which in a way is lost to the star who is as much concerned with panoply as performance, who is forced by his image to be something he is not. Where Elvis is stiff and forced into a mould which is not entirely of his making, Charlie Rich is free to be whatever he likes. He feels none of the terrible constraints of stardom.

He has gained none of its rewards either. He has been not so much underrated as underexposed. He has been taken advantage of, his wife seems to think, almost because of his musical ability. "To me Charlie is a musician's musician. He can play just about anything and it takes him a very short time to pick it up. With most of the musicians you've got to spend a whole lot of time with 'em. But Charlie's thought of as a kind of an afterthought."

His musical background alone would seem to bear Margaret Ann out. First of all, of course, there are very few artists in the country or the blues field who are exposed to the same breadth of music. In addition he has had some training in music theory from his brief stay at the University of Arkansas where, Margaret Ann says, he got

A's in music and F's in English. Most of all his scorings and compositions are marked by a fluency and a natural absorption of influences which is the product as much of native intelligence as of any musical technique. He just seems, as he says, to feel the music and he manages without strain to incorporate all his borrowings into one cohesive whole.

Except for "Sittin' and Thinkin'" (which could itself be a bar-room ballad of the standard variety) the lyrics of his songs frequently seem incidental to the music itself. "Lonely Weekends," of course, served as an archetypal cry of the fifties ("Well, I make it all right/From Monday morning to Friday night/Oh, those lonely weekends"), a good corollary to Fats Domino's "Blue Monday," and "Who Will the Next Fool Be?" — a minor classic which has been recorded by Bobby Bland, Bobby Vinton and Jerry Lee Lewis among others — utilizes the long lines and stretched-out phrasing to which Charlie Rich seems drawn. His lyrics at times seem if anything a little too sophisticated, employing abrupt metrical changes, or internal rhymes along the lines of "Stay," a beautiful soulful ballad which pleads:

> *I don't know*
> *what to say*
> *But I pray*
> *that you'll stay with me now.*

It's the music, though, the voice, the feeling, the piano, which compel attention and, while he will occasionally phrase like Sinatra or rock as good as Jerry Lee. it *is* the soulful ballads which he and his wife write that are his specialty.

For Margaret Ann Rich, a self-admitted frustrated artist, country music is a little "common" ("Don't you dare call Charlie country. Oh, he may be rural, but you can't label him. He just isn't a country artist."), but she does value its honesty. Like Charlie she has a tendency to get a little high-flown. For his cocktail-hour piano she may write lyrics that are "poetic" in a flowery sort of way. At her best, though, there is an incisiveness and a degree of emotional toughness which would do credit to any poet, and perhaps it is only appropriate that it is she in fact who has written the song which best sums up Charlie Rich and their special relationship after eighteen years of marriage. It is the song with which he made his bow on the country charts last year and one which he sings several times this evening, with special feeling, it seems.

> *I don't know how to tell her*
> *   that I didn't get that raise in pay today*
> *And I know how much she wanted*
> *   the dress in Baker's window*
> *And it breaks my heart to see her have to wait*
> *And cancel all the plans she made to celebrate*
> *But I can count on her to take it*
> *   with a smile*
> *And not a frown*
> *She knows that life has its little ups and downs*
> *Like ponies on a merry-go-round*
> *And no one grabs the brass ring every time*
> *But she don't mind*
> *She wears a gold ring on her finger*
> *And it's mine.*

Every time he sings it Margaret Ann is particularly attentive, and she is pleased when I tell her what a beautiful song I think it is. But a distracted look comes over her face. "You know, when he's drinking he reverts to the other music," she says softly. "That's his first love, jazz. It's pathetic, isn't it? He's capable of so much more, but he just can't find anyone who'll turn him loose and let him do what he's capable of doing. I thought this was our year. I really did. I said to myself this has got to be our year. Because it was the revival year for rock 'n' roll. I told everybody, I told all our friends. It's just that it's a little hard to take. Charlie's a very talented man, he has a unique talent." Her voice rises, and an almost desperate insistence comes into her words. "I don't know. You pull for someone eighteen years and..." She never finishes her thought.

His performance improves as the night wears on. He can't really improvise much because of the nature of the band, and his voice is a little ragged compared with the records — "Life's Little Ups and

Downs" is not as flawless in the live version as it is on record — but by the last set he is singing with unmistakable passion and intensity and the shy, reticent, rather inarticulate man of our conversation is transformed into a commanding figure. He isn't really a performer like Jerry Lee Lewis or Carl Perkins or Chuck Berry. To call him a rock 'n' roll singer in the first place may have been a kind of

misnomer, because he has never had any kind of an act. He just sits
behind the piano almost sedately and when he feels the music you
can hear it in his voice, you can feel it through the emotional sparks
he gives off. By the last set even "Lonely Weekends" has become a
kind of cry of pain. He is if anything a soul singer.

> Don't put no headstone on my grave
> All my life I been a slave
> Just put me down and let me be
> Free from all this misery.

Margaret Ann is up at the railing just smiling and nodding to the
music. All her calculations have vanished now, and when she looks
up at Charlie you can see the feeling which has sustained them
through frustration and a lot of hard times.

> Oh, I won't promise the same thing won't happen again
> But I can promise it'll be
>   a long, long time till then
> Cause when I'm drinking
> I am nobody's friend
> Please, baby, wait for me until
>   they let me out again.

At the end of the set Margaret Ann goes off to join friends, and
Charlie and I sit at the table alone. He is drained, and he submits to
this interview meekly, just as he has submitted to all the other
inalterable conditions of his life. A fan comes up to him and he
signs the autograph wearily. "You know, I ain't seen you smile once
all night," she says, folding the paper and putting it in her purse. He
gives her a wan smile and hands me back my pen. A few minutes
later he has to tear himself away, but by then there isn't any more to
ask anyway.

   Out in the parking lot a comfortable middle-aged man says to
his wife, "Well, it looks like the underdog came out on top tonight."
He says it with an air of smug self-satisfaction, as if it were a
cockfight they had just watched or an entertainment devised
especially for their own amusement. Charlie Rich will go up to
Nashville with his lawyer/manager some time tomorrow to pick out
material for his new album. This time, he hopes, he will really get
that hit.

I

Phil Chess is like everyone's Uncle Phil, sharp, aggressive, faintly disreputable, a success. "You a Yiddel, too?" he asked, when he finally caught my name. A sly smile of recognition crossed his face. "You don't cut your hair like a nice Jewish boy."

He reminded me of a dozen other Uncle Phils, all small-time entrepreneurs. Somebody's uncle in the clothing business. Loan sharks. Self-proclaimed shyster lawyers. He had about him that air of the blatant huckster. But Phil Chess, unlike everyone else's uncle, is not in the clothing business, he doesn't sell on easy credit terms, and he never went to law school. Together with his late brother, Leonard, he made records for twenty years for an almost exclusively Negro audience and he remains vice president of one of the largest independent-styled record companies in America today.

"You gotta remember one thing, there's a close tie between the Negro and the Jewish people," says Ralph Bass, an A&R man who has been in the business himself since 1944, who discovered James Brown and has been with Chess since 1960. "See, I'm half-Jew myself, and you gotta understand, there's an affinity between blues and Hebrew music. I hear that blues in a minor key, and hey, baby, I'm back in synagogue."

To Phil Chess it is simpler. "We owned a club," he says. "Yeah, the Macamba Lounge. We heard some of the music and we started recording it."

Phil Chess seems almost out of place today in the company's new corporate set-up. Just four years ago his brother Leonard bought the building which the company presently occupies for cold cash (in 1963 in similar fashion he is said to have plunked down one million dollars in ten-thousand-dollar bills for the purchase of radio station, WVON, now the largest soul station in Chicago) and when he sold the company in 1969 he received in the neighbourhood of ten million dollars.

From the outside the building is unprepossessing enough. It's set in the middle of a warehouse district on the South Side near the lake and looks very much like any one of its neighbours. Inside, however, it houses the whole Chess operation, from studio and executive offices to warehouse and in the basement an entire manufacturing plant. In the lobby a bored white secretary asks you to

215

state your business. Over her intercom she checks with the PR man, and before you can go up in the elevator he must come down and certify that you are who you say you are. On the hard wooden bench there are a few black kids waiting ("Hey, man, what're you keepin' us waiting for?" says one to Ralph Bass, as we pass through the lobby. "We here to make you money."), and when you leave several hours later most likely they will still be there. On the day that I arrive a pouty-looking Koko Taylor is waiting in the lobby, too. She wears a fancy wig and a spangled dress, and she waits

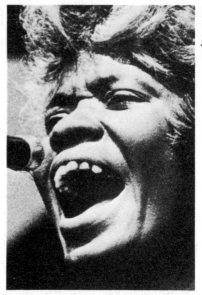

Koko Taylor

all day for someone to see her. She is a fine singer, one of the few female blues artists around, but it is said that she is here on her day off from work. She works as a maid. "Some of the old cats just don't understand," says Bass sympathetically. "In fact they get sullen. A cat like Bo Diddley, he's been around for a long time, he ain't used to all the things we got going on now, he's accustomed to just walking right in."

But Chess is owned today by GRT, which, as any employee of Chess will tell you, is the nation's second largest tape corporation; and although there are advantages (distribution, packaging, publicity, Marshall Chess quickly points out, video tape tie-ins) nearly everyone grumbles about security, accounting, the growing impersonality. "We were like a family," says Willie Dixon. "With Muddy it was more like a father-son or a brother-brother thing than a business relationship," admits even Marshall. "The family thing is gone."

Upstairs the offices are what you would expect of a major corporation. Phil Chess occupies what was formerly his brother Leonard's spacious office. There is a colour picture of his kids on the wall and a row of gold records following the curve of his desk. *Tom Jones* is bound in red leather, there's a built-in colour TV and a discreet stereo console which is in sharp contrast to the functional set-up and giant speakers in his nephew Marshall's office. Phil sits at his desk, looking very much like his pictures, hat tilted back on his head, necktie loosened, shirtsleeves rolled up. He swivels around in his chair to take the phone; there's the sound of soul music booming out of a connected office as he talks to an old business acquaintance from Detroit in a speech liberally sprinkled with "dese" and "dose" and a manner considerably loosened up from the careful air of polite non-committal he has directed at me. "You know we sold the company. Joe, Joe, you know we sold the company," he tells the person at the other end. "No, man, we can't do that. I'm telling you, babe, we can't do that no more. No. I can't give you that kinda bread unless you come across with some shit first." He listens for a while, nodding his head, trying to get a word in edgewise. "You know it ain't like the old days," he says finally. "It ain't like the old days, babe."

Marshall Chess, Leonard's son, is at the time of our interview the president of the company. More than anyone else at Chess he is enthusiastic about the prospects for growth under the aegis of GRT. Marshall is young, energetic, full of ideas. Everyone at the company is proud of him; he earned his position, they emphasize, it wasn't just handed to him. When his father died GRT chose between his uncle and him. They chose Marshall.

Marshall is not reluctant to give his ideas on the subject. The company had not expanded in a big way up till now, he explained, because "you got to remember, you had two men who came over in a boat from Poland. They weren't trained entrepreneurs. We had maximized the possibilities of what we could do under their type of mentality. I'm not putting down their mentality. They just didn't want to get into it any further. Well, who knows? Maybe they were right."

But he doesn't really think they were right. At twenty-eight he's been in the business fifteen years. At thirteen he worked the road with his father, making the regular five-thousand-mile swing through the South to record and promote. He remembers a little from that time. He remembers cutting a session in a cornfield. "Arthur Crudup," says his uncle, then corrects himself. "No. It was Percy Lee Crudup. 'Open up your book, your daddy wants to read with

The Chess Board

you'." He lets out an appreciative chuckle. "I never will forget that song. It's, you know, just a saying, a double meaning."

Marshall recalls certain similar scenes from his past, but he's not really interested in dwelling on them. Nor was he interested in holding a joint interview with his Uncle Phil, as the PR man had originally suggested. "No way," he said emphatically. "Absolutely not. You see, he was a participant and I was like an observer, you know what I mean? And there's a big difference."

And he's perfectly right to be reluctant. He has plans for himself, and he has plans for the company. Chess Records will be as big as Columbia in another few years, everyone around the office is firmly convinced. If Marshall stays with the business. There seems to be some doubt if after fifteen years he hasn't gotten a little bored with it, like his father and uncle before him. But right now he's full of pep and with luck and a little imagination he can see Chess overtaking Atlantic at least as the biggest of the independent-styled companies.

As for Phil he doesn't seem to care how the interview is arranged. He is not a particularly loquacious man, and he says no more than he is willing to give away. Where he could supply a fact he did so, but he showed no interest in offering opinions, no matter how innocent the subject. He was always the younger brother, and he seems to accept the role naturally. You can get a much better picture of Phil from seeing him around the building, pinching receptionists and squeezing secretaries, greeting everyone with an easy familiar wave and being greeted in turn, sometimes openly, sometimes after he was gone, as Uncle Phil.

II

Chess Records grew out of the club business the Chess brothers had operated since 1938, of which the Mocamba Lounge was only the last in a series of bars referred to politely as "jazz clubs" (Leonard) or after-hours joints. "It was a funny kind of place," says Marshall. "It was a big dope hang-out. Dope, hookers, a lot of people used to jam for gin. You know, a shot of gin, they'd get up and blow." "What are you talking about?" Phil huffs up at me indignantly. "There was nothing like that going on. I don't even know what you're talking about." It was in the clubs in any case that they encountered their talent and that they first got the idea for recording. A Hollywood agent came in to listen to a singer named Andrew Tibbs, "so I thought," said Leonard in one of his rare interviews, "if he's good enough for Hollywood I'll put him on record myself." He did that, and the result was a fair-sized hit and a two-sided controversy. The flip side, "Bilbo's Dead," was banned in the South, and the hit, "Union Man Blues," caused union truckers to destroy the record in quantity. "We had to pack the shipping cartons with bricks," says Marshall, "and smuggle out the record ourselves." No, no, come Phil's denials. If any such thing happened it has escaped his memory. The record industry has never been anything but a bunch of nice guys competing for an honest buck.

It was in the beginning, of course, strictly a two-man operation, but soon they were doing well enough to make it into a full-time one. Leonard turned his garage into a studio, which may account in part for the life-long fascination with the echo effect which Chess shared with Sun Records. "I didn't know what I was doing," Leonard told Clarence Petersen of the Chicago *Tribune* shortly before his death, "but I was doing it all myself, working days at the record company, nights at the club. Pretty soon I had to get out of the club and I turned it over to Phil. But then I was on the road so much, three weeks at a time, running up to Detroit and down South because I had to make all the deliveries right to the record stores myself, that I finally told Phil to sell the club and come in and run the office while I was on the road." At the time the label was still called Aristocrat, and it was not until 1950, on the advice of a Southern distributor, that they changed the name to Chess.

The first release on the new label, Gene Ammons' "My Foolish Heart," fell pretty much into the pattern of jazz and jazz-related issues which, despite the success of Tibbs' blues record, had dominated the Aristocrat catalogue. The second was Muddy Waters' "Rolling Stone," and not only did it establish a career for its singer (who had previously had several releases on the Aristocrat label with some local success), it set the tone for the new Chess label and undoubtedly influenced the entire course of post-war blues recording.

"Rolling Stone" was, for its time, a smash hit. That meant that it probably sold sixty to eighty thousand copies, a figure which for a pop hit or even a city blues like Wynonie Harris's "Bloodshot Eyes" or Charles Brown's "Drifting Blues" would have meant little. For an unreconstructed country blues, however, with a real down-home flavour, it was not only an impressive sales figure, it revealed without question that a market for this type of product did still exist. Spurred by the success of artists like Muddy Waters, John Lee Hooker, Howlin' Wolf, many of the independent labels went out in search of home-grown talent, and for the first time since the Depression field recording was being done by commercial companies on a wide-spread basis. Out of all this activity came the last great surge of blues recording and what looks to have been the final flourishing of a form that has persisted for over a century in one guise or another.

Leonard Chess hit the road in 1950. He made a Southern swing which took him five thousand miles every three months. Despite the romantic legends he probably did not do a great deal of selling out of the trunk of his car. According to Marshall by this time there were normal distributing outlets and most of the sales were for promotional purposes or simply to finance the trip. He didn't do a lot of field recording himself either. Phil may recall recording Percy Lee Crudup, and Marshall has vague memories of tracking down

singers in plantation fields, but although he always carried a Magne-chord wire recorder along Leonard probably did not take a great many masters home with him. What he did do was to make contacts. He made contact with artists and distributors and record store owners and within a year he had dramatically expanded his field of operation from Chicago, Gary, Detroit, and St. Louis to take in the entire South.

In 1951 he hooked up with Sam Phillips in Memphis. Phillips, a young recording engineer who had not yet started his own

Sun label, was already tied up with the Bihari brothers in Los Angeles (they had had a nationwide hit with John Lee Hooker's "Boogie Chillen" on Modern even prior to Muddy Waters' success), and together with Ike Turner, Modern's teenage talent scout, he was seeking out and recording some of Memphis's best talent. B.B. King, Walter Horton, Joe Hill Louis, and Bobby "Blue" Bland all appeared on the Modern and RPM labels at that time, while Chess leased masters by Memphis Minnie, Willie Nix, Jackie Brenston, and Howlin' Wolf. Somehow or other Howlin' Wolf ended up on both labels and while he was still flirting with the Biharis Leonard Chess quickly signed him to a contract. That was the beginning of a life-long familial rivalry between Wolf and Muddy Waters and the end of Modern's relationship with Sam Phillips.

There are lots of wild and woolly tales from the old days. Like the time King Records beat Chess to James Brown when Leonard's plane got held up by fog. Or the opportunity that Chess had to sign Elvis Presley, before Sam Phillips peddled his contract to RCA. There are other tales that aren't told. Like what happened to the competition, to the other independent labels in Chicago. For, aside from Veejay, which ended in financial debacle in 1965, Chess has had a virtual monopoly on recording in Chicago since its very earliest days. Its four chief artists — Muddy, Wolf, Little Walter, and Sonny Boy Williamson — all eventually made Chicago their headquarters, and every bluesman in the city has always been anxious to climb onto the label. It's not just the Chess name or reputation which attracts them. It's the power that Phil and Leonard Chess always possessed and never hesitated to use. Johnny Shines tells a story about his recording for Chess in those early days which shows up not only the bad aspects but the good points as well.

"Well, I'll tell you, anybody that Chess fool around with, to me it seems like he was going to get the best out of. He had a knack for getting the best out of musicians. See, I might have hooked up with twenty-five other companies, but I wanted to go with Chess. Cause he had the patience to work with a guy, to find out what made him react, how he react, what he react to. Here's what happened. Chess had a dub on my record, he'd pressed it up, he had the labels and everything, and they call me to come sign a release on my contract. Okay. I go over there and he ain't got nothing for me to sign. Well, this went on for some time. After about four months and nothing happened I just stopped going over there. I told Jimmy Rogers, *You see why he won't release the record.* Well, Jimmy come back, and he told me Chess told him, *Look, we got four or five records out now that're selling. Muddy got a record out, Walter got a record out, you and Eddie Ware got hit records, if we release this 'Joliet Blues' it's gonna kill everything out there. When it gets so you all can't sell then I'll put it out. Cause this is gonna sell whenever it is released. And it's gonna hurt you now.*

"So that's what Jimmy brought back to me. And I believe it was the truth. But anyway two years later I have got me a record with Joe Brown that Joe Brown was fixing to release. Evidently Chess heard that this was good. So he call me to come over and put my name on that old release. Well, this time I cut him down, I told him to forget it and stick it up his ass. So then I called the union hall and told them, *Don't let that record come through here.* Cause I hadn't put my signature on the release. So that was why it have still never been released. But even so the other record was never a hit, it never got played. And I believe Chess did that, too."

"Johnny Shines?" says Phil with that contempt for failure endemic to the self-made man. "He was just a run-of-the-mill blues singer." Ask him anything about the old days and he'll demand a literal factual rephrasing. Names, dates, titles — he can supply you with any of these. Marshall is a little more graphic about it. "You see, my father was a music lover in a very strange way. People used to talk, they'd think he was kind of a freak, because all he'd ever want to do was to go to these little funky clubs that no white person would ever dream of going to, to hear new acts, to buy new talent. I don't think he ever thought of himself as a music lover. But he was in his own way." "No, we never had any trouble," says Phil. "At least I don't think we ever had any trouble. We stayed out of the rough neighbourhoods. In those days you knew everyone anyway. And if they didn't know you I think maybe they thought you were a policeman."

"The clubs?" says Muddy Waters in his meticulously appointed South Side home. "It used to be you could go down this street, just within a few blocks you'd run into four, five clubs. You could find any type of music you'd want just within the space of a few blocks." He turned to his stepson for confirmation. "Ain't that right? You could hear rock 'n' roll coming out of one joint, there was another one for jazz, and then there was the blues clubs. Oh yeah, there are still some clubs operating today. It ain't nothing like the old days, though." He slapped his knee and laughed his short nervous laugh. "It ain't nothing like that."

Big Duke's is one of the clubs that still features blues. A while ago it was known by its previous owner's name, and most of the musicians know it by address. It's easier to remember the clubs by address, because names change so fast.

Big Duke's is not an untypical club. It costs fifty cents at the door. Perhaps to indicate hard times there's a rope instead of a chain to keep out non-customers, and there are holes in the plaster walls and concrete floor. It's not a tourist attraction like Theresa's or Sylvio's, but there's the same Budweiser clock on the wall and it provides the same sense of temporary refuge from the menace of the street outside.

Inside everyone is laughing and having a good time. It's a warm noisy atmosphere; the clientele is all black and lives in the immediate area. For them it's a neighbourhood bar in which the music is background to their conversation. At the end of a number there's no applause, and at the end of a set little notice is taken. Big Duke's does not look like much, but it has recently presented Howlin' Wolf and his band and this Saturday night it features Carey Bell with a band that includes Jimmy Dawkins, Eddie Taylor and a succession of sidemen like S.P. Leary, Lester Dorsie, L.V., and Wolf's drummer W. Williams. Musicians drift in and out. There isn't much work around town, and they seize at any opportunity to sit in.

The music is mostly dance music. There's no P.A. so Carey Bell sings through his harmonica mike. He's got a bad throat and no one listens to the words anyway, but they respond to the cheerfulness of his music and the exuberance of his performance and everyone dances and has a good time. Carey Bell himself is a good-natured genial man who greets old friends and acquaintances from the bandstand and finds it difficult to run a band. Tonight Royal Johnson, his regular lead guitarist, is drunk and drowns out Jimmy Dawkins at every opportunity. Royal has been drunk for the last three weeks and, everyone conceded, something would have to be done S.P. Leary is drunk, too, and different drummers take his place all through the evening.

Up on stage Lee Vera Taylor, a plump pretty woman who is

Eddie Taylor/Watt Casey

Eddie Taylor's wife, is singing and rolling her belly, rubbing the microphone between her legs and scrunching down to show just about everything she can in a gold lame mini dress. "I'm worried about him going away, naturally," confided Carey Bell's wife, Dorothy, about an upcoming tour of England and Japan. "Of course, I wouldn't let him know, because I wouldn't ever do anything to hold back his career. He was out of music for a while, you know, just took it up again recently. Cause it's rough on a man, you know. But anything he want to do I encourage him in." She wipes her eyes tearily and turns her attention to the stage. Just a couple of months ago she and Carey were married in this very club to celebrate a relationship which goes back for some time. Lee Vera Taylor comes off the bandstand, and they start in discussing their kids again.

"You got to really love the blues to put up with these kind of conditions," says Jimmy Dawkins, a melancholy introspective man who has written frequently for the magazine *Blues Unlimited*. "Oh, when everyone gets drunk that's when they call for the blues. But when they're sober they don't want to hear none of that. I used to have a seven-piece group," he recalls plaintively. "But I got used to a trio now. You can't keep 'em. There are more unemployed horn men in Chicago right now than you can count."

"That's right, man," says Carey Bell, coming back to our table. "Keeping a band is a real motherfucker."

Later in the evening about two or three a.m. we're waiting around for Carey to get paid. His part of the take can't come to more than twelve or fifteen dollars, but though there was a pretty good crowd at the bar tonight he has a good deal of difficulty getting even that. While we're waiting, Lester Dorsie, Jimmy Dawkins' drummer and currently unemployed, quizzes me about my book. "Well, tell me this, man, you won't take no offence, but how does a member of the Caucasian race get to have soul?" I blinked a little, struck by the familiarity of the question and the situation. Well sure, I didn't like white blues, I said, because it didn't seem natural, but there was such a thing, I thought, as country soul. "Well, you take this Tom Jones," said Lester Dorsie. "I think he's great. Do you like him?" No, not much, I said. "Well, I wonder why is that? Why do you like Muddy Waters and not Tom Jones?" I explained that I liked the old stuff. "Would you say that is characteristic in general of the Caucasian race?" he said earnestly. I didn't know, I said uncomfortably. I just liked it, that was all.

We were the last ones out. Carey forgot his overcoat, and his wife made him go back in and get it. His throat was worse. Everyone was a little drunk. There was going to be a party at Carey's house, and we drove him there, but when we got there we didn't go in. It was in a burned-out section of town, and all around there were gutted buildings and empty lots. As we pulled up Little Wolf and L.V. and Lester Dorsie piled out of W. Williams' station wagon. They had ladies and bottles with them and would be up partying all night. It didn't matter, though. Tomorrow was Sunday. No one worked tomorrow. No one would be working again until next weekend.

III

These are the places that Phil and Leonard Chess went searching for talent in the fifties — the taverns, the joints — and it is the people who still frequent them who were for the most part their audience. "Man, weekends were the thing," says Marshall. "Friday everyone'd get their paychecks, and Friday night the record stores would be open till two or three in the morning. You could hear the latest sounds blaring out all over the street." They had their own methods of market research, too. "Well, blues, you know, has always been a woman's market. And 'Juke' — you remember the Little Walter single — what prompted my father to put it out, it was a rainy day, we had a canopy over the place and the door was open, cause it gets very hot here in the summer, and he was playing 'Juke,' it had just been recorded a few days before at the tail end of a session. Well, he was listening to the record, and there was this old lady, an old coloured lady, standing under the canopy to keep out of the rain, and he saw her really digging it, you know stamping her feet and really digging it. So he played it again, and then they rushed it into release, and it was one of our biggest hits ever. You know, they didn't really want to admit they dug the blues, but that's the effect it had."

There was more to it than that, of course. Chess had its own production methods. It had a distinct and recognizable sound. By rigging a loudspeaker and a microphone at both ends of a sewer pipe Leonard created the echo effect, and he used a primitive system of tape delay. His big thing, though, was drums. "My father wanted drum, drum, and more drum. I think he was responsible for doing that to blues, to bring out a heavy beat." Sometimes to get the effect he even played bass drum himself. And, as Johnny Shines pointed out, he had a special way of getting the best out of his artists. To Phil this remains the most important part of his job even today. "Blues is nothing but the truth," he volunteered in a rare burst of expansiveness, "truth that at one time or another in his lifetime the singer has felt. Our job was to try to bring out points in his mind that he might have forgotten, to give him ideas, to get him to think about some things that were happening down in Rolling Fork, Mississippi or wherever. It's actually like psychiatry, you try to talk to him for him to bring out the things himself."

"You know, people think there's a magic connected with Chess Records," says Marshall. "They think there's some kind of trick. There wasn't any magic about these sessions. Half the time things that came about accidentally — they think you planned it that way. Kids write to us all the time from England — I don't even think they like blues — they want to know what guitar strings we used, what type of amplifier, how we got that effect. And it was just an accident — a guitar slipped out of tune, something like that."

"The Rolling Stones came here to record," murmurs Phil. "Everyone wants to record here with us. To tell you the truth I liked it better the way it used to be. Mono, just the one track, when we recorded Muddy and the band was cooking and they take a take and you got that groove, boy that was it. Right away you knew you had something. I'll tell you something, The Rolling Stones could record all they want, they couldn't have the feeling of our artists. But," he shrugs, "you gotta go along with the majority."

Willie Dixon/Val Wilmer

IV

Today Willie Dixon has the blues recording scene in Chicago all to himself. If you want to record anywhere you pretty much have to clear it with Willie. And if you want to record for Chess, despite the presence of Marshall and Phil and Ralph Bass, Willie always gets his little taste. A giant lazy-looking man who resembles nothing so much as a stuffed blimp or a beached whale. Willie has been with Chess a long time, and, as has been pointed out by other writers, serves as something of the "house nigger" there. If there are VIPs in town he shows them the clubs. If there are feelings to be smoothed over Willie does that, too. He's a lot more than just a flunky, though. He is a highly intelligent and calculating man who has composed over three hundred songs, among them some of Wolf's and Muddy's biggest hits. He is not particularly well-liked by other blues singers, but he is not disliked either. He is just accepted as a fact of life, to be looked up to, if anything, because he seems to have gotten the better of The Man, and everyone else in the process.

The week that I was in Chicago Willie was just finishing up a new album by Albert King for Stax and recording a singer named Jimmy Jr. under auspices that remain obscure. For his session with Jimmy Jr. Willie was taking his cut not only as producer, but as composer, arranger, and session leader as well. He was also, it was strongly hinted, taking something of a kickback from the singer himself simply for the privilege of being allowed to record.

"I don't know where Willie comes up with them," said the white engineer from the shelter of his soundproof booth. He chuckles, because to him Willie really is a character. "I really don't know where he gets them. The ones he comes up with, you practically got to tap 'em on the back to sing."

Inside the studio the musicians are taking a break. The rhythm guitar and the drummer, studio men for Chess, wander out. The bass player, a white kid named Sid, glances down at the floor while Mighty Joe Young, the lead guitarist, soundlessly picks his guitar. Willie Dixon is giving his singer a pep talk. The names read like a roster of blues greats — Mighty Joe Young, Guitar Murphy, Shakey Horton and Lafayette Leake — but they are all friends of Willie Dixon, and undoubtedly he gets a little taste from each of them, too.

Walter Horton looks in the sound booth. Has the engineer

gotten him a copy of his record yet? Not yet, says the engineer.
Walter Horton sadly shakes his head. He is disturbed about the
session. "Willie wants me to play like Jimmy Reed. Man, I ain't
played like Jimmy Reed in years. Now I got to go home and learn to
play like Jimmy Reed all over again." He goes off down the corridor,
angrily muttering to himself.

The engineer lazily flicks on a switch, and we hear Jimmy Jr., a
slight, dapper, rather boyish-looking young man, complaining to

Chuck Berry

230

Willie, "I don't know what it is. It just ain't together. Now if I could just have sounded like we was sounding in your basement... Then we was really cooking." Willie mumbles some words of reassurance, but Jimmy Jr. does not look convinced. The other musicians smirk and make disparaging remarks among themselves.

In a few minutes they start up again. "The way she walk, it drive me mad/The way she talk, she make me glad/Love that woman..." The band sounds great, too good for the singer, a pale carbon copy of Jimmy Reed whom he sporadically claims to be his father. Walter Horton is really wailing, his arms flapping like some giant bird, but he doesn't sound like Jimmy Reed at all.

"You know," confides the engineer to whom "blues is a music of bare competence," "these guys at least can read. They can give you whatever you want. But the others. Muddy? Wolf? Don't make me laugh. It might surprise you, but there are very few good blues singers. Very few. And most of the records are a joke. Once in a while you might get a good feeling, but that's all."

In the studio they have broken off another take. The engineer calls the bass player in. "Sid, you're playing too white," he says. "Space it out a little more." The bass player, a long-haired kid who looks a little spaced out himself, is hurt. "That's the way Willie wants me to play," he insists. "Usually I play more loose." "Let's hear it back," says Willie to the control booth. The engineer runs back the tape, and all of a sudden the song is booming all through the studio, sounding better than it ever did when Jimmy Jr. was recording it. The engineer is fiddling with the dials — it's a twelve-track machine after all — turning down Walter Horton's solo to the point where you can hardly hear it, bringing up the bass. In the studio Mighty Joe Young is fingering his guitar, playing along soundlessly with the record, embellishing his own performance.

V

To survive in the business you clearly had to be tough. Not just because it was a cut-throat industry readily accessible to union goons, mob influence, Senate investigations, and strong-arm techniques. The artists as well were difficult, strong-willed, independent and erratic men who had grown up in circumstances which demanded cunning to survive and which made them tough-minded and suspicious in their dealings with the white world. Sam Phillips is said to have quit blues recording because of these very difficulties, and undoubtedly their own short-sightedness has contributed to the plights of numerous blues singers. Chess, of course, was fortunate in its artists. Muddy Waters, their first and biggest discovery, is in many ways the model of what a great artist ought to be: intelligent, reserved, dignified and enormously proud. Everyone at Chess speaks of Muddy with great respect, and indeed he is probably the only blues singer with the exception of B.B. King to be able to maintain his dignity even in the most alien of settings. Aside from Muddy there is not much room for the bluesman at Chess today. "A lot of people laugh at me," says Howlin' Wolf, "because I stand out for what I think is right. They put me down for old-fashioned, but I got to do what's right for me, ain't that the truth?" Little Walter was dismissed as nothing but a half-crazy alcoholic who ended up back in the Market playing for spare change. And Sonny Boy? Sonny Boy wouldn't fit at all today into the company's new sense of self-importance.

"Oh, Sonny Boy," recalls Willie Dixon, "Sonny Boy was a sonofabitch. I remember one time, it must have been a little while before he died, the building was all locked up and Sonny Boy was rapping at the window. Well, he seen the girl at the front desk and he say, Let me in there. And she say, I'm sorry, I can't unless somebody sanctions for you to come in. And he say, I don't give a fuck if the building's closed. I built this motherfucker. Open this motherfuckin' door. Well, okay. He's cursing away, trying to climb in through the window, and along comes this rabbi. Well, the girl try to shush him, Sonny Boy, don't you be cursing like that. Don't you see the rabbi? But he say, Motherfuck the goddam rabbi. That there rabbi after the same thing I'm after, and that's money. Oh Lord, I thought. Oh Lord, oh Lord..."

"I've eaten in their homes, they've eaten in ours," says Marshall. "Of course I don't think there was ever any buddy-buddy, because it was a whole different mentality. But we were always close." "That's right," says Phil again, "it was like a family." He's right, it was indeed like a family. To get along with their artists Phil and Leonard Chess had to be tough; without talking down to them they had to speak a language that could be mutually understood, and that language was often crude, direct, and blunt in the extreme. Phil Chess still doesn't talk down to his artists. He can call a bluesman a motherfucker with great aplomb, and when he's conducting business negotiations he can play the dozens without even batting an eye. At times like these he no longer seems the mild-mannered, soft-spoken, almost self-deprecating man who appears in interviews. He possesses instead all the ruthlessness of a Mayor Daley, and if you look away for a moment it is often difficult to distinguish the voices of the two men talking, the black man and the white one, cursing each other out in the harsh, elliptical, almost poetic language of the ghetto.

Chess has not always been overly scrupulous in its business dealings either. Leonard took great pride in the fact that Chess alone deducted payola as a legitimate business expense, and they have stood up to several extensive investigations without ever really getting hurt. Marshall himself admits that there have been discrepancies in their books and deviations from normal business practice. But, he insists, perhaps a little self-righteously, it was always for the artist's benefit. Muddy and Wolf have been with Chess for over twenty years without a contract, and while in the past few years they have obviously been shunted aside more than a little bit they have always been taken care of by Chess. "We paid for Little Walter's funeral. We paid all the expenses, and he was in the red when he died. And when Muddy was in the hospital, didn't have no insurance or nothing — whose fault was that, ours or his manager's, you tell me that — who do you think paid his entire hospital bill? Over six thousand dollars ... Oh sure, we done a little padding. Sometimes when royalty time came around, let's say that he had one group that was very big, my father might cut their royalty by five hundred bucks and add it on to Wolf's statement. But he didn't ever put it in his own pocket."

"Yeah, I'll be with Chess as long as there's a Chess in the company," Muddy admits grudgingly. And Wolf, who refers to Marshall vaguely as "the boy," voices similar sentiments even in the midst of a familiar complaint of mistreatment. "I know as long as there's a Chess in the business they'll remember me." To some extent they may be afraid to venture out into the world after all these years, but there's genuine affection and feeling there, too.

As for Phil he's probably the only one left with any interest in the music as it was. Ask him what he's proudest of, and he will reply promptly, "Building the company." Did he enjoy it? "Enjoy it?" He stares at me incredulously. "Enjoy it? We worked our tails off. It was our job ... Yeah, but, you know, sometimes when you had a real big hit on the market, you'd get that order in and pick the records yourself, then you felt good about. That was the good part."

In 1955 Chuck Berry walked into the Chess offices. "He was carrying a wire recorder," said Leonard, "and played us a country music take-off called 'Ida Red.' We called it 'Maybellene'." "We thought 'Maybellene' was a joke," Berry's pianist, Johnny Johnson, told Michael Lydon. "People always liked it, but it was 'Wee Wee Hours' [the blues that was the flip side] that we was proud of, that was *our* music."

Chess in any case immediately saw the commercial possibilities. "You could tell right away," says Phil, who doesn't bother to conceal a bit his admiration for Berry. "He had that something special, that — I don't know what you'd call it. But he had it." "The big beat, cars, and young love." said Leonard. "It was a trend and we jumped on it."

Bo Diddley/Bill Greensmith

It was a trend all right, and they jumped on it in a big way. Leonard Chess took "Maybellene" to Alan Freed in New York. By the time he got back to Chicago, the familiar story goes, the orders were already backed up. The rest, Leonard told Lydon, was history.

"Maybellene" was Chess's first national hit. Along with Elvis Presley's and Carl Perkins' Sun sides it signalled the beginning of a new era. It signalled as well an inevitable change in the whole Chess outlook and organization. Chess up till then had been a very parochial concern. The music was homogeneous. Distribution was handled under the aegis of the old Aristocrat label. There were probably in 1955 no more than eight or ten people employed by the company, and Leonard and Phil Chess were still doing everything from producing to packing orders themselves. Rock 'n' roll changed all that.

"How did we know it was changing? From our kids," says Phil. "From what they were listening to. You could feel it. You could tell it was crossing over. We just didn't know how big it was going to be." After 1955 all the musical divisions would be blurred. The pop, the r&b market, the country and western field — the distinctions between each would waver and blur, and the race music which Chess had been recording up until that time would suddenly become an anachronism, would without any warning freeze and turn into a museum piece. Chuck and Bo Diddley were not so far removed from the roots. To a great extent they must have considered that they were still singing blues. And Chess obviously did not fully take in the revolution, because when Sam Phillips in a financial pinch offered them the opportunity to buy Elvis Presley and all the other Sun artists they turned it down, according to Phil, without even thinking twice about it. "We didn't consider ourselves a hillbilly label at that time," says Phil, although significantly Berry's first hit was the adaptation of a hillbilly tune. They stuck instead with their stable of established talent — Muddy, Wolf, Sonny Boy, Willie Mabon was big then — supplementing it cautiously with talent that walked in the front door, like Bo Diddley, or came recommended, as Chuck Berry had been by Muddy Waters.

Leonard made his last real field trip some time around 1955. Muddy Waters had his last hit in 1956, and since then has found himself in the increasingly uncomfortable position of being a king without subjects. The company grew while more and more of its energy was directed into promotional activity and other by-products of what was once a feverishly creative scene. The groups, Bo Diddley and Chuck Berry continued to have their hits until just about the time Chuck Berry first got in trouble with the law in 1959 on a violation of the Mann Act; Ramsey Lewis became increasingly popular on Argo, the Chess subsidiary jazz label. The sixties are a blank.

"The Chess identity is over," says Marshall. "Chess was an era. An era of blues. Chuck Berry, Bo Diddley, The Moonglows, The

Flamingoes. It was a period of tremendous creativity and change in the music. But it ended. I hope we're starting into a new era now."

Today Chuck Berry comes into the company and he insists the only person he will work with is Phil. Phil, says everyone around the office, is the only one he'll listen to, the only one who's got any control over Berry, a moody distrustful man to begin with made even more distrustful by his spell in prison. His 1970 single, "Tulane," makes fairly explicit reference to drugs ("Chuck has got the fucking art," says Marshall, "of always keeping up with the times."), and Phil takes considerable pride in having toned the lyric down. "Chuck? Nah, he's never been any problem. We always got along fine." They probably did. Because it isn't even a matter of race anymore so much as that Chuck Berry and Muddy Waters and Howlin' Wolf and the few remaining blues artists that are with Chess all belong to another era, the same generation that could spawn a Phil and Leonard Chess in slightly different circumstances. They understand one another and to a certain extent share a common heritage. "Hail, hail, rock 'n' roll." Chuck Berry said it all right at the start. "Deliver us from the days of old." And that is precisely what time with its inexorable logic has done.

VI

Chess today is an odd assortment of individuals — old and young, black and white, mostly waiting around for the end. Over the years a peculiar kind of ambience has developed, so that white employees adopt a blacker life-style than the black ones. The whites live in the projects with their black wives, lip goatees, and revolutionary rhetoric. The blacks meanwhile are moving out to the suburbs. In Ralph Bass's office an argument develops between Bass and Willie Dixon. "Man, you can fool some of the people," says Bass, a flamboyant, jive-talking hep cat with a bulbous red nose and a penchant for colourful, slightly dated hip talk. "You can fool some of 'em, baby, but you ain't gonna fool that blues audience." For the first time that I have observed Willie is getting a little angry. No, that isn't the way it is at all, he protests. The white kids are sincere in their love of blues. Anyway, "if you play them a little Chopin or *Liebestraum* first, that helps. That way you prove your abilities, and then you say, Hey, man, how about a little afterhours? Why don't you lay some blues on me?"

Soon they are back to reminiscing about the old days, though. "Man, those cats really paid their dues. At one point in my life I wanted to see the black South, what it was like, through the eyes of a black man. So I took a group out on the road. We had Esther with us [Little Esther, a fourteen-year-old Johnny Otis discovery, who at that point was probably the biggest thing in the country], and where the hell can you go, you know? – we used to open the bus door, Willie, in Virginia and the Carolinas on those two-lane highways, you had to go to a place that said for blacks and we couldn't stop on the road. So we used to open the door, we had to be sure the wind was blowing right, and Esther would just squat out the back door. While the bus was going, man, that's right." Bass laughs his high-pitched explosive laugh. "You paid your dues, baby. You got your ass kicked in jail, you got put out of town, somebody'd steal your things from you, man, you paid those dues all over the country. Eating them slop joints and shit, man, eating them sandwiches, go in a grocery store and getting out there and buying yourself a loaf of bread and some salami cause you couldn't eat at no restaurants, couldn't find no restaurant. That was some funny shit, man." He and Dixon chuckle and recall another figure from the past, Harold Ashby or Baby Doo Caston or Sonny Boy.

Hanging around Chess for any length of time is like getting a glimpse of living history. In Bass's office when we come back from lunch is Sonny Thompson. "Sonny Thompson!" Bass prods me. "Do you know who that is?" Didn't he play on some of Freddy King's records, I offer hesitantly. "No, man, Oh sure, he may have played on some of Freddy's records. But that's Sonny Thompson. He did the original of 'Drown in My Own Tears'." Oh, I say chastened. Didn't Henry Glover write that? Bass looks disappointed. "Henry stole that from him."

There are any number of Sonny Thompsons hanging around Chess at any given moment. Little Milton may stop in demanding some publicity and looking sullen in his elegant black fur coat, or Koko Taylor may be in the lobby downstairs; Sonny is doing charts for Ralph's gospel release; Wolf may be rehearsing in the small rehearsal studio, going patiently over the same song again and again, trying to get it right. Even Muddy, the publicity man tells you, dropped by the other day to say hello. First time since his accident. He seems aged.

Meanwhile production goes on, work on new albums and concepts is initiated. T.T. Swann, the coordinator of Chess's exemplary reissue series, a source of great pride to everyone in the company (to them this is where the blues belongs, in a neat expensively wrapped package, safely tucked away in the past), is working on an album by a group which he describes as "the first black rock group." Listening to their tapes and watching them rehearse I can't say that they impress me as very different from a number of other groups which mix a rock beat with soul intonations, but I don't say anything. Everyone at Chess is very enthused about the group, and they're really going to get behind it, they say, in a big way.

Upstairs the warehouse man is taking back returns. "Who put out this stiff?" he says, opening another carton of Muddy Waters' *Fathers and Sons*. "Who put out this fucking stiff?" Told it is Marshall, he nods his head understandingly. Like the security guard and the girl at the desk and a few of the sales people in the offices downstairs he has been with the company a long time, long enough to be indulgent of its owners' foibles. "It's still a fucking stiff," he says, ripping open the cellophane wrapping disgustedly.

Willie Dixon and Ralph Bass are still talking. "I'm fixin' to get the hell out of here," says Willie, stretching lazily but making no move to ease his vast bulk out of the chair into which it has sunk. Someone mentions Leonard Chess's name. "Leonard? Who's that? Oh, was he Chess Records? Pardon me ... You know, this music business is a little like Houdini. There are so many damned things going on behind the scenes, it don't mean a thing what's going on in front. I'm going to write the first honest book about this business, I really am. It's gonna be the first really frank book ... Cause listen, I'm gonna tell you something. So many damn things went down in front that I know, I could give this company the worst record in the world. Shit, man, I remember the Macamba, who was who and what was what, I'm gonna name names..." His voice trails off. Everyone laughs, because that is all a long time ago, it, too, is safely tucked away in the past.

But not quite. In the course of talking with Phil I got something on my tape that he didn't like. "You're not going to use that, are you?" he said to me anxiously. "What are you going to use that for?

You know, sometimes you gotta use that kind of language, but it don't look good. You know, I got a position in the community to uphold."

I wouldn't use it, I assured him, I was sorry for the misunderstanding, it was just good background for the chapter I was going to write. He appeared satisfied with my explanation and walked me up to the PR man's office, where I left him and my tape recorder on the way out to lunch.

"You've got to understand," Loren told me in some embarrassment for his employer, "Phil's a product of his time. He may get a little crude sometimes, but he doesn't mean anything by it." I nodded and tried to explain that I really didn't want to embarrass Phil, that I liked Phil and even admired him for his solidity and tough-minded integrity. Everything about him was clearly of a piece.

When I got back home and looked at the tape, though, I didn't have to wrestle with my conscience, someone had taken care of that for me. The tape was broken off jaggedly in the middle and about twenty minutes of our conversation excised. It was not, it turned out, the right part from his point of view, but in any case the message was unmistakably clear.

POSTSCRIPT

Since this piece was written a lot of things have changed. Chess Records was, first of all, relocated in New York; Phil and Marshall Chess have both left the company, Phil to head radio station WVON exclusively and Marshall to set up The Rolling Stones' label. The offices and pressing plant in Chicago have been closed down, the Vintage Series appears in real danger of extinction, and most of the people I talked to are gone. About all that is left, it would seem, is a name, and that, too, will pass into history. Chess Records will take on the status of legend; all the crassness, the ugliness, the raw vitality which made it happen will be forgotten; and for all that anyone knows it might just as well have been the creation of admen as of Phil and Leonard Chess, those pure products of the American dream. Maybe it's just that reality is too painful to record, but it seems unlikely now that the true achievement of the Chess brothers will be recognized or even that the blues — which was their single most successful product — will be allowed to survive.

EPILOGUE
A FAN'S NOTES

I

In the course of doing this book I became aware of two things. First, that my enthusiasm for the music continued unabated. And second, that I would have to stop writing about it — for a while anyway — if I wanted it to remain so. I consider this chapter a swan song, then, not only to the book but to my whole brief critical career. Next time you see me I hope I will be my younger, less self-conscious and critical self. It would be nice to just sit back and listen to the music again without a notebook always poised or the next interviewing question always in the back of your mind.

It's not easy meeting your idols. Certainly it has always been a painful task for me. From the time that I first forced myself to interview Skip James out of an intense admiration and a feeling that genius such as this would not pass my way again to my latest meeting with Jerry Lee Lewis, I have never found it simple, and the awkwardness, the misunderstandings and self-consciousness which crop up are never lightly disposed of. Imagine presenting yourself at Jerry Lee Lewis's door, even after the most elaborate preparations have been made — it remains in my mind an unnerving experience. And although I tried to explain to him that I was an admirer — I even showed him my Jerry Lee Lewis International Fan Club card — somehow a backstage glimpse, however sympathetic, disqualifies you at least a little as a fan.

Not that any of these glimpses proved disillusioning, really; none shook the firm faith I had in my subject's worth. They were eye-opening, though, if only for the fact that every singer I met, with the single exception of Jerry Lee Lewis, considered himself in some sense a failure. Each one was marked to some degree, white as well as black, by the brutalization of an industry and a society that care very little for his gifts. It was saddening to confront each artist's disappointment with himself and his career, but it was exhilarating at the same time to meet them on their own grounds and to see the source for some of the energy and genius that went into the make-up of their music.

Originally this chapter was supposed to be called "Going Back to Memphis, or You Can't Go to Anyone's Home Anymore." It was going to be about the Memphis Blues Festival, and it was meant to chronicle my disillusionment in a trip which I undertook as a kind of pilgrimage a couple of years ago. Knoxville, Brownsville, Jackson, Tennessee; Beale St., W.C. Handy Park, the Peabody Hotel – driving down, place names became realities, and my brother and I threw song lyrics at each other. "If you're going to Memphis stop by Minglewood." "From Memphis to Norfolk is a thirty-six-hour ride." And at the exit to Sleepy John Estes' hometown: "I'm going to Brownsville, take that right-hand road."

We had never been South before, and everything was strange to us. The language, the heat, the social customs, the Negro road gang that we saw in their striped convict's suits somewhere in Virginia or North Carolina. The Festival itself, however, was the same old shuck. It was contrived, it was disorganized, and it was geared irremediably towards a white audience. So that most of the time the bluesmen were overshadowed by the very groups that had come to pay them homage (Canned Heat failed to show, but Johnny Winter appeared with twenty-two amplifiers and assorted equipment), and when they did get to play there was a musty flavour to it, as if the music had been embalmed and specially trotted out for this occasion. These were, in fact, many of the same problems which have plagued every blues "concert" I have attended since I first saw Lightnin' Hopkins at Harvard twelve years ago: a stiff, unnatural atmosphere, an un-bridgeable gulf between performer and audience, and a tendency to treat the blues as a kind of museum piece, to be pored over by scholars, to be admired perhaps but to be stifled at the same time by the press of formal attention. It was a depressing realization and one that left me on the whole with the feeling that even in its own backyard blues had ceased to be a living experience.

Well, I no longer feel that's true. Certainly blues is the property of an older generation whose days are just as certainly numbered. Then, too, there is little question that the sense of regional isolation which gave rock 'n' roll as well as blues much of its original impetus is fast dying out, to be replaced by a form of cultural homogeneity which denies local differences or distinctions. All across the country the radio announcers have the same bland voice, and I couldn't help thinking as I drove down to Memphis how different it must have been for Elvis or Johnny Cash or Carl Perkins, growing up listening to B.B. King and Howlin' Wolf and Sonny Boy Williamson on the radio, seeing Muddy Waters and Junior Parker and Joe Hill Louis as popular artists of the day. It's almost as if they were living in another world. And yet doing this book taught me that world still exists, and that despite the fierce assault of time upon it the music has an ongoing vitality.

Seeing Hound Dog Taylor at Florence's a few blocks from the University of Chicago playing for a crowd that has no more idea of the existence of twentieth century comforts than it did before leaving Mississippi. Listening to Buddy Guy relaxed and singing for his own people in a way that was altogether different from any of the countless times I have seen him perform for white audiences. Couples dancing and life surging around the pounding relentless beat. Robert Pete Williams at home in rural Louisiana, playing his guitar for himself and his friends with a confidence and a sense of place that no frequenter of jazz festivals or blues concerts will ever sense. Charlie Rich singing from the depths of his soul for an audience of boosters and parvenus – native Memphians who want to make good in an ad agent's world. The girl who selected "Dust My Broom" on the jukebox of one of the Chicago clubs and then sang along with lyrics that had been composed before she was born. The atmosphere of any one of the South Side joints where heads turn when you walk in not so much out of hostility as real curiosity that a white should venture into their sealed-off world. A man named Honey offers to buy you a drink, his girl wants to dance, and you look for the catch, you wait for the delayed explosion. There is none; it is just manifest good will, people are glad to see you somehow and after a while you, too, begin to feel part of a community that has been created almost as a shelter against the storm outside.

All these glimpses add up to a picture which is not necessarily coherent but which puts me back in touch with the feeling that originally drew me to the music. It was, when I first heard it, an emotional experience which I could not deny. It expressed for me a sense of sharp release and a feeling of almost savage joy.

II

Since these pieces were written I have run into several of the artists in a number of different settings. Muddy Waters is back on the road, off crutches and sipping champagne again while his band runs through their interminable warm-up sets. Still as regal as ever he takes more frequent advantage of the prerogatives of the star and is visibly pleased at all the attention he has gotten in the past year. When I went back to see him shortly after his first comeback concert he wanted me to know how elated he was at the response of his young fans and to a neighbour who called on the phone he boasted that "I got a friend of mine from Boston here to see me. I got a reporter from *Rolling Stone.*"

Robert Pete Williams we put on in concert at Harvard, and the result was a mixed success. He had been practising bottleneck since I visited him in May, and he played a typically odd and eccentric set in this newly acquired style. In many ways he seemed absolutely the same: he repeated the same stories virtually word for word to an audience of rapt admirers, and his sad liquid eyes conveyed the same look of sorrowful trust as he told of indignities heaped upon him ("I *like* Robert Pete Williams," said Johnny Shines, who was so amused by the story of our attempts to locate him that he repeated it on educational TV. "I mean, he's definitely masculine, but there's something almost feminine about his sensibility."). His music remained strikingly original in any case, but somehow at Harvard it seemed also forced and constrained.

Johnny Shines, too, appeared in our Harvard concert series, and as much as anyone could have he helped to restore my faith in the value of such an undertaking. His performance was brilliant in every respect. The music was superb; his sensitivity and ability to manipulate his audience equalled the achievement of any theatrical performance; and the degree to which that audience was involved was greater than I have ever seen at a blues concert. But then Johnny Shines to my mind is very different from any other blues performer I have ever met. More than any other bluesman of my acquaintance he is firmly entrenched in the twentieth century, and he comes to the blues now as much through choice as necessity.

"Because, you see, I almost feel like I got to carry it on. I wants to remind people, black people especially, because if you forget your beginnings you can't do much with the future.

"You see, I guess I'm different from the average fellow. Now when I was small my mother and father separated, and I was being handed around between 'em quite a bit. And that's when I realized I was gonna need an education. So I started in, I had the opportunity to go to school about three months of the year, the other nine I worked out in the country on my father's farm. But by being determined to get it, that's how I got promoted in my studies, and then after I got to be thirty-one years old I went back to school, and that's what really helped refreshing my memory.

"Oh, I used to read all the time. I guess that's why I got no eyes now. When I'd be travelling with Robert I'd go out in the moonlight or if we was staying in a rooming house I'd raise the sheet and read by the streetlight. Robert? No, Robert didn't have no education at all so far as I could tell. I never saw him read or write, not even his name. He was just a natural genius."

About ten months after I spoke with him in Boston, The Chicago All Stars broke up, and Johnny Shines moved to Alabama. There he lives in a comfortable ranch house in a suburb outside of Tuscaloosa. He plays at a few local clubs, he enjoys the hunting and fishing and relaxed social climate (in Chicago he was concerned that his sixteen-year-old son would be forced to join one of the gangs), and alone among blues singers he seems to have formulated an explicitly radical point of view. "Well, you know something good is going to come out of this. All this mess is the best thing that ever happened to the poor person in America. Because it is showing the young people just what it is like to be a black person in this country. And regardless of what you think about it, one day these students that they are brutalizing and misusing will be running the country. Because this place is all over here in America, by jingo. And they're gonna find out sooner or later that being the head of a country is something like a unicycle rider. You got to be very well-balanced. Cause if you don't you gonna lean the wrong way."

He is fairly well off financially, he is now successfully launched on a new solo career, and he is even writing a book based on his own experiences and developing an elaborate theory of the blues back to African origins. It is called *Success Was My Downfall*.

Chess Records, of course, collapsed shortly after my second trip to Chicago and was subsequently sold to All Platinum (in 1976), who showed as little idea of what to do with their purchase as GRT. Howlin' Wolf died in January of 1976, two months after a typically heroic final performance in which he struggled to outdo B.B. King, Albert King, Bobby Bland, and Little Milton at Pervis Spann's International Blues Festival in Chicago. Charlie Rich improbably enough went on to achieve the stardom and international acclaim which had been predicted for fifteen years and found that it only presented an entirely different set of problems. And Jerry Lee Lewis has sadly fallen on hard times, careering chaotically from one excess to another, briefly forswearing rock 'n' roll for the church after the death of his mother, showing bitter remorse following his divorce and the death of Jerry Lee Jr. in an automobile accident in 1973. In November of 1976 he was arrested outside of Graceland, Elvis' Memphis mansion, for shouting obscenities, brandishing a gun, and demanding to see Elvis at 3 o'clock in the morning. Elvis, the recluse king, a victim of spiritually hard times himself, was reported to have suggested over the intercom that Jerry Lee go around back with the rest of the trash.

Well, it's an ongoing story and not always a happy one. It's a constant struggle for a buck, and many performers crack under the strain. Perhaps their attitude towards this unwarranted intrusion on their lives is best expressed by Johnny Shines. "I don't give a damn what you say about me," he said at one point. "You can call me a DOG, but use my name first. Say, you a dog, John Shines," And my attitude is best summed up in the pages of this book.

Val Wilmer

SELECTED
DISCOGRAPHY

DISCOGRAPHY

Obviously a selection of this sort is bound to be arbitrary. I have confined myself to artists covered in this book, and as a result many of my own favourites (Furry Lewis, Sleepy John Estes, Blind Willie McTell, Butch Cage, and Willie Thomas) are missing. It is intended purely as an introduction, however, and I hope readers will go on to make their own discoveries and choose their own favourites. With the invaluable help and expertise of Frank Scott, I revised the discography in the winter of 1997–98, trying to take into account the revolution of reissues that has taken place on CD without being drawn into the mania for completism which at times seems to animate it. Where there has been a new CD release that truly reflects the artist or the music, I have so indicated, with the latest catalogue number of the most widely available album of which I am aware. Where I know records to have gone out of print with no suitable substitute available, I have simply listed the original, or most familiar, version with an asterisk to indicate its antediluvian (pre-CD) status. I have *not* substituted what I consider to be an inferior, relatively anomalous selection simply because it is available. In any case, the idea is simply to provide a starting point, and if you want to pursue the matter further, the best mail-order sources that I know are Roots & Rhythm (formerly Down Home Music), P.O. Box 837, El Cerrito, CA 94530 and Red Lick Records, P.O. Box 3, Porthmadog, Gwynedd, Wales, UK LL48 6AQ.

Chapter 2 Blues in History
For collections and anthologies of early country blues material, the Yazoo label offers a selection of almost breathtaking scope. *Mississippi Moaners, Lonesome Road Blues, Tex-Arkana-Louisiana Country,* and *Frank Stokes' Dream* (Yazoo 1009, 1038, 1004, 1008) are just a few that will introduce the listener to the work of Bukka White, Son House, Robert Jr. Lockwood, Skip James, Texas Alexander, Henry Thomas, Frank Stokes, Furry Lewis, and Memphis Minnie. Sound and presentation are exemplary, and virtually the entire catalogue would make an invaluable addition to anyone's record library. Also providing a good overview, and a fine introduction to the full gamut of blues styles, are *The Blues: A Smithsonian Collection of Classic Blues Singers* (Smithsonian 101), a well-programmed 4-CD set, and Rhino's 15-volume *Blues Masters* series (Rhino 71121–71135), a somewhat more haphazard, but consistently enjoyable, selection.
The following are albums by individual artists cited in this chapter.

Blind Lemon Jefferson
King of the Country Blues (Yazoo 1069). Fine selection, probably the best sound that will
    ever be gotten out of Blind Lemon's Paramount recordings.
Lightnin' Hopkins
The Gold Star Sessions, Vols. I and II (Arhoolie 330, 337). Probably the best overall selection (perhaps because it's the earliest) from an indefatigable recording artist. *Lightnin' Hopkins: The Complete Aladdin Sessions* (EMI 96843), from much the same period, shares many of the same themes (and even lyrics and melodies) but is overall a less arrestingly idiosyncratic program. Also well worth seeking out is the out-of-print *Blues Train* (Mainstream 901), beautifully remastered (the Gold Star are not, and the Aladdin are uneven) from 1950 and '51 sessions.
Charley Patton
Founder of the Delta Blues (Yazoo 2010); *King of the Delta Blues* (Yazoo 2001). Definitive; beautifully remastered with informative notes. In addition, check out *Masters of the Delta Blues: The Friends of Charlie Patton* (Yazoo 2002) for perhaps the best selection of Patton-influenced Delta blues available.
Son House
Delta Blues — Original Library of Congress Sessions (Biograph 118). The epochal 1941–42 Library of Congress recordings. Son House solo, Son House with band (!), Son House in all his vocal majesty and glory.
Father of the Delta Blues (Columbia/Legacy 48867). First recordings upon rediscovery; with Al Wilson (not yet of Canned Heat) on harmonica and guitar. The second CD consists of outtakes and does not add a whole lot, but the first is the original album and has moments

of real inspiration. The *Original Delta Blues* (Columbia/Legacy 65515) is a single CD with all nine original cuts plus two altogether unnecessary additions. Take your pick.

Robert Johnson

The Complete Recordings (Columbia/Legacy 64916); *King of the Delta Blues* (Columbia/Legacy 65211); *King of the Delta Blues Singers* (Columbia/Legacy 65746). The first is, of course, the complete work (with one exception, noted below), alternate takes and all; the second, with just sixteen classic tracks, is, I think, more listenable; the last is a replica of the still-astonishing 1961 album (with the addition of a recently discovered alternate take of "Traveling Riverside Blues" not included in *The Complete Recordings*) with which Robert Johnson's blues were ushered into the modern age. Indispensable in any form (I think my selection might be the last) — but for a sentimental choice let me propose the vinyl version of this original LP (Columbia 1654), which to me still has the best sound, though that may be nostalgia talking.

Elmore James

The Sky Is Crying: The History of Elmore James (Rhino 71190); *"Let's Cut It": The Very Best of Elmore James* (Flair 86257); *Elmore James: The Classic Early Recordings* (Flair/Virgin 3-CD box 39631). The first is a wonderful survey of James' career, from start to finish. The second is the best of the early years, while the third offers as complete a survey of those same years (1951–56) as we are ever likely to want or get.

Elmore James: King of the Slide Guitar (Capricorn 42006). Later and maybe even greater; the height of his emotion-laden style in a comprehensive 2-CD set from Bobby Robinson's '60s recordings. *Rollin' and Tumblin': The Best of Elmore James* (Relic 7026); *Dust My Broom* (Relic 7040); and *The Last Sessions* (Relic 7097) include all of the Capricorn cuts, plus some additional alternates. You can't go wrong with either set.

Bukka White

The Complete Bukka White (Columbia/Legacy 52782). The Vocalion sessions in their entirety. Rivals even the Robert Johnson.

Big Joe Williams

Big Joe Williams, Vols. I and II (RST Records 6003, 6004) is more or less complete from 1935 to 1949. Brilliantly rhythmic, idiosyncratic, and not to be missed — from one of the most underrated of the master bluesmen.

Shake Your Boogie (Arhoolie 315); *Piney Wood Blues, Blues on Highway 49* (Delmark 602, 604); *Mississippi's Big Joe Williams and His Nine-String Guitar* (Smithsonian/Folkways 40052). His first and best after rediscovery. Fully the equal of the early sides.

Tommy Johnson

The Complete Recorded Works (Document 5001). Lyrically and melodically lovely.

Chapter 3 Muddy Waters

The Complete Plantation Recordings (Chess 9344). The Library of Congress recordings in their entirety, including interview segments with the young McKinley Morganfield. Something of a miracle.

Chicago Blues: The Beginning (Testament 2207). Both Muddy's and Johnny Shines' previously unissued sides for Columbia. Muddy's are presently available on *First Recording Sessions: 1941–1946* (Document 5146), which also includes the Library of Congress recordings.

Muddy Waters: His Best 1947–1955 and *1956–1964* (Chess 9370, 9380). These two albums supplant all previous "Best Of" collections.

The Aristocrat of the Blues (Chess 9387). Virtually all of Muddy's great early sides, from the time he first set foot in the Chess (né Aristocrat) recording studio to his first hit in 1950. In addition you get wonderful tracks by Sunnyland Slim, Robert Nighthawk, Baby Face Leroy, and Little Johnny Jones, as well as Andrew Tibbs' inflammatory "Bilbo Is Dead."

Fathers and Sons (Chess 92522). An experiment uniting Muddy and Spann with Paul Butterfield and Mike Bloomfield. At this point perhaps more of a curiosity than anything else.

Hard Again (Blue Sky 34449). Muddy at sixty and back on top, rocking in the company of James Cotton and Johnny Winter.

Various albums are available by band members Little Walter (*His Best, The Essential, Blues with a Feeling,* and *Confessin' the Blues,* Chess 9384, 9342, 9357, 9366); Jimmy Rogers (*Chicago Bound,* Chess 9300, or *The Complete Chess Recordings,* Chess 9372 [so long as you ignore the second CD]); and Otis Spann (*Down to Earth,* MCA 11202; *Live the Life,* Testament 6001) — all of which show the artist and the Muddy Waters band to advantage.

Chapter 4 Johnny Shines

Dust My Broom (Paula 14). Johnny's great 1952 and '53 recordings for JOB, along with five tracks each by Sunnyland Slim and Robert Jr. Lockwood. Johnny's are as good as it gets.

Chicago/The Blues/Today! Vol. III (Vanguard 79218). His first after rediscovery.

Masters of the Modern Blues, Vol. I (Testament 5002). Traditional material in a band setting; includes "Tom Green's Farm."

Johnny Shines with Walter Horton (Testament 5015). Brilliant original compositions; great harp.

Last Night's Dream (Sire 9 45285-2). My favourite, along with the Vanguard. Amplified slide with rhythm; more original compositions.

Hey Ba-Ba-Re-Bop (Rounder 2020). The 1971 Boston Blues Society recordings.

Chapter 5 Skip James

*Blues at Newport 1964, Part II (Vanguard 79181). The historic live recordings. (*Blues at Newport, Blues with a Feeling,* and *Great Bluesmen — Newport,* Vanguard 115/116, 77005, and 77/78, among them include two of the three performances from the above, plus several more.)

Skip James: The Complete Early Recordings (Yazoo 2009). In the Yazoo tradition. All eighteen of James' classic 1931 recordings, with the best possible sound.

Blues from the Delta (Vanguard 79517). A good combination of Skip's two Vanguard albums, *Skip James/Today!* and *Devil Got My Woman* (Vanguard 79219, 79273), with two pretty ephemeral previously unissued cuts. Includes well-thought-out reworkings of many of his best-known songs as well as less-familiar cuts and new compositions. *She Lyin'* (Genes 9901) is a looser, more playful, but less fully realized set from a year or two earlier (not long after Newport), and *Skip's Piano Blues* (Genes 9910) has similar limitations and similar appeal.

*Goin' Up the Country (Rounder 2012). David Evans field recordings, including brilliant examples of the Bentonia style by Jack Owens and Cornelius Bright.

It Must Have Been the Devil (Testament 5016). Wonderful stomps, two-steps, and blues by Jack Owens in the inimitable Bentonia style.

Chapter 6 Robert Pete Williams

Robert Pete Williams, Vols. I and II; *Angola Prisoners' Blues* (Arhoolie 394, 395, 419). His prison legacy, plus some bonus tracks on Vol. II. *Angola Prisoners' Blues* is an anthology with only three Williams cuts, but these include the absolutely essential "Prisoner's Talking Blues."

Free Again (Prestige Bluesville OBC 553). An almost equally amazing declaration of artistic independence, recorded on parole.

*Blues at Newport 1964, Part I (Vanguard 79180). His first appearance outside the state. (*Blues at Newport* and *Blues with a Feeling,* Vanguard 115/116 and 77005, between them include two of the three performances from the above.)

NB: David Evans' recordings of Robert Pete from the late '60s still remain to be issued and may well represent his finest post-parole work.

Chapter 7 Howlin' Wolf

Memphis Days, Vol. I (Bear Family 15460); *Howlin' Wolf Rides Again* (Ace 333). The early Memphis sessions; crude, raucous, overamplified, powerful.

Howlin' Wolf (Chess 9332); *Ain't Gonna Be Your Dog* (Chess 9349). Can't be beat. Brilliant, comprehensive 3- and 2-CD collections. If you just want to dip your foot in, try *His Best*

(Chess 9375), but really you can't go wrong buying the first, then the second — and at that point I defy you to stop!

The Back Door Wolf (Chess 9358). Wolf at the end. Some great moments, not the least of which is a heartfelt "Coon on the Moon."

Chapter 8 Sun Records

The Sun catalogue has proved even more fertile than anyone except for Sam Phillips could possibly have imagined. There have been any number of celebrations of the Sun era embarked upon over the years in, literally, hundreds of configurations. The most common, and the most commonly available for many years, came from Shelby Singleton's reconstituted Sun label and its English licensee, Charly, which worked its way up to a catalogue of well over a hundred albums of Sun material. Most of these albums are no longer available, and I must confess I am at somewhat of a loss to distinguish among the various compilations, and am particularly wary of the mania for completeness which sometimes supersedes matters of judgement and taste. The following, however, I believe are the best places to start, even if you have to go to a secondhand record store to do it.

The Sun Records Collection (Rhino 71780). A relatively comprehensive and altogether wonderful survey of all the Sun styles, from blues and country to rockabilly, gospel, and rocking r&b in a single 3-CD set.

The Blues Came Down from Memphis (Charly 67); *Blue Flames: A Sun Blues Collection* (Rhino 70962); *Mystery Train* (Rounder SS38). Three variants on a single blues theme, in my descending order of preference. They're all good — but you'd probably want just one. For an alternative approach, try *Sun Records: The Blues Years* (Charly Sun Box 7), a compellingly idiosyncratic 8-CD set for any true blues aficionado, not just the completist.

The Complete Sun Singles, Vols. I and II (Bear Family 15801, 15802), may be a little much for the casual listener but provides a fascinating view of the evolution of the label. There are innumerable other collections and single-artist sets, but the above will at least provide you with a starting place.

Sunrise (RCA 67675). All the titles, most of the alternate takes and studio conversation, the two original acetates (all four sides) that Elvis recorded at his own expense in 1953 and early 1954, all the experiments and all the dogged failures, plus six rare Hayride sides and two additional r&b numbers (recorded at a Lubbock radio station) on a 2-CD set. About as close as we're ever likely to get to what Elvis and Sam Phillips were really driving at, both individually and collectively, at the beginning.

The Million Dollar Quartet (RCA 2023). The Rosetta Stone, Part 2. Over an hour of Elvis, Carl Perkins, and Jerry Lee Lewis fooling around in the Sun studio in 1956 on gospel, country, blues, and rock 'n' roll. Talked about for over thirty years before it finally saw the light of day, the revealed moment is less apocalyptic than might have been imagined, perhaps, but no less engaging.

The Classic Carl Perkins (Bear Family 15494-95); *Up Through the Years* (Bear Family 15246). The second is a wonderful 24-track survey of the Sun years. The first, a 5-CD box, is Carl close to complete through 1964. Carl is creative enough (and more than antic enough) to sustain this kind of attention.

Chapter 9 Jerry Lee Lewis

Jerry Lee Lewis said at one point that he had recorded enough material at Sun for forty separate albums to be issued, and he may well have. By now more than that number have come out, though with a considerable amount of duplication. You can scarcely go wrong with any of them, but here are the best not just of the Sun sides but of his later work as well.

Classic Jerry Lee Lewis: The Definitive Edition of His Sun Recordings (Bear Family 15420). An 8-CD, 246-song set, complete with some of the most amazing music, thematic variations, and incidental dialogue ever recorded. The one boxed set that no rock 'n' roll record collection should be without. Either *Original Sun Greatest Hits* (Rhino 70255) or *Up Through the Years* (Bear Family 15408) would be a good place to get a taste — but I can't emphasize too much how transcendent an experience the boxed set can be.

DISCOGRAPHY

Greatest Live Shows on Earth (Bear Family 15608). It is (they are).
Live at the Star Club (Bear Family 15467; Rhino 70268). Even better.
*Another Place, Another Time; *She Still Comes Around; *She Even Woke Me Up to Say Goodbye (Smash 67104, 67112, 67128). As far as I know, none of these is currently available, but they are by far the best of his innumerable and good country albums. For a fine selection of his Smash work, try the out-of-print CDs *Killer: The Mercury Years,* Vols. I–III (Mercury 836 935, 938, 941), which cover country, rock, gospel, r&b, and Jerry Lee's unique ventures into any territory he deems worthy of exploration. For country only, *Killer Country* (Mercury 526 542) goes considerably further than I would go (up to 1977, and 55 tracks!) but remains a powerful (and entertaining) statement overall.

Chapter 10 Charlie Rich

Feel Like Going Home: The Essential Charlie Rich (Epic/Legacy 64762). An overview going from his first Phillips hit to 1992's *Pictures and Paintings*. Includes the original demo version of "Feel Like Going Home."
Lonely Weekends: The Sun Years (Bear Family 16152). The issued Sun sides are fine, with some classics and some duds, but the "midnight demos" are the real treat in this extraordinary 3-CD set, which includes 62 rare and unissued recordings. For the less dedicated Charlie Rich fan *The Sun Sessions* (Varese 5695) would be the more predictable (and more economical) way to go — but I keep going back to those demos!
The Complete Smash Sessions (Mercury 512 643). The sessions that Charlie was most satisfied with from the early part of his career. Brilliant original material.
Big Boss Man (Koch 7971). Includes all of his RCA Groove album, produced by Chet Atkins, plus five additional tracks. Nearly as good as the Smash material, not quite as moody but jazzier in places and a little more swinging.
Charlie Rich Sings the Songs of Hank Williams, Plus . . . (Diablo 810). It's the plus that is of greatest interest to me. Includes dramatic soul ballads and a heartbreaking demo of a song for his daughter Renee.
*Silver Linings (Epic 33545). The gospel side of Charlie Rich. Beautiful and heartfelt (if occasionally gimmicky) versions of old favourites, sung in the inimitable manner.
Pictures and Paintings (Sire 26730). I've got to admit to more than a soft spot in my heart for this particular collection. This is the album that Charlie wanted to make from the time I first met him — blues, jazz, soul, and beautiful new originals from Charlie and Margaret Ann in 1992. Because of my own involvement, I can't even pretend to be objective. "You Don't Know Me" was the original title.

Chapter 11 Chess Records

The Chess catalogue is currently available in a splendour, comprehensiveness, and diversity that could never previously have been imagined. It includes indispensable albums by Sonny Boy Williamson (Chess 9116 and 9324), Elmore James (9114), Lowell Fulson (9394), and J. B. Lenoir (9323), among others. *Drop Down Mama* (93002) is a brilliant anthology of early sides by Johnny Shines, Robert Nighthawk, Honeyboy Edwards, Blue Smitty.

The real gems of the Chess collection are *Chess Blues* and *Chess Rhythm and Roll* (Chess 9340, 9352), two 4-CD anthologies which give as substantial and entertaining an overview of the label as the Rhino, Bear Family, and Charly Sun boxes, while *The Aristocrat of the Blues* (Chess 9387), cited in the Muddy Waters section above, gives a wonderful insight into the evolution of the Chicago style. Marshall Chess once claimed that he was going to have an entire library of vintage Chess recordings bound in leather for his children, but Andy McKaie, the head of the MCA Chess reissue program, has in effect done it — if in a more democratic, jewel-box kind of a way.

Chuck Berry's work is available in different forms, most notably in *His Very Best,* Vols. I and II (Chess 9371, 9381). Bo Diddley's similar *His Best* (Chess 9373) just about covers it, but there's a wealth of listening out there. You can't ever run out.

Val Wilmer

GENERAL
BIBLIOGRAPHY

BIBLIOGRAPHY

The magazines, *Blues World* (22 Manor Crescent, Knutsford, Cheshire, England); *Living Blues* (2615 North Wilton Ave., Chicago, Illinois 60614); and *Blues Unlimited* (36 Belmont Park, Lewisham, London, England) have proved invaluable sources of information.

The following is a selective list of works of general interest. Many, if not all, were used specifically for this book, but all have contributed to whatever understanding I may have of this seemingly inexhaustible field.

William Broonzy and Yannick Bruynoghe. *Big Bill Blues: William Broonzy's Story*. London: Cassell, 1955.

Samuel Charters. *The Bluesmen*. New York: Oak Publications, 1967.

———. *The Country Blues*. New York: Rinehart, 1959.

———. *The Poetry of the Blues*. New York: Oak Publications, 1963.

R.M.W. Dixon and J. Godrich. *Recording the Blues*. London: Studio Vista, 1970.

Jonathan Eisen (ed). *The Age of Rock*. New York: Random House, 1969.

David Evans. *Tommy Johnson*. London: Studio Vista, 1971.

John Fahey. *Charley Patton*. London: Studio Vista, 1970.

William Ferris. *Blues From the Delta*. London: Studio Vista, 1971.

Phyl Garland. *The Sound of Soul*. New York: Regnery, 1969.

Karl Gert zur Heide. *Deep South Piano: The Story of Little Brother Montgomery*. London: Studio Vista, 1970.

Charlie Gillett. *The Sound of the City: The Rise of Rock and Roll*. New York: Outerbridge and Dienstfrey, 1970.

J. Godrich and R.M.W. Dixon. *Blues and Gospel Records 1902-1942* (discography). London: Storyville, 2nd ed., 1969.

John Grissim. *Country Music: White Man's Blues*. New York: Paperback Library, 1970.

Bob Groom. *The Blues Revival*. London: Studio Vista, 1971.

Woody Guthrie. *Bound for Glory*. New York: Dutton, 1943.

W.C. Handy. *Father of the Blues*. New York: MacMillan, 1941.

Paul Hemphill. *The Nashville Sound: Bright Lights and Country Music*. New York: Simon and Schuster, 1970.

Nat Hentoff. *The Jazz Life*. New York, 1962.

Billie Holliday. *Lady Sings the Blues*. New York: Doubleday, 1956.

Jerry Hopkins. *Elvis*. New York: Simon and Schuster, 1971.

Leroi Jones. *Black Music*. New York: William Morrow, 1968.

———. *Blues People*. New York: William Morrow, 1963.

Charles Keil. *Urban Blues*. Chicago: University of Chicago Press, 1966.

Mike Leadbitter and Neil Slaven. *Blues Records 1943-1966* (discography). London: Hanover Books, 1968.

Mike Leadbitter (ed). *Nothing But the Blues* (BU anthology). London: Hanover, 1971.

Alan Lomax. *Mister Jelly Roll*. New York: Duell Sloan and Pierce, 1950.

Michael Lydon. *Rock Folk*. New York: Dial Press, 1971.

Albert McCarthy, Alun Morgan, Paul Oliver and Max Harrison. *Jazz on Record: A Critical Guide of the First 50 Years*. London: Hanover, 1968.

Bill Malone. *Country Music U.S.A.: A Fifty-Year History*. Austin: University of Texas Press, 1968.

George Mitchell. *Blow My Blues Away*. Baton Rouge: Louisiana State University Press, 1971.

BIBLIOGRAPHY

Paul Oliver. *Bessie Smith*. London: Cassell, 1959.

– – –. *Blues Fell This Morning*. London: Cassell, 1960.

– – –. *Conversation With the Blues*. London: Cassell, 1965.

– – –. *Savannah Syncopators: African Retentions in the Blues*. London: Studio Vista, 1970.

– – –. *Screening the Blues. Aspects of the Blues Tradition*. London: Cassell, 1968.

– – –. *The Story of the Blues*. London: Barrie and Rockliff, 1969.

Bengt Olsson. *Memphis Blues*. London: Studio Vista, 1970.

Harry Oster. *Living Country Blues*. Detroit: Folklore Associates, 1969.

Johnny Otis. *Listen to the Lambs*. New York: Norton, 1968.

Frederic Ramsey. *Been Here and Gone*. New Brunswick: Rutgers University Press, 1960.

Jerry Rivers. *Hank Williams: From Life to Legend*. Denver: Heather Enterprises, 1967.

James Rooney. *Bossmen: Bill Monroe and Muddy Waters*. New York: Dial, 1971.

Tony Russell. *Blacks, Whites, and Blues*. London: Studio Vista, 1970.

Eric Sackheim. *The Blues Line: A Collection of Blues Lyrics*. New York: Grossman, 1969.

Nat Shapiro and Nat Hentoff. *Hear Me Talkin' to Ya*. New York: Rinehart, 1955.

Robert Shelton and Burt Goldblatt. *The Country Music Story*. New York: Bobbs Merrill, 1966.

A.B. Spellman. *Four Lives in the BeBop Business*. New York: Pantheon, 1966.

Derrick Stewart-Baxter. *Ma Rainey and the Classic Blues Singers*. London: Studio Vista, 1970.

Roger Williams, *Sing a Sad Song: The Life of Hank Williams*. New York: Doubleday, 1970.

BIBLIOGRAPHY

The following articles and monographs were specifically helpful in the preparation of this book.

Chapter 2 Blues in History:
Julius Lester. "Interview with Son House." *Sing Out,* Vol. XV, No. 3 (1965).
———. "Interview with Bukka White." *Sing Out,* Vol. XVIII, No. 4 (1968).
Frank Scott, John Holt and Paul Oliver. "Lightnin' Hopkins." Texas Blues Society, December 1965.
Al Wilson. "Son House." *Blues Unlimited.* Collector's Classics No. 14, 1966.

Chapter 3 Muddy Waters:
Don DeMichael. "Father and Son: An Interview with Muddy Waters and Paul Butterfield." *downbeat,* August 7, 1969.
Sheldon Harris. "An Otis Spann Record Date." *Jazz & Pop,* 1968.
Paul Oliver. "Muddy Waters." *Blues Unlimited.* Collector's Classics No. 1, 1964.
Pete Welding. "Interview with Muddy Waters." *American Folk Music Occasional No. 2.* Oak Publications, 1970.

Chapter 4 Johnny Shines:
Johnny Shines. "Remembering Robert Johnson." *American Folk Music Occasional No. 2.* Oak Publications, 1970.

Chapter 5 Skip James:
Bruce Jackson. "The Personal Blues of Skip James." *Sing Out,* 1965.
Jacques Roches. "Henry Stuckey: An Obituary." *78 Quarterly,* No. 2, 1968.

Chapter 6 Robert Pete Williams:
Harry Oster. Liner notes and transcriptions.
Pete Welding. "Interview with Robert Pete Williams." *downbeat,* August 6, 1970.
Al Wilson. "Robert Pete Williams: His Life and Music." *Little Sandy Review,* 1966.

Chapter 7 Howlin' Wolf:
Bruce Iglauer. "Interview with Howlin' Wolf." *Living Blues,* Vol. 1, No. 1, 1970.
Pete Welding. "Interview." *downbeat,* December 14, 1967.
Paul Williams and Peter Guralnick. "Interview." *Crawdaddy!,* No. 5, 1966.

Chapter 8 Sun Records:
Stanley Booth. "A Hound Dog to the Manor Born." *Esquire,* February, 1968.
Claude Hall. "Phillips, Presley, Cash, Sun." *Billboard,* December 27, 1969.
Mike Leadbitter. "Memphis." *Blues Unlimited.* Collector's Classic No. 13, 1966.
Michael Lydon. "The Top Beats the Bottom: Carl Perkins and His Music." *Atlantic,* 1971.
Jules Paglin. "Lousiana Disc Jockeys." *Blues World,* No. 31, June 1970.
Paul Vernon. "The Sun Legend," 1969.

BIBLIOGRAPHY

Chapter 9 Jerry Lee Lewis:
John Grissim. "Jerry Lee Lewis: Higher Than Most." *Rolling Stone*, September 17, 1970.

Chapter 11 Chess Records:
Ray Brack and Earl Paige. "Chess and the Blues." *Billboard: The World of Soul*, June 24, 1967.
Michael Lydon. "Chuck Berry." *Ramparts*, 1969.
Clarence Petersen. "The Chicago Sound." *Chicago Tribune Magazine*, May 11, 1969.

INDEX

Note: Pages set in italics represent photographs

Dick Waterman

CHARLIE PATON - PONY BLUES
SONNY HOUSE - -"-
ROBERT JOHNSON

Also by Peter Guralnick

LOST HIGHWAY
Journeys and Arrivals of American Musicians

"Guralnick understands so well and expresses so eloquently the forces that grind many of America's greatest artists to dust [and yet] never loses sight of the dream that set them all on that highway in the first place." LESTER BANGS

"A book not just for fans, but for anyone interested in music, American popular culture, and quietly eloquent writing." *New York Times*

"Guralnick deploys a master's touch and a lover's intensity to the simultaneous depiction of the character of the individual subject and the world in which he moves." Charles Shaar Murray, *NME*

ISBN 1 84195 282 6, £12.99, www.canongate.net

SWEET SOUL MUSIC
Rhythm and Blues and the Southern Dream of Freedom

"No one I've read writes as well about musicians and their music as Peter Guralnick . . . Magnificent – as clear and as joyful as the music that inspired it." RODDY DOYLE

"Buy this book! In years to come it will seem like a bargain compared with all the wonderful records which you will have to buy after reading the vivid accounts of *Sweet Soul Music*." ELVIS COSTELLO

"The best history of '60s soul music anyone has written or is likely to write, but it is much more than that." *News York Times*

ISBN 1 84195 240 0, £12.99, www.canongate.net

PETER GURALNICK has written extensively on American music and musicians. His books include the prize-winning two-volume Elvis Presley biography, *Last Train to Memphis* and *Careless Love*; the biographical inquiry *Searching for Robert Johnson*; and the novel *Nighthawk Blues*.